# Sermons On The First Readings

## Series II

### Cycle C

**Mary S. Lautensleger**
**Frank Ramirez**
**Stan Purdum**
**Lee Ann Dunlap**
**John Wayne Clarke**

CSS Publishing Company, Inc., Lima, Ohio

Copyright © 2006 by
CSS Publishing Company, Inc.
Lima, Ohio

Some scripture quotations are from the New Revised Standard Version of the Bible, copyright 1989 by the Division of Christian Education of the National Council of the Churches of Christ in the USA. Used by permission.

Some scripture quotations identified (KJV) are from the King James Version of the Bible, in the public domain.

Scripture quotations identified (CEV) are from the Contemporary English Version of the Holy Bible. Copyright © The American Bible Society, 1995. Used by permission.

Some scripture quotations are from The Message by Eugene H. Peterson, copyright © 1993, 1994, 1995, 1996, 2000, 2001, 2002. Used by permission of NavPress Publishing Group. All rights reserved.

Some scripture quotations identified (TJB) are from The Jerusalem Bible, copyright © 1966 by Darton, Longman & Todd, Ltd., and Doubleday, a division of Bantam Doubleday Dell Publishing Group, Inc., Reprinted by permission.

Some scripture quotations identified (REB) are from The Revised English Bible, copyright © Oxford University Press and Cambridge University Press, 1989.

**Library of Congress Cataloging-in-Publication Data**

Sermons on the first readings. Series II / Mary S. Lautensleger ... [et al.].
   p. cm.
  ISBN 0-7880-2368-3 (Perfect bound : alk. paper)
  1. Bible. O.T.—Sermons. 2. Sermons, American—21st century. 3. Church year sermons.
I. Lautensleger, Mary S., 1947-. II. Title

BS1151.55.S475 2005
252'.6—DC22

                               200508082

For more information about CSS Publishing Company resources, visit our website at www.csspub.com or email us at custserv@csspub.com or call (800) 241-4056.

Cover design by Barbara Spencer
ISBN 0-7880-2397-7

# Table Of Contents

**Sermons For Sundays
After Pentecost (First Third)
*Wisdom's Delight*
by Stan Purdum**

## Sermons For Sundays
## After Pentecost (Middle Third)
### *The Hard Task Of Truth-telling*
## by Lee Ann Dunlap

## Sermons For Sundays
## After Pentecost (Last Third)
### *Profiting From The Prophets*
## by John Wayne Clarke

# Sermons On The First Readings

## For Sundays In Advent, Christmas, And Epiphany

### *Shoots Of Tomorrow*

**Mary S. Lautensleger**

*To honor
Ruby Townsend and Jackie Webb,
two significant others in my ministry.
"Cheerleaders" from my first parish
who are always there for me.*

# Preface

For centuries, the people of God have dreamed of and planned for the time when a Messiah, a new king, would come to bring salvation, institute justice, and affect peace in their land. Today finds us still waiting and dreaming those same dreams. During the season of Advent, we join with God's people of all times and places in waiting for our Messiah.

The First Testament still has great relevance for us in the twenty-first century. Our long-awaited Messiah tells us he has come, not "to abolish the law and the prophets, but to fulfill them." He reads from the prophet Isaiah and announces, "Today the scripture has been fulfilled."

The season stirs our hearts as the light of the world enters once again. Culture pulls us in many directions as we prepare to worship a newborn king. Prophets speak to us of proper worship and appropriate actions toward our fellow humans. The prophetic voice calls us to prepare ourselves and to rejoice.

> Mary S. Lautensleger
> Concord, North Carolina

15

# Foreword

More often than not, books of sermons are not the most stimulating materials to read, perhaps because sermons are best heard and not read. The exception, however, are those written sermons in which the preachers or authors paint in words their ideas and imaginative thoughts with such lucidity that they capture the imaginations of the readers. This is precisely what the reader will encounter in reading this book of sermons by Reverend Mary Lautensleger.

Here are sermons that combine a comprehensive understanding of the biblical texts on which they are based with a wide breadth of knowledge born of the preacher's education, readings, and imagination. Here are sermons whose relevance to our contemporary situation arrests the reader from the beginning to the end. Here are sermons whose illustrations are pertinent, amusing, and thought-provoking at the same time. Here are sermons that will comfort and disturb, inform and challenge, amuse and provoke the readers all at the same time. Having read these sermons prior to their publication, I desire some day to hear Reverend Lautensleger preach.

In addition to their spiritual insights and inspirations, this collection of sermons will provide pastors with insights into a fascinating homiletical style of sermon construction that might best be described as faceting the texts. It will also illustrate the delivery of sermons as story, and be a rich resource for sermon illustrations. The laity will find these sermons to be an invaluable source for private devotions, group fellowship and discussion, and study sessions. Altogether, I highly commend this collection of sermons to these readers.

Reverend Dr. Albert J. D. Aymer

# Shoots Of Tomorrow

In the parable of *The Giving Tree*, a young boy would gather his favorite tree's leaves on mild autumn afternoons. He fashioned them into a crown for his head and played king of the forest. The tree was fun to climb, and he loved to eat its delicious apples. The boy enjoyed swinging from the tree's branches, and discovered a shady resting place beneath those same branches on hot summer days.

As the boy became a teenager, he visited the tree less frequently. He did stop by once to carve his initials, and those of his girlfriend, on the apple tree's trunk, framing them with a heart. As the boy matured and his interests changed, he found that he needed some spending money. So, he picked the tree's luscious apples and sold them at the farmers' market in town.

As an adult, he cut off many of the tree's branches to provide lumber for his young family's new home. During his middle years, he found himself with leisure time, and cut down the tree's trunk to fashion a sailboat's hull. Where a magnificent tree had once stood, spreading its leafy branches toward the heavens, all that remained was a stump. In his final years, the boy, now an old man, returned to the remaining stump to sit and rest his weary bones and to reminisce of days gone by.[1]

But, that stump wasn't the end of the memorable old tree. From stumps that have seemed long dead, new shoots can spring to life and become trees once again. God can make the dead come alive. God is making all things new, when an old stump is "reborn" into shoots of tomorrow.

As we stand at the threshold of a new church year on this first Sunday in Advent, we find ourselves waiting once again for the birth of a baby. Our prophets, among them Jeremiah, Malachi, Zephaniah, Micah, and Isaiah, join with shepherds, angels, Wise Men, and our gospel writers to retell the never-ending story of salvation. This is a season of preparation, of watching and waiting as we look to God for signs of hope and new life.

Prophets are people who speak for God. They hear God speak in this world, and then share with the rest of us what they have heard. The world is inhabited by many people who feel that God is far away, paying no attention to the things of our realm. Prophets are sent for folks just like that, for the multitudes who don't hear God speak, who don't see the wonders of God's presence. Prophets use their own eyes and ears for the sake of many others with ears that do not hear and eyes that fail to see.

Through the prophet Jeremiah, God speaks a word of promise and hope to the people of Judah, and to us. Jeremiah has already announced a new covenant to be written on our hearts instead of on stone tablets. The people of Judah are suffering under an oppressive system of exile in a foreign country. They have lost almost everything — families separated, land plundered, homes taken, livelihood destroyed, temple plundered, and king gone.

Then, like the first hints of a spring thaw, Jeremiah's words warm the hearts of his listeners and give them hope that they will return home. King David's lineage is to be restored and the land repaired. Those days are surely coming, promises Jeremiah.

The future is in God's hands, a future that is redemptive, joyous, and just. God promises to "raise up a righteous Branch" who will govern properly and fairly. Redemption is drawing near. From a budding branch, Jeremiah sees an image of hope — the promise of spiritual renewal, of a just society, and of peace on the horizon. The message of Advent has one recurring theme: Things are going to change!

"The days are surely coming, says the Lord, when I will fulfill the promise I made to the house of Israel and the house of Judah." Maybe you have said similar words to your children: "The days are surely coming when you will have children of your own and then your hair will turn gray, just like you're doing to me. The day will surely come, just you wait." And we admonish our children: "Stop wishing your life away," as they anxiously await Christmas, or their birthday, or the last day of school.

From the very beginning of scripture, the tree has been a symbol of life. The tree's "branch" became a biblical symbol for newness growing out of hopelessness, and was also a way of speaking about the expected Messiah (Jeremiah 23:5). Our earthly lives are branches that continue to grow and bear fruit. As we bear fruit, the kingdom's branches spread throughout the world.

Advent is the time of year when many trees have lost their leaves. Our deciduous trees can certainly pass for dead at this time of year. Metaphorically speaking, we also "lose our leaves" in the autumn of our lives, and it might be easy to give up hope.

In a *Peanuts* comic strip, Lucy looks up to see one solitary leaf clinging to a tree branch. "Stay up there, you fool!" she orders. A gentle breeze lifts the lone leaf from its branch and Lucy watches as it spirals downward toward the ground. "Oh, good grief!" she exclaims. "You wouldn't listen, would you? Now it's the rake and the bonfire. You just can't tell those leaves anything!"

Jeremiah must have felt at times that the people of Judah were like the last remaining leaves on a tree, desperately hanging onto the branch. They were dried up and without sustenance or hope. And, like Lucy, he could not tell them a thing, not about covenants, or faith in God, or even worship. The hope of Judah seemed to be crashing down like a mighty tree. From the Tree of Life, each leaf must, in its own time, fall — all colors, shapes, and sizes, both the great and the insignificant. God then lovingly gathers each leaf and calls it by name.

With God, we know to look past the falling leaves and stark branches of winter. Within each tree, there is dormant new life. Beyond winter, the rebirth of spring awaits. Life within that old stump is ready to spring forth and sprout anew. In death, there is resurrection. People again will have hope for new life from God. Winter has not officially arrived, and already Jeremiah is looking

21

toward spring, when leaves begin to sprout and buds burst into bloom. Jeremiah has told of a day when God will again plant and build (31:28). God will cause a new shoot, a new king, to spring from the cut-off stump of the lineage of Jesse, David's father. Many of us are familiar with the Advent Calendar, used in counting the days until the Messiah arrives. The Jesse Tree is another option for numbering these days. The Jesse Tree, the family tree of our Messiah, illustrates many of the people and events that God uses over time to bring Jesus into the world. Resplendent in its colorful symbols, the Jesse Tree grows and branches out as the Nativity of our Lord approaches, bringing hope and light into our winter bleakness.[2]

The children of Israel had always gathered to tell and retell the Jesse Tree stories of how God brought them from slavery in Egypt to the promised land. Generation gaps shrank as they shared their common life through their old, old stories. They would begin with Adam and Eve, the gardeners, and relate the story of Noah, the boat builder, and the rainbow. Abraham and Sarah are travelers who journey to a distant new land to make a home for God's people.

Isaac has a close call, but God always keeps promises and comes through for us. Jacob's own sons trick him, the trickster, as his favorite son, Joseph, becomes a missing person. Moses is a basket case until a burning bush calls him to deliver the slaves from Egypt. The Israelites walk through the Red Sea and God lays down the law at Sinai. Joshua takes over where Moses leaves off, and the wanderers finally settle down.

Little Samuel grows up to anoint kings, and King David proves himself a good shepherd to God's people. God calls prophets to remind the people of who they are and whose they are, but the people have become deaf. Their land is invaded and defeated by other countries, and they are scattered to the four winds. Prophets offer comfort and hope, again reminding God's people that they are God's people.

God has spoken of a time when God will cause a new shoot, a new king, to spring from the cut-off stump of the lineage of Jesse. The new king will rule with compassion, bringing justice to the world. The prophet Jeremiah relates God's message: "Someday I will appoint an honest king from the family of David, a king who will be wise and rule with justice. As long as he is king, Israel will have peace, and Judah will be safe. The name of this king will be 'The Lord gives Justice' " (Jeremiah 23:5-6 CEV).

With the great interest genealogy has generated today, tracing our roots and getting to know our family trees seems more important than ever. Your family tree includes parents, grandparents, and ancestors as far back as you can track. Our biblical family tree stretches back through centuries.

The Israelites are the family tree of Jesus. This "family tree" that God planted and raised was chopped back to a stump. But repeatedly, God restored it to life. The Jesse Tree is our story, too, of how we are at times our own worst enemies. It is the story of how God chooses to bring life once again even to those who take too much pleasure in chopping life down.

This Advent season, as we prepare for the birth of a Savior, we await the event Jeremiah and the people of Judah waited and hoped for. We also prepare our hearts and minds for Christ's "Second Advent." The season of Advent is not just to prepare us for Christmas. It is to prepare us for eternity.

Once Jewish theologian, Martin Buber, addressed an audience of priests, explaining the difference between Christians and Jews. "We all await the Messiah. You believe he has already come, while we don't. I propose that we wait for him together. When he appears, we can ask him if he was here before. And I hope I'll be close enough to whisper, 'For the love of heaven, don't answer.' "[3]

The Messiah is still branching out into human history today. As a branch of Jesse, Jesus enters our lives through our baptism. We continue to grow in him through word and sacrament. Once again, hope is blossoming in Bethlehem. The days are surely coming when Christ will return in glory. We wait in eager anticipation of the kingdom of God. Christ has come. Christ will come again.

1. Shel Silverstein, *The Giving Tree* (San Francisco: HarperCollins, 1964), pp. 6-56.

2. For suggestions on making a Jesse Tree, see Dennis Bratcher, "The Jesse Tree," *The Voice*, http://www.cresourcei.org/jesse.html [Accessed September 1, 2005].

3. Elie Wiesel, *All Rivers Run to the Sea* (New York: Alfred A. Knopf, Inc., 1996), pp. 354-355.

# Preparing The Way

Preparing the way can become an all-consuming endeavor. Unforeseen obstacles often have a way of getting in our way to hamper progress and sidetrack us. Then, Murphy's Law goes into effect: "If anything can go wrong, it will." Plans for the Paris subway system were begun in 1845, but the actual work was not begun until much later. A civil engineer, Fulgence Bienvenue (1852-1936), was assigned the task of preparing the way. His first big task was to dig the network of underground tunnels for the trains.

The workers hit many unexpected problems along the way. A few of the obstacles they ran into included underground springs, rock quarries, layers of chalk and sand, underground caverns, and prehistoric swamps under the a city that was inhabited by millions of residents.

The Seine River flows through the middle of Paris, so the subway lines also had to be routed under the river. Removal of the riverbed mud became one of their greatest problems. The solution they arrived at was quite clever, though. The workers froze the mud solid, then cut it into manageable chunks with picks and axes, and hauled it away before it thawed.[1]

The project lasted forty years, and that persistent engineer in charge stayed on the job until the subway system was up and running. The French government recognized his talent, perseverance, and leadership by presenting him with the Legion of Honor award on four different occasions. Today, the Paris subway system is one of the finest in the world. Millions of commuters depend on it daily to transport them to their destinations, but few know of the civil engineer and the other dedicated workers who toiled long and hard to bring its construction to fruition.

They were the ones who prepared the way for countless citizens and visitors to move about the city of Paris much more conveniently. Preparing the way is not an easy task. Trailblazers are frequently subjected to ridicule and threats, and the prophet Malachi is no exception.

Malachi is declaring to the Hebrew people that a messenger is coming to prepare the way for a new covenant, one that will be written on the hearts of the people. God is enlarging the promises made to the descendants of David with an everlasting covenant because God loves all people with an everlasting love.

Just as God prepared the way through the Red Sea and out of Egypt, God has provided release for the Hebrew people from captivity in Babylon, and the return to the land of their ancestors. The people are now back in their homeland of Judah, where Malachi is concerned because both the priests and the worshipers are not taking their religious responsibilities seriously. The physical exile has ended, but a spiritual exile seems to permeate the hearts of the people. Their devotion is noticeably half-hearted, and contributions to the offering plate have fallen off dramatically.

The priests, who are descendants of Jacob's son, Levi, and of Aaron, are cheating the sacrificial system. They have become complacent and corrupt. Moral standards are practically nonexistent, resulting in a deceptive and selfish people. Those living immoral lives appear to be prospering and enjoying the good life, while others are asking, "Where is the God of justice?" "Why do good things keep happening to corrupt individuals?"

The people are disappointed that, with restoration of the temple in Jerusalem, the glory days of Solomon have not returned. After all this time, their messianic dreams have not materialized, and appear to be more and more remote as time passes by. The embers of their faith are growing cold, but God is about to stir those smoking remnants and heat things up. A hot God is about to strike a match to the frozen chosen of Judah.

In addition to denouncing religious practices of the day, Malachi also provides a word of encouragement. By the same method that an advance team precedes contemporary politicians on the campaign trail, God will have a crier moving ahead to prepare the way for the new messenger. One is coming who will cleanse the priests with a refining fire and a powerful soap, resulting in a purified priesthood. The white-hot coals of the refiner's fire will change people in the same way iron is changed into steel.

The Day of the Lord will be no Sunday picnic. God's cleansing power will be more like going through an automated car wash on a bicycle. Malachi calls for a return to faithfulness because the Lord, whose coming is their hope, will not come until the temple and priesthood are purified. When the Lord comes, he will burn as a purifying fire, but first he will send a messenger to carry out reform, and to bring about repentance.

Malachi tells of the messenger sent to prepare us for God's coming, who will purify the unfaithful and rebellious. John the Baptist is a road-builder destined to prepare the way for the coming of the promised Messiah. John's mother, Elizabeth, and Mary, the mother of Jesus, celebrate together as they await the births of two very special babies.

Zechariah, father of John, is serving as a temple priest when confronted with a very pregnant pause. He is rendered speechless for the duration of his wife, Elizabeth's, pregnancy. When he finally regains his speech, he is deliriously happy over the birth of his son. Zechariah speaks to this newborn infant, knowing that John's destiny will be intertwined with that of one who is even greater.

The Gospel of Luke tells of powerful earthly rulers, stretching from imperial Rome to the holy city of Jerusalem, but they will pale in comparison to the one God has appointed. John the Baptist will burst forth into a corrupt world like a cannonball crashing through a stained-glass window, proclaiming a baptism of repentance for the forgiveness of sins.

Advent practices focus on the themes of reflection and repentance, and John's vocation is to call the world's attention to the one coming, who will save the people from their sins (Matthew 1:21). The ministry of John the Baptist is concerned with purification and righteousness, and Jesus will take up where John leaves off.

John thunders a revolutionary message of the one greater than he, who is coming to baptize with the Holy Spirit and with fire. This one will separate the wheat from the chaff and will burn the chaff with an unquenchable fire.

Today, we are called to face the future that God promises and into which God calls us. The future that beckons us is to the promised day of the Lord when God in Christ Jesus will establish the divine rule in justice and righteousness and give salvation to all people. Our readiness for the coming of God is witnessed in the love and commitment we have for one another. To love and care for others is a sign of our readiness to face the future in meeting new situations and various people.

You and I are here today because someone else prepared the way for us. That may well include several different individuals and span many years, but we usually can pinpoint one or two special individuals who have touched our lives, making the path easier to travel.

Those who have prepared the way for our faith walk may include the biblical characters whose stories we identify with, as well as the saints throughout history who have built and reformed the church on earth. Those who raised the funds and built this house of worship are included, as well as those who made sure we attended Sunday school and worship as young people, even when we didn't want to.

There are strong connections between preparing the way of the Lord and evangelism. You and I are the twenty-first-century prophets who make the paths straight for other sojourners. You can be a life-affirming source of guidance and inspiration for fellow travelers on the roads of life.

As the age of the prophets draws to a close, it does so in the person of John the Baptist. Malachi and John have prepared the way for a new world order. The great and powerful will be humbled, and the lowly and faithful will be exalted, just as every valley will be filled and every mountain and hill made low. Malachi and John are messengers who are leveling the road, preparing the way for the coming of the Messiah.

It is time for repentance, for a change of heart and mind. In one sense, all of life is a preparation for the coming of the Messiah. Preparation does not mean grim, fearful living, but celebration of the grace of God, and recognition of our need for continual repentance and renewal. Whatever lies in the future, we know that God comes to us in Christ with understanding and forgiveness.

Malachi and John remind us of our vast Judeo-Christian heritage, which comes to us through scripture and the church, and of the many ways God enters our lives. We must then relate our understanding of spiritual truth to this new cybernetic, nuclear, automated, impersonal, computerized age, or we are likely to lose our humanity as new knowledge engulfs us.

We are here to prepare the way of the Lord and make the path straight. Right here where we live is now where the action is. That requires the dedication and discipline the prophets have called for. It requires regular worship and constant effort to be sure we are following the Christ of the church and scriptures, and not the Christ of culture or of our own invention.

In this Advent season, brilliant sights and sounds rush us too quickly toward Christmas, without adequate time for preparation. The world promises bright lights and tinsel, which, like the flowers and grass of summer, will all too quickly fade and wither. We need to take time to listen to the wilderness messengers, who direct us again to the powerful Word of God, which endures forever. The wilderness voice points us to the one far greater and more important than anything else the world has to offer.

The voices of Malachi and John are crying in the wilderness. Listen! There is a message for us, the road builders of today. Prepare the way of the Lord. Make the paths straight. The kingdom of heaven *is* at hand.

---

1. Pascal Desabres, "The Parisian Subway, 1880-1900: A Local or a National Interest Line? On the Concept of Globalization," *Business and Economic History On-Line*, Vol. 1, 2003, online at http://www.h-net.msu.edu/~business/bhcweb/publications/BEHonline/2003/Desabres.pdf [Accessed September 1, 2005].

# An Invitation To Joy

Stan Freberg has written a musical farce parodying the commercialization of the Advent season, appropriately naming it *Green Chri$tma$*. That is green as in money, with dollar signs in place of the letter "S" in Christmas. In starring roles are two of our old seasonal favorites, Bob Cratchet and Ebenezer Scrooge. You may as well spell Scrooge with a dollar sign, too, because he is typecast as a greedy, unscrupulous Madison Avenue advertising executive who is out to exploit Christmas in every way imaginable.[1]

On the other hand, Bob Cratchet, who understands the real reason for the season, is up against incredible odds. Cratchet is the owner of a small spice company in East Orange, New Jersey. He wants to mail his customers Christmas cards picturing the three Magi bearing gifts to the Christ Child with, of all things, a Bible verse inside.

Scrooge, dreaming of a green Chri$tma$, tells Cratchet that the Magi on the card should be portrayed carrying the spices Cratchet's company is selling instead of their traditional gifts of gold, frankincense, and myrrh. How else can the card promote Cratchet's spices, expand sales, and increase revenues? After all, that is the purpose of Christmas cards, Scrooge believes.

During their meeting, Cratchet endures Scrooge's Musak, hearing several traditional tunes with altered words, such as "Deck The Halls With Advertising." We can only hope that, rather than this "mercantile Messiah," old Scrooge will finally see the light of Christ, as he does at the hand of Charles Dickens.

31

Christmas cards, which once were sent to wish others peace on earth, goodwill, and blessings of the season, are now serving more commercial purposes. I love the story about an apartment building in New York City. It was early in December when all the residents awoke to find a greeting card taped to the outside of their apartment doors. The cards read, "Merry Christmas from the custodial staff."

"Well, isn't that nice," one of the new residents thought to herself. "What a lovely, caring staff we have at our service." Then she promptly forgot all about the card. A week later, she came home from work to find another card taped to her door. This one said, "Merry Christmas from the custodial staff. Second notice."

December is often criticized as a time of overindulgence and excesses, with too much shopping, eating, drinking, and self-gratification. Each person searches for happiness in his or her own way, with many believing that the more things they can accumulate, the happier life will be. Things get old quickly, though. Shopping is enjoyable for some, but today's acquisition is old by tomorrow.

A rabbi once asked a prominent man, "Why are you always hurrying?" He answered, "I'm running after success, fulfillment, and rewards for all my hard work." The rabbi responded, "You assume those blessings are somewhere ahead of you, and if you chase fast enough you may catch them. But what if those blessings are behind you, are looking for you, and the more you run, the harder you make it for them to find you?"[2] If money can buy happiness, it is a short-lived happiness, one that must be continually replenished with more stuff.

God is leading us toward a deeper spirituality where we can find true joy and peace, but isn't it odd that, of all times, we are too busy for God this time of year? We will have much more time for God in January. Spirituality and worship will have to wait for a more convenient time.

In the time of the prophet Zephaniah, the people of Judah have forgotten to make time in their lives for worship. They have become caught up in the cultures of foreign nations and no longer practice a worship or a lifestyle that is pleasing to God. The prophet

Zephaniah proclaims judgment, while at the same time calling for a new moral and religious order, and telling the people to rejoice. The prophet's tools are words, and not ordinary, smooth words that are easy to understand or easy to dismiss. They are sharp, divinely honed two-edged swords. With these words, Zechariah announces God's intentions and challenges the people's complacency. He announces that later their distress will be turned to rejoicing because the oppressor will be overthrown, and a new king is coming to the throne of David.

Zephaniah also underscores the importance of an external expression of faith. Formal worship is a means for increasing awareness of God's presence in all areas of life. External acts of worship must proceed from a strong faith that results in obedience to the law, in righteous living, and in doing justice.

Zephaniah envisions a new day when God will purify the speech of the people so "that all of them may call on the name of the Lord." The purpose of judgment is not destruction, but redemption. Judah and the nations are judged so that God can gather the humble and lowly, those who will call on the name of God and serve with one accord. This is the prophetic hope that accompanies the purpose of salvation (3:9).

There will be a sorrowful time when Jerusalem is captured by the Babylonians. The people will be driven from their homes, cities, and land into a foreign country. They will be deep in sorrow in faraway Babylon. Now, even before the captivity begins, Zephaniah invites God's people to rejoice because their salvation is near. The faith of a few will result in the transformation of many, and rejoicing will certainly follow.

God's people again will celebrate, sing, shout, be glad, and rejoice. God promises to save the lame, change shame into fame, gather the outcasts, and restore the fortunes of the people. But, the hope in God's future requires radical change and reshaping of the people's lives for this foreseen future to become a present reality. There is still time to repent and reform. Repentance will free the people from emotional pain, unfulfilled dreams, broken relationships, and moral failures.

The third Sunday of Advent is traditionally "Rejoicing Sunday," as we remember and give thanks for God's great gifts to us. Imagine Zechariah and the people of God celebrating, and God is there in their very midst. All are singing and dancing in the streets, and God is singing louder than anyone else. There is rejoicing because the people have been forgiven. They were imprisoned in sin, but all is forgiven and their sentence is commuted. God is their salvation. God has come into their midst to save them.

Zephaniah speaks in past, present, and future tenses. His words are fulfilled in the coming of Christ. He also points us to Christ's coming again. Christ is in our midst now, of that we can be assured. There will be a time still to come, when we will have our final homecoming with God. That will be the greatest celebration of all.

With uplifting words for a troubled world, the prophet Zephaniah looks beyond judgment to a day of hope and restoration. He calls for rejoicing in Jerusalem, since it will be once again a city in which God delights, and which delights in God's presence. Zephaniah says, "Sing aloud, O daughter of Zion ... Rejoice and exult with all your heart."

The Apostle Paul echoes Zephaniah's command to rejoice, even while Paul is imprisoned at the hands of the Romans: "Rejoice in the Lord always; again I will say, rejoice!" That is a most unusual mandate coming from a prisoner who may be about to lose his life. Paul tells us that God is nearby. Christ will come again, bringing a peace that passes all understanding. Peace will then spread across the land (Philippians 4:4-7).

Several years ago, a thirteen-year-old Japanese girl named Sadako died of radiation-induced leukemia, often referred to as atomic bomb disease. She was one of many who suffered the after-effects of the bomb dropped on Hiroshima during World War II. During her illness, Sadako was able to entertain herself and raise her spirits by making origami cranes.

There is an old Japanese legend that says cranes live for 1,000 years and that the person who folds 1,000 paper cranes will have any wish granted. With each paper crane she made, Sadako wished that she would recover from the fatal illness. On one paper crane she wrote, "I will write 'peace' on your wings and you will fly all over the world." She was only able to fold 644 cranes before her death. To honor her memory, Sadako's classmates folded 356 more cranes so that she could be buried with 1,000 paper cranes. Later, her friends collected money from children all over Japan to erect a monument to Sadako in the Hiroshima Peace Park. It is a statue of a girl standing with her hand outstretched, and a paper crane flying from her fingertips. Inscribed on the base are these words: "This is our cry, This is our prayer, Peace in the world." People continue to place paper cranes at the base of the statue to recall the tragedy of war and to celebrate humanity's undying hope for peace.[3]

This season is all about peace, a commodity that has always been in short supply in our world. We're not merely talking about the absence of conflict, but rather the calming inner certainty that all is well. This peace is born out of a harmonious relationship between the Creator and the created, and has its foundation in a faithful allegiance to Jesus.

The coming Messiah was believed to be an economic liberator, but all the scrooges in the world cannot accumulate sufficient funds to buy peace and joy. Peace and joy are priceless. This season is all about reconciliation of the spirit, and the peace that Paul preaches. May "the peace of God, which surpasses all understanding, guard your hearts and minds in Christ Jesus," our Lord. Amen.

1. Stan Freberg, *Green Chri$tma$*, available online at http://freberg.8m.com/text/greenchristmas.html [Accessed September 1, 2005].

2. Harold Kushner, *When All You've Ever Wanted Isn't Enough, The Search for a Life that Matters* (New York: Kushner Enterprises, Inc., 1986), p. 146.

3. David Krieger, "Remembering Hiroshima and Nagasaki," *The Blackaby Papers, No. 4*, August 2003, pp. 12-14, available online at http://www.wagingpeace.org/articles/2003/08/00_krieger_blackaby-papers.pdf [Accessed September 1, 2005].

# A Little Town
# Of Great Renown

The name Johann Sebastian Bach has been familiar in church music circles for many years. Bach inscribed all his compositions with the phrase, "To God Alone The Glory." Professor Peter Schickele of the fictitious University of Southern North Dakota discovered an obscure relative, P.D.Q. Bach, known as the most bent twig on the Bach family tree. The name Bach had always been associated with fine music until P.D.Q. appeared on the scene. This fabled genius, P.D.Q. Bach, was referred to as "the worst musician ever to have trod organ pedals," "the most dangerous musician since Nero," and other things even less complimentary.[1]

P.D.Q. composed works that were sure to catapult him into obscurity, not the least of which was "O Little Town Of Hackensack." Phillips Brooks, the nineteenth-century Episcopal priest and bishop who penned the words to "O Little Town Of Bethlehem," could never have imagined the cultural changes that have transpired in our country during the last century. I doubt that Hackensack, or any little town in New Jersey, will ever achieve quite the stardom of Bethlehem, the city of David.

We are all aware of the powers music exercises over the human spirit. It communicates to the soul what no academic study of theology ever can achieve. Music reaches where words cannot, ritualizing the emotions deep inside us for which there are no words. Christmas carols encourage us to worship, to hope, and to expand the horizons of our vision so that we can see the light of truth and dare to live justly in a troubled world.

No matter how often we sing them, the simple words of "O Little Town Of Bethlehem" always transport us to the night on which the Christ Child comes to earth. Through a gentle, quiet tune and pictures painted with words, we enter the time and place when God is born into human history and the Word becomes incarnate.

We have a "greeting card" picture in our minds of how Bethlehem must have looked 2,000 years ago. Bethlehem appears to spring up from the middle of a desert oasis. Quaint domed houses line gently rolling hillsides sprinkled with palm trees. Overhead, a cerulean sky features a bright and shining star. An extraordinary light is streaming from the star, leading some stargazers to travel toward Bethlehem.

Bethlehem, one of the little towns of Judah, is legendary in both story and song. Not many great cities are as well known as the little town of Bethlehem. An insignificant village, it became the birthplace of our Savior. God was indeed at work, and in Bethlehem of all places, not in imperial Rome! As Bishop Will Willimon has observed, "The Word was made flesh in Bethlehem before it ever went to Washington, London, or Paris."[2]

Whenever we think of Bethlehem, we always seem to think "little," possibly because of the carol so named. Our society is programmed to believe that bigger is better, but the best things often come in small packages. Bethlehem has been a center of action throughout history, attesting to the fact that bigger is not necessarily better.

It is here in Bethlehem that Rachel gives birth to Benjamin, the last of Jacob's twelve sons. Later, Naomi, her husband, and their two strong sons leave a famine-stricken Bethlehem to seek sustenance in a foreign land. Years later, she and her beloved daughter-in-law, Ruth, return to Naomi's hometown of Bethlehem, where Ruth gives birth to Obed, King David's grandfather.

The prophet Micah tells of a great ruler who is to come from Bethlehem, King David's hometown. Bethlehem is mentioned several times throughout the life of David. While David is growing up, Bethlehem is dominated by the Philistines and their weapons of iron. Goliath is one giant of a Philistine with an ego to match. David is bringing supplies to his brothers in the service, when he discovers that the Philistine giant is no match for his trusty sling-shot and the power of God.

It is in Bethlehem that the prophet Samuel first anoints David King of Israel. God tells Samuel to quit lamenting the demise of King Saul, who has fallen from grace, and to head for Jesse's house in Bethlehem. Jesse introduces a fine assortment of sons to Samuel, but the youngest son, David, lovingly referred to as the runt of the litter, is away tending the sheep and singing sweet psalms.

Who would have thought David to be the apple of God's eye, and a king of God's own choosing? At Samuel's insistence, Jesse sends for his youngest son. At God's instruction, Samuel anoints and appoints David to become the future king. At that moment, like a rushing wind, the Spirit of God enters David, and at the same time departs from Saul (1 Samuel 16:1-13).

Later, when David is fleeing from the wrath of the maniacal King Saul, who is after his hide, David hides in a cave near Bethlehem. While there, he becomes very thirsty, and requests water from the well by the city gate of Bethlehem. Unfortunately, the town is still under the control of those less-than-neighborly Philistines.

This is not a problem for three of David's hearty men, who break through the Philistine line and draw water from Bethlehem's well for David. Yet, when David is presented with this precious commodity, he realizes his men have risked their very lives in order to get this water. He then pours out the water before God as an act of worship and gratitude for God's goodness to him (2 Samuel 23:13-17).

Two thousand years ago, Bethlehem was situated in a country occupied by foreign troops and administered by Roman officials, who had little interest in the humble folk who lived there. During the century before the birth of Christ, the Roman Empire had gobbled up the ruling Greek Empire. In the Luke's Gospel, the Roman Emperor, Augustus, has ordered a census, requiring Mary and Joseph to travel about 75 miles from Nazareth to Bethlehem. The town is overcrowded; packed with travelers arriving to register for the emperor's census. The little town, literally, is bursting at the seams.

God is at work, even through governmental decrees, preparing for the birth of the Messiah in Bethlehem, the city of David. The people are expecting the Messiah to be a descendant of King David. Matthew's Gospel quotes our scriptural promise from Micah 5:2: "And you, Bethlehem, in the land of Judah, are by no means least among the rulers of Judah; for from you shall come a ruler who is to shepherd my people Israel" (Matthew 2:6). God fulfills promises, using all kinds of people, even emperors.

Bethlehem becomes the center of our universe at this time of year. Bethlehem is where everything comes together, where a child is born and laid in a manger, a child who will grow strong in faith and in obedience to God. He will love and heal, teach and mentor. He will die our death, and in return, give us the greatest of gifts, everlasting life.

Hope in the Messiah is a hope for peace, and the prophet Micah is celebrated for his vision of peace. Micah explains that, "They shall beat their swords into plowshares and their spears into pruning hooks. Nations shall not lift sword against nation, and never again will they train for war" (Micah 4:3). Saint Luke, who records the message of Jesus as Messiah, also records a song about peace that is sung by the angels after the baby Jesus is born. "Glory to God in the highest and peace on earth among those whom he favors" (Luke 2:14).

People who don't know any other songs know the words to Christmas carols. People who are reticent to sing at any other time of year will lift their voices to join in the songs of Christmas. This is music that we know and love, songs we can't wait to sing at this time of year.

The name Bethlehem means "House of Bread." On the night when Jesus was born, the village lives up to its name. The "Bread of Life" comes down from heaven to enter human history in Bethlehem, the "House of Bread" (John 6:35, 51). There had been some big events in the life of Israel: The Exodus, Moses and the Ten Commandments, David anointed king, and the return from exile in Babylon. But none are bigger than the events in the little town of Bethlehem. This is not another in a long series of God's actions in shaping world history. This is God in the first person singular.

Luke tells the story of those who travel the road to Bethlehem on the first Christmas. Some people travel that road under duress. This is certainly true with Mary and Joseph. The trip was required by governmental decree. Some people walk the Bethlehem road today out of a sense of obligation. "Here it is Christmas time, and we really should to go church." That is what Christians do this time of year.

Once the philosopher, Josiah Royce, was sitting in his study at Harvard University talking with a young student. In the course of the conversation, the student asked the professor, "What is your definition of a Christian?" The great philosopher replied, "I do not know how to define a Christian ... But wait," he added, looking out the window, "there goes Phillips Brooks."[3]

What he was saying is that you cannot define Christianity in words. It must be embodied in a life, and Phillips Brooks so lived the life of faith that he had become part of God's plan to establish the reign of love and righteousness. He was an Advent person. Early in his ministry, Phillips Brooks visited the Holy Land and was in Bethlehem on Christmas Day. As a result, Christians throughout the world, who know nothing of his historic ministry in Boston, are blessed by the poetry about the little town of Bethlehem he was moved to write while there.

Our Messiah is firmly rooted in the prophecy of the First Testament, fulfilling all that God requires of the Savior, the Anointed One. The Christ Child gives us roots, a past steeped in tradition, and a place to plant our feet. There is a permanence in the child given to us at Bethlehem. Through this child we become heirs of the long history of God's people.

Roots of yesterday become shoots of tomorrow. As we wait anew for the birth of a baby in Bethlehem, we recall that we are also awaiting the coming again of Christ at the end of time. Through Jesus, we have a future filled with hope, both in this world and for the next. Through this gift, we know that nothing can ever separate us from God's love, not death, political power, not the present, and not the future. The manger is that place where we can lay down the hopes and fears of all the years, knowing they will be borne by *the one* who came for that very purpose.

1. Peter Schickele, "O Little Town of Hackensack" from *Consort of Choral Christmas Carols*, text is available online at www.schickele.com/composition/consortchristmas.htm [Accessed September 1, 2005].

2. William H. Willimon, "First-Year Bishop: Dispatch from Birmingham," *The Christian Century*, Vol. 122, No. 19, September 20, 2005, p. 28.

3. Leonard Griffith, *What Is a Christian?* (Nashville: Abingdon Press, 1962), p. 21.

# The Light Of Christ

Isn't it wonderful to be part of a candlelight Christmas Eve worship service? It's truly breathtaking to see so many people holding candles, preparing to be bearers of Christ's light in the world. One of the special moments of a candlelight service is watching people pass the light through the congregation. One person gives the gift of light to another whose candle is dark and cold.

But, the light is unlike a gift that when given, leaves the giver with less. Instead, after the light is shared, both candles glow with equal brightness. The light multiplies exponentially as it is passed down each row. Just as a single candle sheds light and illuminates an entire room, the life of one person, Jesus Christ, casts light on all the darkness of the world.

We are very much aware of darkness this time of year. Days are short and nights are long and cold. An overcast sky and the nip in the air combine to make it feel darker than it actually is. Living in darkness is difficult and challenging. We may stumble over hazards in our path. We are sometimes fearful of who or what may be lurking in the dark shadows. In darkness we can easily become disoriented and lose our sense of direction.

Have you even noticed how a problem of any kind seems so much worse at 3:00 a.m. than it does at 3:00 p.m.? Darkness seems to hold an ominous power over us. There is a game children play blindfolded. They try to negotiate a path through objects strewn around the floor by listening carefully as others direct them. There are many challenges to living in darkness. But, we can take heart because days are becoming longer now.

If you have ever driven in a snowstorm or through dense fog where visibility is poor, you may have felt much more secure being able to see and follow the taillights of the vehicle in front of you. That vehicle was in essence blazing a trail for you to follow. But, it is possible to follow the wrong lights and get into trouble. Nags Head is a location on the North Carolina Outer Banks where hundreds of ships have run aground. In colonial days, land pirates lured ships by leading horses with lanterns tied to their necks up and down the beach during stormy weather. Merchant captains, trying to find their way in the storm, mistook the bobbing lanterns for the stern lights of ships in a safe harbor. Following those lights, they ran aground in the shallow water, where their ships became pickings for the thieves who plundered them.

Lights point the way and direct our attention to something specific. Many new buildings are surrounded by floodlights and are beautifully illuminated at night. The owner of the building may have spent thousands of dollars on floodlights, but no one ever says, "Look at those magnificent floodlights." Instead, they say, "Look at that magnificent building." The lights call attention to another, not to themselves.

"The book of Genesis begins with darkness covering the face of the deep. The exodus from Egypt begins in the darkness of the Passover. The life of Jesus begins in the darkness of the stable. Advent also begins in darkness: the darkness of this present age."[1]

Long ago, several prophets had given clues that the Messiah would not be just an earthly king, and not an extraordinary human, but truly God. The prophet Isaiah is preaching to prepare us for the arrival of the light. Isaiah is expressing hope and expectation for the one who is to come.

The words of Isaiah remind us again that the light which shines in the darkness is the Christ Child. The light of Emmanuel, God with us, is more brilliant than any light we can imagine. Jesus is the light of God's personal encounter into human history. Isaiah gives the Messiah extraordinary titles such as "Wonderful Counselor, Mighty God ... the Prince of Peace."

On a night back in 1741, composer George Frederick Handel was walking down a dark London street. A series of misfortunes had befallen him, and his mood was every bit as dark as the night. His age had caught up with him, leaving him in poor health, and with failing eyesight. He was partially paralyzed. He had writer's block and was not composing. Consequently, there was no income. He felt depressed and despondent, broken in body and in spirit.

Cold and despairing, he returned to his run down little house. In the lamplight he could barely see the package leaning against his front door. Stooping over and ripping open the package, he discovered the text for a new piece of sacred music, and a note from a friend asking Handel to set the words to music.

Handel took the package inside and lit a lamp to read by. Still disheartened, Handel began to turn clumsily through the pages. Then his weak eyes fell upon a passage he could identify with. It read:

> *He is despised and rejected of men; a man of sorrows, and acquainted with grief ... Surely he hath borne our griefs, and carried our sorrows: yet we did esteem him stricken, smitten of God, and afflicted. But he was wounded for our transgressions, he was bruised for our iniquities: the chastisement of our peace was upon him; and with his stripes we are healed.*
> — Isaiah 53:3-5 (KJV)

Handel understood what the prophet Isaiah was saying. He could identify with the words about Christ. Handel himself felt despised and rejected, a man of sorrows, acquainted with grief. He anxiously read on and found the words, "He trusted on the Lord that he would deliver him ... seeing he delighted in him" (Psalm 22:8). Feeling comforted, Handel continued, seeing these words: "I know that my redeemer liveth" (Job 19:25), and "Hallelujah."

By this time Handel was rejuvenated. His creative juices had once again begun to flow. Magnificent melodies and harmonization flowed freely into his head and then onto his manuscript. He worked nonstop day after day, hardly even stopping to eat or sleep. He was overcome by the power of the scriptures, and afire with unquenchable energy. Handel finished his greatest oratorio, *Messiah*, in only 24 days, and then collapsed into his bed for a lengthy and well-deserved rest.

Handel himself was a new creation after his experience with *Messiah*. A different person emerged from the work on this composition. He had experienced firsthand the light of Christ in his life. Christ was born anew in Handel's heart as Handel experienced the peace that passes understanding. Handel's *Messiah* is an integral part of this season as scripture comes alive through music and the arts.

Thomas Kinkade, hailed as the "Painter of Light," is a committed Christian who gives hope and inspiration through his art: He understands the power of light to transform our world, especially candlelight. He explains that of all the colors of light, the warmest is the color of candlelight. When Kinkade paints light coming from the windows in his Christmas paintings, he tries to capture the color of candlelight. It is warm, welcoming, an amber glowing. Nothing transforms the feeling in a room the way candlelight does.[2]

Once there was a holy spot in the country, and every week, people would meet to enjoy each other's company, to raise their common prayers, and to read scriptures. And in their time of meditation, it seemed as if someone was always inspired to share a thought that more often than not found a spot in some hungry heart.

It was very interesting to watch these people grow in spirit and commitment as the years passed. And it happened all because of the light. You see, this rural spot in the middle of nowhere had no electricity. The only heat was that which was gently drifting from the old pot-bellied stove sitting right in the middle of their "sanctuary," and the only light was that which was shed by the candles.

Everyone in that small fellowship was responsible for bringing their own light. Upon leaving home, each worshiper would remember to check for two things: their Bible and their candle. Arriving, they would set their candles in a candlestick, light them, and sit under their mellow glow. And as so often happens when people come together to worship, each family had their own special spot.

Now it got to be that a person would always know when someone was missing in that quiet gathering. And do you know why? It was because of the light. It seems that as the candles shed their soft glow across the church, the darkness was dispelled, but if someone was absent and their spot remained unlighted, the little room was darkened. Over the years, the folks grew to understand that they were really needed because their presence brought light into the darkened fellowship.

We are living in a world that often seems dark. Long shadows extend across our community, shadows that will loom larger unless we all bring our lights from far and near to dispel the darkness. One small light can pierce the darkness. And Jesus, whose birth we are celebrating, tells us that we are the light of the world. Long ago, "God said, 'Let there be light,' and there was light. And God saw that the light was good" (Genesis 1:3-4). Countless generations later, God spoke again through the prophet Isaiah to say, "The people who walked in darkness have seen a great light" (Isaiah 9:2; Matthew 4:16).

The first time God spoke to light up the world, the second time God's Word came to light up our hearts with the promise of a coming king, a Savior. How important it is to have that light within. When we've got it on the inside, our whole world is a brighter place. Bring your light to church each week. Brighten the corner where you are by worshiping the God who created you and the Christ who saved you.

As we stand at the threshold of the Christ Child's birth, the manger already stands in the shadow of the cross. Jesus died for the sins of the entire world so that all nations might turn from darkness to light. Jesus is the light of the world (John 8:12), and so are we, his people. Just as Isaiah brought the message of God's light and salvation to his dark times, so may you as God's people today, bear witness faithfully to Jesus, the holy child born within your hearts this night.

You are the light-bearers who have answered the call of the gospel and whose task it is to "proclaim the mighty acts of him who called you out of darkness into his marvelous light" (1 Peter 2:9). As we leave here tonight, we become light-bearers to a dark and troubled world. Keep your lights burning brightly so others can follow as you illuminate the path to salvation. May others find Jesus, the light of the world, through you. Go shine.

1. Mary Anna Vidakovich, *Sing to the Lord* (Nashville: Upper Room Books, 1994), p. 15.

2. Thomas Kinkade, *Christ, the Light of the World* (Nashville: Thomas Nelson Publishers, 1999), p. 29.

# The Boy Grows Up

Each of us faces the choice of who and what we will become. Sometimes, we don't really know what we want to be when we grow up until we are forty-something. Our earliest models for making that choice are the people who raise and nurture us. Although we identify with the adults whom we admire most, each of us is unique and intended to become "our own person."

Occasionally there is a family-owned business and we are expected to carry on in that tradition, or to choose the vocation of one of our parents. Heredity and environment influence who we become, but they do not determine it. Ultimately, we must make the choices about how we will live.

Children benefit greatly from contact with other adults, including friends, relatives, and teachers who show love and model appropriate behavior for them. The child who receives the love and care of adults beyond his or her own home is truly blessed. And, blessed are the adults who recognize that it does take a village to raise a child.

Every adult is responsible for nurturing and mentoring the next generation. Corrie ten Boom once remarked that, "God has no grandchildren." Each of us is responsible for bringing children to church and sharing with them that old, old story. Some adults, like teachers and coaches, provide nurturing formally. Others do it informally as trusted friends who never hesitate to stoop to greet a child, just as Jesus would have.

Before the days of widespread formal education, families frequently apprenticed their children to skilled workers who taught them a trade. Today, many companies and churches have intern or mentoring programs modeled on those very relationships. These programs prepare our young people to adapt to their changing world by providing unique experiences and opportunities. They develop our youth morally, intellectually, socially, and spiritually in a way that is consistent with becoming responsible and productive individuals.

Saint Benedict designed a set of rules for ordinary young Christians to live by, not necessarily for those who chose a cloistered lifestyle. The rules are patterned on living out biblical values such as prayer and service to neighbors within our community.

> *Listen carefully, my* [sons and daughters], *to the master's instructions, and attend to them with the ear of your heart. This is the advice from* [one] *who loves you; welcome it, and faithfully put it into practice. When you begin a good work ... pray earnestly to bring it to perfection.*[1]

The words of Saint Benedict could well have echoed the words of the priest, Eli, to his young charge, Samuel. Eli is present in the temple at Shiloh when Samuel's mother, Hannah, is praying for her heart's desire, a son. Her inability to have a child is breaking her heart. She promises God that if she has a son, she will give him back to God to serve in the temple at Shiloh. Hannah and her husband, Elkanah, would journey annually to Shiloh to worship and to offer their sacrifices, since God is present in a special way in worship.

Hannah does give birth to a son and names him Samuel. When he is old enough, she brings her son, an immense personal sacrifice, to live in Shiloh to be mentored by Eli. The sons of Eli had none of their father's honorable qualities, but God provides Eli with a second chance through his relationship with Samuel.

Every year, Hannah makes a little robe for Samuel, complete with a linen ephod, a symbol of the holy office of the priesthood. She and her husband, Elkanah, take the robe to him when they go to Shiloh for their yearly sacrifice. For Hannah, this is also a renewal of her sacrifice of Samuel to God's work.

Centuries later, another family travels from Nazareth to the Jerusalem temple every spring for the Passover Festival, to remember how God had saved his people from slavery in Egypt. Passover lasts seven days and is a great break from school and work. Jesus, Mary, and Joseph join the throng of Passover pilgrims. Jesus is twelve and old enough to participate in the ritual bar mitzvah. At age thirteen, he will be considered a young man.

Leaving Jerusalem, Mary and Joseph assume that Jesus is with friends or other relatives who are traveling companions. When this proves wrong, they return to Jerusalem and discover Jesus discussing scripture with teachers in the temple. While he is giving his parents the fright of their lives, Jesus is amazing these teachers with his knowledge. Jesus must be in his Father's house. Like Hannah, Mary understands that her son's life will be dedicated to God, and to bringing reconciliation and peace.

In contemporary society, both adults and young people are unbelievably busy. Never have there been so many choices when it comes to activities and use of our time. In the 1970s song, "The Cat's In The Cradle," a boy continually requests time with his dad. At various stages of his childhood and teen years, the son asks, "When're you coming home, Dad?" Each time the father replies, "I don't know when, but we'll get together then." When the dad finally has time for his son, the son is busy and has no time for his father. Then, when the father asks his adult son, "When're you coming home, Son?" his son replies, "I don't know when, but we'll get together then."

Unfortunately, this tragedy happens with mothers, too. They are so busy with careers, social, or volunteer activities, or making the home perfect, that they have no quality time for relationships. Deciding what is ultimately important in life can make all the difference in the world.[2]

Melanie was awakened by a phone call in the middle of the night. It could only be bad news at that hour. When the medical examiner identified himself, she expected the worst. She felt her world had ended when he told her that her teenage son had been murdered. The horrifying childhood memories of watching her mother and older sister being shot to death flooded back.

Dragging herself through months of pain and heartache, Melanie fielded calls from the police department about various suspects until the news of the killer's apprehension finally came. Eventually she found it in her heart to forgive the young murderer and wrote a letter telling him that she had forgiven him. He responded to her correspondence, and a relationship was begun. Today, that young man calls her "Mom."[3]

As a part of her grief work and healing process, Melanie began a program called "Mentoring A Touch From Above" for teens who have been in trouble with the law and are at risk. She encourages them to finish their education and teaches them the "people skills" they will need for getting along with others in this world. She gives constant encouragement and hope to young people who may never have experienced a caring adult before. And, there are many more young people today who call Melanie "Mom."

Melanie has mentored many troubled youths, giving them a chance at opportunities they would never have had otherwise. In turn, the young people she has ministered to have helped her in the healing process as she discovers and lives out God's call on her life. She also has the reward of seeing her mentees becoming productive members of society.

On another front, Jason was frequently in trouble, and was ordered to perform ten hours of community service. He ended up at Tree Musketeers, a youth environmental and leadership organization. Jason had sinking grades, feelings of depression, and an attitude a mile wide. Let's just say that the staff at Tree Musketeers endured Jason for his ten hours of work, and breathed a great sigh of relief after he was gone.

It wasn't long before the organization received a call that Jason was being punished with five more volunteer hours. Reluctantly, they took him back as they were launching a community-wide recycling program. Jason was assigned to a sixteen-year-old "volunteer supervisor." They had to give the supervisor double credits for volunteer hours in order to get him to work with Jason.

During those five hours, Jason learned how to explain recycling to residents and worked as a team member with the other kids. Much to everyone's surprise, Jason began to enjoy working at Tree Musketeers. He felt he had something to contribute and announced that he wanted to come back. The executive director said, "Sure, Jason, come back whenever you want to," but doubted he would.

A week later, there was Jason on their doorstep. The staff sat down with him and drew up a plan and schedule for him to volunteer for tree plantings and community education. Amazingly, he stuck to it and proved to be an enthusiastic worker. He adopted a desk as his own and frequently "hung out" in the office.

For the first time in his life, Jason felt like a responsible person who had something to contribute to society. Tree Musketeers was founded by eight-year-olds in 1987, and the organization believes that kids can do anything they set their minds to.

Jason helped care for trees, became a tree-planting supervisor, did data entry, ran errands, responded to children's letters, and even assisted with fundraising. He wrote the cover letter in support of a government grant for $63,000, which Tree Musketeers received. Jason's first speaking engagement was to city council. Everyone cheered as he finished, and the mayor said he expected Jason to hold his office in the future.

Jason was elected president of Tree Musketeers and even flew to Seattle to present a workshop at a national conference. There had been a time in the not-too-distant past when Jason felt he was worthless, and he acted like it. But, what had begun as punishment for a troublemaker turned into 787 hours of volunteer service that changed both a community and a young life.[4]

True mentors are a life-affirming source of guidance and inspiration. They are "artists of encouragement," who help us discover what is unique about our lives and encourage us to pursue it. These spiritual guides are all around us, waiting to give generously of themselves. God has gifted you with talents and abilities you can share with others. Reach out to another individual and change a life. One person at a time over your lifetime will ultimately change the world we live in. God is calling you to make a difference in the new year, right where you are planted.

1. Jerome Theisen, "About the Rule of Saint Benedict," http://www.osb.org/gen/rule.html [Accessed September 1, 2005].

2. Glen Martin, *Beyond the Rat Race* (Nashville: Broadman & Holman, 1995), p. 24.

3. Melanie Washington, "Mentoring A Touch From Above," http://www.matfa.org/about.htm#founder [Accessed September 1, 2005].

4. Jack Canfield, et. al., *Chicken Soup for the Volunteer's Soul: Stories to Celebrate the Spirit of Courage, Caring and Community* (Deerfield Beach, Florida: Health Communications, Inc., 2002), pp. 237-239.

# Walking In The Light

Walking in the dark is difficult, even in the familiarity of your own home. Furniture has a way of rearranging itself in the dark so that you can whack your shins a little easier. Small, sharp toys crawl out from their hiding places to park themselves in your path. Your dog or cat is stretched out on the carpet, sleeping blissfully until your foot makes contact with a tail or a paw.

At one time or another, most of us have been plunged into darkness involuntarily because of a power outage. Suddenly, we are unable to locate what we need or to accomplish any task or activity, other than catching up on our sleep. All our movements seem painstakingly slow as we grapple with the impediment of unwanted darkness. We can't remember where the flashlight is, and have to feel our way through drawer after drawer, searching for candles and matches.

Darkness robs us of our sight and leaves us vulnerable to attack. Our imaginations can run wild amid frightening thoughts of what lurks in the darkness of our surroundings. Then, relief and thankfulness flood over us when power is finally restored.

Children are sometimes afraid of the dark and lose their sense of security when it's time for lights out. Nightlights prove to be a tremendous blessing for our young ones at bedtime. Many of these nightlight bulbs resemble Christmas tree lights. There is something about seeing the glow of Christmas tree lights in a dark room that lifts our hearts and gives us hope. In the same way, there is something about one small nightlight in a dark room that gives a child peaceful rest.

As comforting as they may be, nightlights are not a satisfactory substitute for a 100-watt light bulb on the ceiling. But, nightlights do serve to remind us that there is a brighter light in existence. As Christians, we are called to glow like nightlights in the midst of a dark world, witnessing to the fact that there is a much greater light. Jesus is indeed the light of the world, healing our spiritual blindness, so that others might see the light through us.

The Israelites, as descendants of Abraham, were chosen by God to be a light to the nations. Christ has come into the world as the light no darkness can overcome (John 1:5). The early church intended for all the world to know that Christ was its light, as God's message proclaimed salvation to all people and nations. Christ, the light of the world, is represented by the star which led the Magi to Bethlehem.

Light is an attention-grabber. Just as many flying insects are attracted to light, bright or unusual lights also attract people. Neon lights with their peculiar shapes and colors, strobe lights, and even candlelight, all have a distinct fascination, especially when seen against a backdrop of darkness. And, who hasn't been wowed by a spectacular laser light show? "Lasertainment" is here to stay.

On a clear night in Chile, the stars of the southern hemisphere glisten brightly. The wonder of God's creative power is fully displayed in the innumerable luminaries flung across the limitless reaches of space. On a starry night one January, Chilean missionaries had gathered near the ocean for a retreat. During a break, they all watched as two luminaries moving in opposite directions crossed in the velvet black sky overhead and then disappeared.

Were they a sign from heaven? Were they two comets speeding through the cosmos? No, they were two space satellites, one American and the other Russian, racing around the earth in their orbits. Eerie, beautiful, mysterious, and silent in their journey, they captivated the missionaries who were watching.[1]

The Magi must have experienced that same awe and excitement 2,000 years ago as they observed a most unusual star moving in the western sky. This "star of wonder, star of light, star of wondrous beauty bright" led them westward toward Bethlehem in search of a new king. By contrast, that same star greatly troubled and unnerved King Herod.

In Mark Twain's story of *The Prince and the Pauper*, the crown prince and a peasant trade places. The exchange of roles between the future king and another young man who looks like him is easily accomplished because of our preconceived expectations surrounding royalty. Princes live in palaces, and paupers live in poverty. Princes wear regal attire, while paupers wear peasant apparel. Princes act with assertiveness in the limelight, and paupers move largely unnoticed in the shadows of their everyday tasks. If we fail to look beyond what seems obvious, we may miss out on what is actually taking place.

To find a child who will become king, of course, we look toward a palace. When the Magi arrive in the city of Jerusalem, it is only natural they would go to King Herod. They expect to find this new infant king in the palace, but King Herod knows nothing of the birth. Herod learns from those in the know that God's prophet, Micah, had said the king would come from Bethlehem, so he sends the Magi there.

The star they had seen earlier leads the Magi from the palace in Jerusalem, to the place where the young child is. Without God's leading through scripture and star, they could not have found the king whom they sought. If they had not trusted the revelation given to them, they would have continued to inquire in the wrong place.

The prophet Isaiah offers encouragement to us today with his prophecy of the coming light. Jesus, the light of the world, appears in the black night of our sin and despair, showing us the way out. Indeed, he was, and is the only way out. This light continues to attract all nations, because forgiveness and hope are found in Christ. When we follow this light, we don't move toward our destruction, but instead toward salvation.

Amid the darkness that threatens to engulf the world, among the lost that we encounter every day, God has set perfect light. In the confusion of a million clamoring claims on our hearts, God has set perfect light. In places where people live distressed or desperate lives, God has set perfect light.

Jesus reminds us again, "I am the light of the world. Whoever follows me will never walk in darkness but will have the light of life" (John 8:12). The light breaks into darkness as God's grace comes into the world to offer hope and joy to those trapped in the darkness of sin. The saints of God are assured that "... there will be no more night; they need no light of lamp or sun, for the Lord God will be their light" (Revelation 22:5).

Many churches have placed a vigil candle in their chancels. This light burns 24 hours a day, seven days a week, all year long. In other words, it is an eternal flame. Christ lights our paths to one another, even when our dreams and our very lives seem to plunge into darkness. Broken relationships, illness, and grief from losses are as disorienting to our everyday lives as trying to walk through unfamiliar darkness.

On a quiet, somber night, Sam walked into the darkened church. He found his way down the center aisle easily. Over the years, he had come to know this building well. In countless times and ways, he had heard and shared the Word of God there.

Tonight, Sam came alone. He had lost his job and was devastated. Let go after almost twenty years with the company, he had grown increasingly discouraged in the months that followed. His prospects were few, and he felt he was letting his family down. Angry about his circumstances, he was losing self-confidence.

Sam entered the sanctuary, welcoming its silence and darkness. As much as he enjoyed and appreciated his friends at the church, he had hoped not to meet any of them tonight.

In the darkness, only one small point of light gleamed, the glow of the vigil candle, the eternal light. This light, which hung above the chancel, gave him focus. As he walked forward, comforted by the familiar smell and feel of the room, he lowered the weight of his body and life into a pew near the front. There, he sat and wept. In the comfort of God's house and in the anonymity of darkness, he let himself be honest and hurting before God.

In the darkness, he remembered the Word of God, "I will not leave you comfortless." The candle in the front of the church, with its steady glow, reminded him of the constant light of God's presence that had shone in the lives of faithful believers throughout the centuries. The light shone in the darkness to remind him that God would always be with him. He would be able to go on.[2]

"Arise, shine, for your light has come." Follow God's light to the manger, to the cross, and the empty tomb, to find the one who alone qualifies to be the king of our lives. May your life be a light, a flame that burns so brightly that it also kindles others.

The world is a dark place for so many of God's children. Put your time and talent to work for the good of the community. In doing so, you are helping the world by letting your light shine. There is a great deal of injustice and violence in the world, as well as darkness. Make it your personal mission to light a candle. Any positive action you take adds more light and dispels some of the darkness. The world needs all the illumination it can get, and you, my friends, are the sparks that will light our way to a brighter future.

The Epiphany season is upon us. God's signs and God's Word still beckon us to come to Jesus and to worship him as our king. Walk in the light. Come, you starry-eyed stargazers. Come to the inextinguishable blaze. Once you have seen this star, the memory will not fade. Our surprising God still remakes our impossible into new possibilities, enabling us to "shine like stars in the world" (Philippians 2:15).

---

1. Woodrow Phillips, "The Wise Men Worship Jesus," in *Standard Lesson Commentary* (Cincinnati: The Standard Publishing Company, 1994), p. 148.

2. Augsburg Fortress Weekly Church Bulletin, Second Sunday after Christmas (Minneapolis: Augsburg Fortress, 1991), 9211-C.

# What's In A Name?

"What's in a name? A rose by any other name smells as sweet." Or does it? This well-known line from Shakespeare's *Romeo and Juliet* is true, but only up to a point. A rose named hydrogen sulfide might remind us of that unmistakable rotten-egg odor, causing us to avoid an otherwise lovely flower that emits a delicate fragrance.

The names we are given carry a tremendous influence throughout our lives. The names we are called frequently become synonymous with our identity. A nineteenth-century governor of Texas, James S. "Big Jim" Hogg, named his baby girl Ima.[1] He did not discover the significance of this choice until days later, when he received a copy of her birth certificate, which read "Ima Hogg." I cannot help but wonder if he named his next child "Ura."

Many celebrities have been pressured into changing their original names. In earlier days, their studios laid down an ultimatum: no name change meant no movie contract or no recording contract. Leonard Slye thus became cowboy Roy Rogers, while Betty Joan Perske changed her name to Lauren Bacall. We knew Frances Gumm as Judy Garland. Actor Kirk Douglas was originally Issur Danielvitch Demsky and singer John Denver began life as Henry John Deutschendorf, Jr.

We must even pay careful attention to what the initials of our baby's name spell. No child will be pleased to wear a monogram such as C-O-W, D-U-D, or P-M-S.

People make judgments about us by the names we have been given before they even meet us. Names have become stereotyped and may reveal our approximate age. Although many names are time-honored classics, your name may indicate that you are either a senior citizen or a youth. It may also reveal your nationality, ethnicity, or gender.

Boys are teased for having girls' names, but girls can usually get away with having boys' names. Country singer, Johnny Cash, recorded a song called "A Boy Named Sue," telling all about the trials and tribulations of a guy growing up with a girl's name.

Most twenty-first-century parents know the gender of their baby ahead of time, and usually have a name ready at birth, but customs were very different at the time Jesus was born. Then, boys were named eight days after their birth, and girls, fifteen days after. Of course, the angel Gabriel had already told Mary to give her baby that name above all names, "Jesus." Gabriel also informed Zechariah of the name for his son, a cousin of Jesus, who would be John the Baptist.

Customs changed again after the Christian church was established. Babies often were not named until the time of their baptism. This naming rite became know as christening, after Christ, or being given a Christian name to add to one's family name. Today christening, or naming, is no longer a function of the church. Instead, christening is reserved for the naming of watercraft.

Through baptism, you are connected with Christians around the world, and become part of one big family. God chose you, before the world began, to be a child of God. We find our identity in relationship to God, others, and to the world. Just as we are initiated into clubs and organizations that humans have created, baptism is our initiation into the Christian church. Our faith journey begins as God calls us by name and says, "You are my child. I delight in you."

Our baptismal liturgy includes words spoken over the water that we refer to as "The Flood Prayer" because of its many water images. The flood, the pillars of cloud by day and fire by night, and the promised land are some of the other significant images mentioned. When we hear of Noah, the exodus through the Red Sea, the baptism of Jesus, and other stories mentioned in the flood prayer, we can rejoice in our own baptisms and give thanks for this gracious gift from God.

In the book of Acts, baptism is regarded as important and life changing. Baptism is not seen as an event that takes only a moment, but as the redirecting of an individual's life. The powerful movement of the Spirit revealed in baptism led the young church in many unexpected directions. The unleashing of the Holy Spirit in baptism led to radical changes in both the individual believers and in the early Christian community. Contrary to what some folks believe, the Spirit is still doing so in the church today.

We Americans are a "feel-good society," and tend to weigh our experiences emotionally. When we don't feel warm and fuzzy all over, we believe something is wrong with a relationship, whether it is human or divine. God has given us our intelligence and the ability to reason. We know that God is present with us at all times and in all places, even when we don't "feel" God's presence in the way we would like.

Water can feel warm and soothing, or as freezing cold and discomforting as a polar bear swim in January. Water is an element that cannot be destroyed by normal means. It can only change form, from liquid to solid to gas. It has even been known, on occasion, to cause great destruction, by flood or tsunami. The psalmist reminds us that, "The Lord sits enthroned over the flood; the Lord sits enthroned as king forever" (Psalm 29:10). God is in control, and carries us across the floods of this world.

On the other hand, water seems to be quite gentle and purposeful. It meanders downhill, finding its own way, respecting obstacles in its path until it finds a way around or through them. With one little drop at a time, over millions of years, water can form a huge canyon. Covering most of the earth, water represents both power and serenity. Water heals, cleanses, and nourishes, and is the primary component of our own bodies.

In baptism, God speaks to Jesus with water and with words, "You are my Son, the beloved" (Luke 3:22). The psalmist advises us that, "The voice of the Lord is over the waters ... over mighty waters" (Psalm 29:3). God's voice is "powerful and full of majesty, shaking the wilderness." Jesus belongs to God. Through baptism, Jesus is revealed as human, as one of us. Jesus was born, lived, and died just as any other person. God names Jesus "beloved."

God also names you "beloved." You are God's beloved sons and daughters. Through Christ, God comes in person to tell you face-to-face that God is for you, with you, and concerned personally about you. The prophet Isaiah reminds God's people that God was with them as they passed through the waters of the Red Sea (Isaiah 43:2).

Baptism is tenderly personal, but it is also communal, taking place in a much broader context. You are baptized into a community, the church, into the company of people who care for and about you as well as one another. This is the family of God. Symbolically, you are buried with Jesus in your baptism, and raised to new life with him.

Baptism is a drowning, a putting to death of the old self, and a raising up of a different self to new life. You become a new creation in Christ. However, you do not emerge from the waters of baptism as a mature Christian. You are always in process, growing and maturing in the faith.

Celebrating the baptism of our Lord, we hear God's voice speaking to us. We hear God's voice affirming our essential identity as children of God. God calls you by name, saying, "You are precious in my sight, and honored, and I love you" (Isaiah 43:4). God knows each of you by name. God knows your special gifts, your needs, your hurts, and concerns.

The prophet Isaiah envisioned a healed, transformed world on the horizon. The name Isaiah means, "the Lord gives salvation." Isaiah was born into a world enmeshed in war, injustice, and corruption. God's people living in Judah had been defeated and carried away to the far country of Babylon. They were living as refugees by the waters of Babylon.

Isaiah preserved for God's people a vision of who they were as sons and daughters of God. This vision provides a challenge and hope for those who live in God. Isaiah opened the floodgates for a thirsty world so people could feel the splash of God's grace and forgiveness. God's people were again given hope in a world that had seemed ready to self-destruct.

In her spiritual autobiography, *Holy The Firm*, Annie Dillard is surrounded by waters as she describes her vision of Christ being baptized. The setting is an island in Puget Sound, where several spectators are gathered to watch. Jesus and John are bare to the waist as they enter the water. John immerses Jesus, who then rises from the water with beads of water on his shoulders. They appear to be planets, "A billion beads of water as weighty as worlds, and he lifts them up on his back as he rises."[2] Inside each bead of water, Dillard sees a world, and all the faces of that world.

All time, past, present, and future is contained within the beads of water. All that has been or ever will be is visible in the transparency of the water. There are no words to describe adequately the brilliance of holiness that scene portrays.

The baptism of Jesus signals the beginning of his ministry here on earth. Jesus is set apart as the chosen servant who will bring justice and healing to Israel and to all other peoples of all times. Your baptism is your commissioning to service in the kingdom of God here on earth. You are baptized in the name of the Father, and of the Son, and of the Holy Spirit, into this great adventure of following Christ. Your ministry is to be explicit, visible, and active in the world today. Your ministry is both a blessing and a responsibility.

In our baptism, the holiness of God touches us as God comes to each of us in a special and personal way. God initiates the beginning of a relationship with us, bringing us into God's family. God says to you today, "I have called you by name. You are mine. Child of God, through your baptism, you have been sealed by the Holy Spirit and marked with the cross of Christ forever." Remember your baptism and give thanks. God has "redeemed you and called you by name."

---

1. "Ima Hogg," Famous Texans, http://www.famoustexans.com/imahogg.htm [Accessed September 1, 2005].

2. Annie Dillard, *Holy The Firm* (San Francisco: Harper and Row, 1977), p. 67.

# Called By A New Name

Two or three generations ago, the only women who did not take their husbands' names after marrying were movie stars and a handful of professional women. Today, many women choose to retain their maiden names, so as not to lose identity with their families of origin. Husbands and wives also combine their names. I know one person who refers to these couples as "the hyphenated families."

Some couples even become creative, combining syllables of both surnames in order to form an entirely new name. Children who are adopted, take their new family's last name. Regardless of the reason for acquiring a new name, it usually implies a change in our circumstances or status.

We are also known by the names of what we do to earn a living, and where we belong. Teacher, salesperson, truck driver, coach, nurse, and guitarist are names we respond to, names that identify a particular skill, interest, calling, or talent that is ours.

Some of you may also be called Rotarian or Kiwanian. Others are in Boy and Girl Scouts, on athletic teams or golf leagues, bands or choruses, fraternities or sororities. When you are a leader within an organization, you may be called by yet another name such as chairperson, treasurer, scoutmaster, quarterback, pitcher, or concertmaster.

All the clubs and organizations we belong to were established by people to carry out worthy goals. But unlike those organizations, the church, this community of faith that we are a part of, was not instituted by human beings. It was created by the Holy Spirit to guide us in serving God's purpose here on earth.

The disciples were first called by the name "Christian" at Antioch by those who did not believe in the resurrected Christ (Acts 11:26). It began as a somewhat derogatory name for this new-fangled religion that was to sweep much of the known world.

Followers of Christ in the early church referred to one another by more endearing descriptive names such as brethren, faithful, elect, saints, or believers. Today, Christians identify themselves by many names, including United Methodist, Presbyterian, Baptist, Lutheran, Pentecostal, or Roman Catholic.

As Moses answered his call to ministry, he had a particular interest in discussing God's own name with God. In the ancient world of Israel, to know someone's name was to know something about the center or deepest part of that person. Moses wanted to know who God was at the most intimate level.

We are synonymous with our names, in the sense that they identify who we are. People have been known to change their names precisely because they want the new beginning they hope a new name will bring. To change your own name is one thing; but having your name changed by God is quite remarkable.

God initiated name changes for several of the important forebears of our faith. Abram and Sarai become Abraham and Sarah. Then Jacob becomes Israel. Saul takes the name Paul, and Simon becomes Peter.

God promises that Abraham and Sarah will become the parents of many nations, and from them even kings will descend (Genesis 17:4-6). Their descendants are to be as numerous as the stars in the sky or the grains of sand along the seashore (Genesis 22:17). The name Abraham means "ancestor of a multitude," and Sarah means "princess," every girl's dream, since Sarah is to be the fore-mother of royalty. Sarah is the only woman in the Bible to have her name changed by God, a significant fact in itself that a new day is dawning.

Abraham and Sarah's grandson, Jacob, becomes "Israel," the embodiment of a nation and benevolent father of twelve tribes.

Jesus' disciple known as Simon becomes Peter, the "rock," destined to represent the solid foundation of Christian teachings. By changing their names, God is calling our attention to these individuals whom God has chosen to accomplish specific tasks and has blessed in the process.

In the Greek language, the name Paul means "small." Paul exchanged the name of Saul, the first Hebrew king, a name associated with power, to a less important Gentile name. Paul then became an evangelist to the Gentiles with a more appropriate name for his calling, a name the Greeks could easily identify with.

Mary George is named after her mother and her grandfather. She would have greatly preferred to be named Claudia, after her father, Claude. For a short while in elementary school, she convinced her close friends to call her Claudia. She was elated at the idea of being called by a new name, one of her own choosing. She even thought she looked like a "Claudia," not a "Mary George."

Claudia felt like a different person with her "new" name. It was the easiest extreme makeover imaginable. Almost overnight, she seemed to gain self-confidence and poise. Her own self-image was transformed into what she hoped to become.

Then Claudia's mother caught wind of the name change, and phoned the parents of Claudia's friends, as well as her teacher at school, instructing them to call her Mary George. Her Cinderella stint was over, and she felt like a charmaid in rags once again.

A clergy couple, pastors Mark and Johanna, were raising three teenage sons they had named Matthew, Mark, and Luke. Then, oops, they found themselves parents again of a baby daughter. The name they chose for her was Heaven, to be a daily reminder of a glorious eternal paradise. Once Heaven was well into her terrible twos, Mark remarked to his wife, "You know Johanna, I think we missed the mark with Heaven's name. It should have been Helen."

Faithful people are called upon by God to change. It has been so throughout the biblical story. From the calling of Abraham and Sarah to the conversion of Saint Paul, faithful people have had to change. And not just changed on the surface, either. In the Bible, a change of name is deeply significant. It alerts us to a radical transformation, a new identity, a change of course that is unalterable.

Almost 600 years before the birth of Christ, Babylonians defeated God's chosen people in an unholy war. The Babylonian army toppled the walls of Jerusalem and desecrated the temple. They then deported many of the Hebrew people to Babylon. The homeland, the promised land, was left desolate and forsaken.

The prophet Isaiah speaks words of hope and encouragement to the Hebrews living in Babylon. As these exiles return from Babylon, Isaiah tells the people that God will be calling Jerusalem by a new name. A new day is dawning. The names Forsaken and Desolate will no longer be valid. Jerusalem will be rebuilt in all her former glory. A celebration is in the air. The people will instead be called by new names.

Faithful people will not only have to change — we shall have to change and be changed at the very heart of who we are. And for faithful people, that change does not happen all at once. Faithful people will be called on to change over and over.

In Annie Proulx's Pulitzer Prize-winning novel, *The Shipping News*, the central character is named Quoyle. Although it is spelled with a Q-U, it is pronounced the same as a coil of rope. The author defines "quoyle" as a coil of rope, a spiral coil of only one layer that is made on a ship's deck and can be walked on. Quoyle is decidedly walked all over, as well as called by a variety of unflattering names.

Born in Brooklyn and raised in a shuffle of dreary upstate towns, Quoyle is called "failure" by his abusive father: Failure in swimming, failure in ambition, failure in sitting up straight, failure in speaking clearly, failure at everything. In adulthood, he is called distributor of vending machines, fired, car wash attendant, fired, all-night clerk in convenience store, fired, newspaper reporter, fired.

Partridge, a Christ-figure in the novel, meets the bungling Quoyle in a laundromat and makes small talk. As Quoyle frets about ink stains in his clothing, Partridge tells him how to remove the stains, and then extends to Quoyle an invitation for dinner in his home. He then suggests that Quoyle apply for a position on the newspaper staff where he himself is employed.

Quoyle suffers through the suicide of his parents, his philandering wife who sells their little girls and then dies in a fiery car crash, and losing his job once again. He, Aunt Agnis, and his daughters, move to Newfoundland, their ancestral home, and Partridge again intervenes to help him land a job at a newspaper. Over time, Quoyle's potential emerges as he comes to terms with his abusive father, his bodily self-image, grief, and loneliness. He is transformed through relationships that extol his value as a person. Children, family relationships, and a successful career bring a new dignity and new names to Quoyle's life. His new names include beloved husband, dad, nephew, faithful friend, and managing editor.

What is your name? Now, I'm not talking about Anna, or Elizabeth, or James. I don't mean the name your friends address you by. What would you name yourself? What is your self-image? *(pause)* God has already chosen a name for you. God calls you Beloved. God calls you My Own. God calls you Special.

# Home At Last

One of the more colorful eras of our country's past is the old Wild West. We can visualize cowboys chasing stagecoaches over rough, barren terrain, and sheriffs swaggering down dusty main streets. Towns sprang up virtually overnight around regions rich in natural resources such as lumber, borax, silver, and especially gold, the glitter that inflamed a continent.

These thriving little communities "out west" revolved around a general store, blacksmith shop, livery stable, prospectors' office, saloon, jail, sawmill, and a doctor's office. There was even the occasional white clapboard church, complete with adjoining cemetery. Sometimes these small settlements on the open range vanished as quickly as they had burst upon the scene, leaving a ghost town full of abandoned buildings where once there had been a community of vibrant commercial enterprises.

Jerusalem may have resembled a ghost town of sorts to the Hebrew people upon their return from being held captive in Babylon. More than 500 years before the birth of Christ, Babylonians had conquered Jerusalem and carried the more prosperous, better-educated residents of the region back to Babylon with them.

Only a small number of peasants had remained in the Holy City to hold down the fort. Ancient cities surrounded by their protective walls, usually several feet thick, were very much like forts. The walls, complete with massive gates and watchtowers, inspired feelings of security.

After enduring more than a fifty-year absence as captives at the hands of the Babylonians, the Hebrew people found their old home place to be a sight for sore eyes. The Holy City had become dilapidated, with crumbling walls, and streets full of potholes. The narrow streets, which had once held bustling market traffic and international trade, were now strewn with rubble.

Yet, it was home, the land God had given to their ancestors. Most of the returning exiles were poor and had few resources for rebuilding their land. But, the people of God made some important accomplishments during their homecoming time.

One immediate need in Jerusalem was to rebuild the city walls. Without the advantage of modern power tools, the building team accomplished most of the work in 52 days. In spite of opposition from Israel's enemies, they were successful in rebuilding the wall around Jerusalem. Thus, the rebuilding and restoration of Israel had begun.

Nehemiah is one of the Hebrews who had actually prospered while residing in Babylon. As personal valet to the king, he had become a leader who was respected by both his own people and those in powerful positions in Babylon.

Nehemiah is a man of prayer, and a man of action, devoted to God as well as to his people and their native land. While living in Babylon, he had received disheartening news from the remnant of Hebrew people left behind in the promised land. With most of the leading citizens in exile in a foreign country, the city had fallen upon hard times. Can you imagine a city without its business leaders, teachers, artists, musicians, engineers, computer professionals, health-care professionals, and lawyers? Jerusalem had found itself in a similar predicament.

With the blessings of the Babylonian government, Nehemiah had organized the building team to travel back to their beloved Jerusalem on a mission trip. The Hebrew people journeyed 500 miles, returning to the land God had promised their ancestors. Travel was largely on foot, since the camels and donkeys were needed to transport precious supplies.

Nehemiah also recognizes the need for spiritual reform, and makes plans for a city-wide revival. Ezra, the preacher for the revival, happens to be a former resident of the area, who also traveled from Babylon back to Jerusalem. Ezra gathers the people on the plaza by the Water Gate, which now is securely embedded in their newly refurbished city wall.

The Water Gate is not restricted to "men only" like other gates, so women and children can also participate in this revival. It is a most appropriate location to receive the living water of God's Word.

As the revival begins, Ezra rolls out the scroll of Moses and begins to remind the people who they are as members of the family of God. He advises this congregation that the Law of Moses is not a burden, but a gift, one they can receive with gratitude.

Long ago, Moses had met with God on Mount Sinai. God gave Moses laws, instructions, and guidance to pass on to the people of Israel. Carrying on the ministry of Moses, Ezra reads scripture from early morning until midday, about six hours. During this time, the people, so hungry for God's Word, listen intently. The Word of God is explained in light of their present circumstances, so they will be able to apply it to their daily lives.

They are reminded that their covenant with God involves promises and responsibilities on both sides. God has chosen to enter into relationship with them. They are moved to tears and begin to reclaim their understanding of themselves as the people of God.

The reading of God's Word inspires repentance, praise, thanksgiving, and action. Once again the people are becoming a "people of the book," or rather, a "people of the scroll." They believe that God has provided all they need through God's Holy Word in the law, the prophets, and the writings of the First Testament. The community of returnees is reorganized around the requirements of the law. God's Word is able to change hearts and shape behavior today, just as it did in Nehemiah's time.

The law shows us how God's people are supposed to act and how we are to relate to one another. According to the prophet Jeremiah, people will know in their hearts right from wrong and want to keep the law. A Savior is coming who will atone for all our sins.

The psalmist declares, "The law of the Lord is perfect, reviving the soul, and giving wisdom to the simple. It is more valuable than gold and sweeter than honey" (Psalm 19:7, 10). Martin Luther reminds us that the law is also full of God's grace. "The law says,

'Do this,' and it is never done. Grace says, 'believe in this' and everything is already done."[1]

Before sending his disciples out, Jesus gathers them to give them instructions. He advises them to be "wise as serpents and innocent as doves" (Matthew 10:16). Nehemiah would have understood this advice of Jesus. He has already employed this strategy with those who are trying to undermine his work on the wall. Nehemiah shows us how to put Jesus' words into actions.

Our reading and study of scripture instructs us in virtuous living, but reading is not enough. We read to learn God's will, and to be equipped for God's work in our world. Then we are to respond by serving others and by carrying out God's purpose here on earth.

Just as the Hebrew people were carried away to Babylon so many years ago, Africans were captured and torn from their homeland, only to be carried thousands of miles away to the United States and enslaved. Removed from their families, their faith practices, and their way of life, Africans were forced to learn the English language and adapt to unfamiliar customs.

Freedom to choose was a thing of the past, and injustices surfaced at every bend in the road. The rights to life, liberty, and the pursuit of happiness were only a pipe dream. Africans longed for their homeland, or their heavenly home. An uncivil war granted an illusive freedom, while most African Americans were still held in the captivity of segregation.

Prophetic voices rose once again in protest. Martin Luther King, Jr., and Desmond Tutu represent contemporary prophetic voices, like those of Nehemiah and Ezra. King proclaimed God's Word and worked for justice in the southern United States during the 1950s. As an African-American pastor serving congregations in Georgia and Alabama, King could not ignore the injustices he witnessed in civil and human rights.

The Hebrews, exiled to Babylon, had dreamed of a day when they could return to their homeland. Similarly, King envisioned a new world order where people of all colors and religions could learn how to live together, treating each other as brothers and sisters. He had a dream that people would put an end to hatred, injustice, and violence, and a new spirit of kindness, sharing, and unity would spread across our land. He believed that his dream could become a reality if only we would commit to forgiveness, justice, and love for one another.

King shared the dream of the prophet Isaiah (40:3-5), also proclaimed by John the Baptist (Luke 3:4-6) that

> *... one day every valley shall be exalted, and every hill and mountain shall be made low, the rough places will be made plain and the crooked places will be made straight and the glory of the Lord shall be revealed and all flesh shall see it together.*[2]

Archbishop Desmond Tutu is a South African clergyman and activist who rose to worldwide fame in the 1980s through his opposition to Apartheid, a term for legally sanctioned segregation. Apartheid enables a white minority to rule and oppress the black population.

Echoing King's words, Tutu writes that God also has a dream where God might speak these very words to us:

> *I have a dream of a world whose ugliness, squalor, and poverty, its war and hostility, alienation and disharmony are changed into ... joy, and peace, where there will be justice, compassion, and love. I have a dream, that My children will know they are members of one family, My family.*[3]

The voices of King and Tutu met with resistance, and they themselves became targets of anger and abuse as they called society to accountability, speaking on behalf of the poor and disadvantaged. They were not "appointed" by God to be prophets as such, but were guided by God's Word to strive against great odds, like Nehemiah, to bring about justice and peace in our world.

Persia had become the world's new superpower during the Babylonian captivity of God's people. King Cyrus the Great of Persia conquered Babylon and released Nehemiah and the captives to return to Jerusalem and their promised land. Cyrus, a benevolent ruler with a keen sense of justice, authored history's first declaration of human rights.[4]

The prophetic message for all times is one of justice and advocacy for the powerless, and accountability for the powerful. As people of faith, we are called to shine a light on economic and social injustice. We are called to stand up for the needs of the poor and marginalized in this country and around the world.

Our faith calls us to shine light on unprecedented levels of women and children living in poverty, workers without insurance, unemployment of African-American men and other minorities, and global spread of HIV/AIDS. Our faith calls us to shine a light on the inequality of civil rights for all people, declining wages, and the rise of the working poor.

As disciples of Christ, you are today's prophets. Prophetic justice means speaking truth to those in power, as the biblical prophets spoke truth to the kings of Israel. Speaking God's Word rebuilds and plants newness of life where once there was only rubble. Prophetic justice demands public policies that meet a rigorous standard of fairness and truth, providing liberty and justice for all of God's children.

As a nation blessed with extraordinary resources and wealth, we are called to remember those who have been left behind in this progress. Scripture opens our eyes to the pain of our sisters and brothers who are poor, unemployed, underemployed, homeless, hungry, or living on the edge.

Biblical prophets worked unabashedly to change the conditions of the world in which they lived. We are heirs of those prophets, who challenge us today to follow in their tradition to make a difference in our world.

---

1. Martin, Luther, "The Heidelburg Disputation," May, 1518, online at http://www.augustana.edu/religion/lutherproject/HEIDELBU/Heidelbergdisputation.htm [Accessed September 1, 2005].

2. Martin L. King, Jr., "I Have a Dream," *Afro-American Voices*, online at http://www.toptags.com/aama/voices/speeches/speech1.htm [Accessed September 1, 2005].

3. Desmond Tutu, *God Has a Dream: A Vision of Hope for Our Time* (New York: Doubleday, 2004), pp. 18-19.

4. David Ussishkin, "Big City, Few People: Jerusalem in the Persian Period," *Biblical Archaeology Review*, July/August 2005, 31:4, p. 29.

# Risky Business

Su Xueling (pronounced ZOO-ling) is a different breed of entrepreneur, delivering instant noodles on her bicycle to satisfy fast-food appetites in central China. She wanted to use her business acumen to spread the gospel message in a land where religion has been controlled or suppressed by the government for decades.

Ms. Su's father is a communist revolution veteran, and religion has always been considered a leading threat to Communist rule. A Christian revival of sorts had already begun to sweep through China's peasantry when Ms. Su's life hit rock bottom.

Until she was thirty something, Su had never even heard of Jesus. Her husband, after months of suffering, died of brain cancer, leaving her with young sons to raise and astronomical medical bills to pay. She had sought peace of mind through several different avenues, when a nurse who had cared for her husband suggested that she explore Christianity.

While walking in the snow one day, she "heard a voice" calling her to church, where she experienced a conversion. She began attending the state-run Protestant church in her hometown.

Her newfound faith gave her great solace, in addition to enough self-confidence to step outside the box in one of the world's fastest emerging economies. She renamed her product "Gospel Noodles," and fellow Christians began purchasing her noodles to the extent that she needed a production line for noodles and six vans to deliver them.

Ms. Su wanted to do something more for God, so she decided to invest her profits in a seminary to train leaders for spreading

Christianity across China. This bold undertaking set Ms. Su on a collision course with Chinese government officials.[1] There is nothing unusual about using private funds for religious purposes here in the United States, but it is risky business in China.

Chinese officials actually appreciate the contributions, financial and otherwise, that Christians have made to their communities, but they still eye Christians as a potential threat to government. They allowed the seminary to operate for four years before shutting it down in 2004. After its closing, students and faculty alike scattered throughout the country evangelizing.

On the back of Ms. Su's business card was printed, "Turn China into an aircraft carrier for spreading the gospel." God often chooses people to do God's work that others consider unlikely candidates. Throughout scripture, God selects the young, the weak, outcasts, the poor, single parents, and the sinful to carry out special tasks.

Scripture tells us that God chose and consecrated Jeremiah for ministry even before his birth. When God approaches Jeremiah as a young teenager, he thinks God had to be mistaken. "Me a prophet, God? Why, you surely must be joking. I can't do that. I'm not ready for something like that. I'll think about it for a few years, and you come back when I'm older."

Jeremiah wondered how anyone as young and inexperienced as he could be expected to influence powerful adult leaders. It seems that only a handful of people know what their life's calling is at an early age. Others are middle-aged before they discover what they want to be when they grow up.

Jeremiah was a P.K., a preacher's kid. He had been born into a priestly family, so there would have been a set of expectations awaiting him regardless of God's intervention. In today's more upwardly mobile circles, I hear that the children of clergy are referred to, not as P.K.s, but as T.O.s — theological offspring.

However Jeremiah may have thought of himself, he still felt very much like a fish out of water. He learned quickly, though, that God does not call the equipped. Instead, God equips the called. God promises to be present and to supply Jeremiah with the words that will accomplish God's purpose.

The task before Jeremiah is frightful. As a youth, Jeremiah is charged to foretell the devastation of Israel, as well as to preach hope for a new way of life. His own words are to be as powerful and effective as fire, or as a pounding hammer. While his message will separate the prophet from family and friends, God will never leave him alone. In God's service, Jeremiah can be assured of God's continuing presence.

Jeremiah is not alone in his reticence to proclaim the Word of God. Many folks are terrified of public speaking. Surveys say that most people, if they have a choice between public speaking and death, will choose death. Janet was a card-carrying member of the latter group. During her college years, she somehow ended up with the assignment of giving devotions for her sorority. Never in a million years would she have volunteered for this.

Janet was so terrified, even among her peers, that when the time came for her to present her devotional, she passed out. Her sorority sisters thought she was on a starvation diet like some of them, and that was the cause of her fainting. Janet just let them think that, too. She felt that starvation was a much more respectable excuse than simply being scared to death.

Janet knew she was a person who deserved to be voted "most likely *not* to succeed" in the area of public speaking. But when God calls, God also equips us with the skills we need in order to answer that call. Today Janet is a successful pastor who gets up in front of her congregation every Sunday and preaches without notes.

God has brought Jeremiah and each of us safely through birth, and rebirth. Our psalmist declares, "I depend on you, and I have trusted you since I was young. I have relied on you from the day I was born. You brought me safely through birth, and I always praise you" (Psalm 71:5-6).

Jennifer was being ordained into pastoral ministry when she told her congregation that she was *in utero* a quarter century earlier when her mother was ordained. Therefore, she considered herself to be "preordained," just like Jeremiah. Each of us is called to ministry and "ordained" for that ministry by virtue of our baptisms.

Jeremiah is called to be a prophet against his will, given a message he does not want to deliver, and is sent to a people who are not

83

going to take his advice seriously. He will be punished and persecuted, risky business indeed. In spite of the odds, he becomes a courageous and passionate proclaimer of God's message.

At the age of eighteen, Tom was shocked when Miss Lucy, the Sunday school superintendent, asked him to become a teacher, and horrified when she told him which class she had in mind for him. The fourteen-year-old boys! Tom knew all about that class. After all, he had been one of its ringleaders four short years ago.

No teacher had ever stayed with that class more than a month, and most didn't last that long. He told Miss Lucy, "No," several times, but she was persistent. Finally, Tom gave in, becoming a Sunday school teacher against his will and against his better judgment.

Tom began the task with more stamina than wisdom. During the first class, he literally picked up a defiant student and sat him in a chair so forcefully that the chair shattered into a pile on the floor. The boys laughed uproariously. That chair had been broken previously, and pieced back together. The boys had planned to offer that very seat to their new teacher.

When the joke backfired, even Tom joined in the laughter. The boys accepted him immediately, and the class came under control for the first time in years.

Erik Weihenmayer (pronounced VI-en-mai-er) was about Jeremiah's age when he also found himself facing insurmountable odds. Erik was born with an eye disease that gradually unraveled his retinas, resulting in total blindness by the time he was thirteen. His mother died in an automobile accident around the same time.[2]

After a brief pity party, Erik was determined to rise above his disability, and to dream big. He struggled to overcome the limits visual impairment placed on him and "see" the world with different senses. His mother had always prayed for him, and his father encouraged him to set sky-high goals, striving for mountaintops.

Through perseverance and hard work, Erik became a school teacher, acrobatic skydiver, skier, marathon runner, bicyclist, ice climber, rock climber, and wrestler. Even more amazing, he was the first blind person to reach the summit of Mount Everest, the world's highest mountain. At an altitude of 13,000 feet on Mount Kilimanjaro, he married his childhood sweetheart, Ellie.

Young people such as Jeremiah and Erik are a powerful inspiration to those who are older. Jeremiah delivers God's message to a people who had not kept covenant faith with God. God wants his people to repent, to turn from their evildoing, and return to the ways of the covenant. Jeremiah has a message of doom, which is followed by hope. The Hebrew people will be defeated and carried away to Babylon, but a remnant will return to rebuild the promised land, with God's help.

The prophet Jeremiah was called to address an audience that thought of itself as religious, even though it had failed to apply its faith to issues of justice and honorable living. Jeremiah noted that the leaders and people had placed more trust in gaining prosperity than in seeking justice in their land. He is concerned with helping them replace their old values and taking on the new standards that a godly life demands.

Even in the midst of disaster and defeat, Jeremiah speaks a word of promise to the people. Their troubles will end, and God will make a new covenant with them. The law will no longer be an external set of rules on tablets or scrolls, but an internal set of values and directives. The people will know in their hearts what is right, and want to be obedient. The coming of the promised Messiah will bring about still another sweeping change in the rules.

Being chosen by God is an awesome responsibility. In *The Lord of the Rings*, Frodo asks Gandalf, "Why was *I* chosen?" Gandalf replies, "Such questions cannot be answered. You may be sure that it was not for any merit that others do not possess. But you have been chosen, and you must therefore use such strength and heart and wits as you have."[3]

God created you and walks with you from birth to death, reminding you that, "I was there to hear your borning cry." God has prepared a destiny for each of us. We may feel overwhelmed and inadequate, just as Jeremiah did. We are chosen and called to carry out God's mission and ministry here in this place at this particular time.

Making and marketing noodles is certainly an unusual form of ministry, but God can use your God-given talents and abilities in marvelous and remarkable ways. When you step out in faith in response to God's call, God will direct your steps, no matter how difficult the path we are to follow.

---

1. Charles Hutzler, "Mixing Religion and Noodles Lands Ms. Su in Hot Water," *The Wall Street Journal*, 245:107, June 2, 2005, A1.

2. Erik Weihenmayer, *Touch the Top of the World: A Blind Man's Journey to Climb Farther than the Eye Can See* (New York: Dutton, 2001), p. 72.

3. J.R.R. Tolkien, *The Lord of the Rings* (New York: Houghton Mifflin Company, 1994), p. 60.

# Who Will Go?

Ken had not realized there was a shoplifter in the supermarket. He had been standing in the checkout line, "blissfully unaware" of any suspicious activity going on nearby. That all changed dramatically as a security guard, "300 pounds of corpulent fury, came barreling like a cannonball out of the security surveillance room" and down the next aisle.

That human behemoth of a security guard swooped down on the culprit, grabbed him by the belt at the small of his back, and lifted him off the floor. With his prey in tow, he vanished beyond the pickled okra, back into the secret recesses of the doors marked "Employees Only."

What security force would not be delighted to have such a huge embodiment of dedicated loss control on its staff? Later as he was reliving that disturbing scene, Ken thought to himself, "Shoplifting is a serious crime, but that security guard is a man uniquely suited to his calling."[1]

We are all aware that a call does not always come at a convenient time in our lives. Think about those annoying sales calls. Three things give away telephone solicitors. First, they call during a meal, or at some other equally inconvenient time. Second, if your name isn't Smith or Jones, they will probably mispronounce it. Third, they don't understand phrases such as, "No, thank you," or "I gave at the office." They are persistent, and have a prepared counterattack to any excuse we offer for not buying their product.

The national "Do Not Call" Registry has helped that situation somewhat. Unfortunately, people also place God's name on their "do not call" list and block God's address from their email in-box. But, unlike the telephone solicitors and spammers, God knows our name and acknowledges our right to say, "No." God has our best interests at heart instead of someone else's bank account.

Just as God called the prophet Isaiah, God also calls us and can be very persistent. We may try explaining to God that this is not a convenient time for a call. We offer all manner of excuses to God, too. "But God, I like my current job." "I have young children still at home." "I can't afford it." "I simply cannot do *that thing*." "I don't have the right training, background, experience, education...." The excuses go on and on.

God has a special job for each one of you. Fringe benefits include on-the-job training, impressive growth opportunities, and an extravagant retirement in a unique paradise. Experience is not required, but you will find all prior experiences to be helpful.

There are no age requirements, since you are never too young and never too old. Having physical impairments is no obstacle whatsoever. And, the Son of the top boss is in charge of job training and human relations. He will help you attain the skills and abilities you need to accomplish what you are called to do.

Although your call will probably not be recorded the way Isaiah's is, being chosen by God is an awesome responsibility. Some 700 years before the birth of Christ, Isaiah is serving as a court priest, a position comparable to today's Senate chaplain. Isaiah's call comes in temple splendor, preceded by a six-winged rustling in the air.

Isaiah feels a strange numbness in his lips as he watches the seraph descend with a live coal in its hand. Isaiah's lips are unclean because he, like the rest of his people, has been guilty of deception.

God wants Isaiah to speak only the truth of God's own word. The live coal is like the fragment of a meteor, and Isaiah knows at once that his lips are to be purified by fire. His impurities of speech will be burned away by the seraph who has two wings over the eyes, two over the feet, and two with which to fly. Even the seraph is blinded and rendered impotent by God's holy radiance.

Isaiah, who would be the prophet and servant of the most high, bends his mouth upward as though a lover awaiting a kiss and closes his eyes. His lips burn with cosmic, creative pain, and then the coal is taken from his charred lips. The seraph places the dying ember in Isaiah's hands and it becomes an ordinary coal.

The seraph returns to the air and the six-winged rustle, like a gentle breeze through an oak tree, disappears. Isaiah has not yet proclaimed the Word of the Lord. Then, from his black lips and tongue, he begins to speak the words of a poet — holy, holy, holy words. Smelling the burning flesh of his own face, he goes to his people to speak.[2]

More often than not, prophets call us to accountability through a message we would just as soon not hear. No prophet has ever never been known to win a popularity contest.

The call of Isaiah excites us because it is stimulating to see someone so dramatically caught up in the purposes of God. God calls all of us to be ministers. It is indeed an honor and a privilege to be called by God and to serve God.

The ones you call "Reverend" are actually those who give order to our common ministries. An individual's suitability and competence cannot always be measured, even through testing and interviews. The disciples Jesus chose would be unlikely candidates for ministry in today's world, just as they were in their own.

In the matter of seeking our calling, the "destination" is not always clear as we begin our journey. Our calling is, by definition, an expression of our spirituality, and occurs in the context of living out our faith. Ways of fulfilling our calling are as varied as the individuals who are called.[3]

Today, most people don't think of their work as a Christian vocation. They refer to it as their "profession," their "career," or simply their "job." For some, their work is a means of making a living, putting food on the table, and a roof over their heads. You do not have to be employed by a church in order to serve God in this world. God expects you to be of service in whatever vocation you choose to follow. Your work, whatever that may be, is also caught up within God's work.

In the midst of a dejected and lonely existence, Helen felt the call of God on her life. Helen had suffered from depression and alcoholism for years, and was finally institutionalized for several months. After being discharged, she was sober, but also frightened and lonely. She sat alone in her mobile home in despair, without work or friends, with nowhere to go and nothing to do. She feared that it would only be a matter of time before she would be worse off than before.

With nowhere else to turn, Helen began to pray. Hands in her pockets, she felt her car keys and pulled them out. In that moment she knew where God was leading her. "I can drive a taxi!" she exclaimed. Helen organized a taxi service in the little town where no public transportation was available.

Many people, especially the elderly, had no way of getting around. Her taxi service developed into a fleet of old, but reliable, cars driven by people much like Helen. The taxis would pick up prescriptions at the pharmacy and deliver them, take people to senior citizens' activities and shopping, enabling many to get out who could only sit at home before.

Helen's story reminds us that God is still speaking to us today, as God spoke to Isaiah in the temple. In such holy moments, ordinary people hear their names called, and their lives are given purpose and direction.

God doesn't tell us "the rest of the story" to begin with. That is where faith comes in. God tells us to walk by faith and not by sight. If we could see the entire picture, faith would be unnecessary. We don't know what may happen next year, or even next week. In all likelihood, we will not see a burning bush or even a six-winged seraph.

We all have a calling to which God has summoned us. God uniquely equips each of us with gifts and graces for the special calling that is ours. This is how we actively fulfill God's plan for our lives as we work among God's human family members.

At a young age, Rick Curry felt called to be a Jesuit priest. As he pursued holy orders, he was told that the priesthood was not open to him. The reason? He had been born without a right hand and forearm, a handicapping condition that would render him incapable of elevating and breaking the communion bread during mass. The Jesuits did welcome him as a monk, however.

While studying for his Ph.D. at New York University, Brother Curry was surprised to learn that several of his classmates were supplementing their incomes by acting in television commercials. This was in the old days when you did not have to be a famous superstar to act in commercials. An "average Joe or Jane" could get paid to brush their teeth on national television.

Curry was living in New York City under a tremendous financial strain. After obtaining approval from his Jesuit superior, Curry scheduled an appointment to audition for a mouthwash commercial. He thought he would be wonderful gargling nationally.[4] Arriving at the agency prepared to audition for a mouthwash commercial, he was greeted by a receptionist who burst out laughing at the man with the empty right sleeve. She was sure her boyfriend had put Curry up to this as a joke on her.

When Curry assured her that he was a serious applicant, she replied, "Please leave. I couldn't possibly send you upstairs to audition. If I send you upstairs, I could lose my job."[5] Curry felt deep hurt and anger. Painful as it was, that moment of looking directly into the face of prejudice changed his life. "Nothing had prepared me for this rejection," he said.

Two days later, Brother Curry decided to begin the "National Theatre Workshop for the Handicapped," which has now been in existence for over thirty years. This theater experience has been transforming the lives of performers and audiences alike for over three decades.

Brother Curry urges all people to celebrate their differences and to use their imaginations to change the world. "Artists," he explained, "have the gift of imagination, and imagination has no physical boundaries." Prophets are like artists, helping us to see what we had been looking at but had not noticed.

Jesus did not call any rabbis or priests to be his disciples. He called laypersons exclusively. God calls disciples from all walks of life to seek justice, love kindness, and walk humbly with God. The church is called to equip disciples and to send them into the world to accomplish God's work.

Some of you, I know, have found your ministry among us, while others are searching for a way to use your gifts. Some of you even believe you don't have any gifts God can use, but let me assure you that God *can* use you.

God empowers and equips us for the work within the church and community. Prayer is important. Take time to pray and take time to listen. Each one of us is an integral part of the body. God's work in our lives is not entirely contingent on our knowledge or even our agreeing to work for God. Throughout your lifetime, God has always been at work within you. Examine your skills, interests, the needs of the Christian community, and even the needs of the world. Each of you is invited to participate in God's work of reconciling the world to God.

When holiness comes calling, what will be your response? God is calling you right now with a special job that only you can do. Is your spiritual cell phone turned on? Listen to God's call. Along with Isaiah, we hear the question, "Whom shall we send, and who will go for us?" And, can you say with Isaiah, "Here am I, Lord. Send me!"?

---

1. Kenneth L. Waters, *I Saw the Lord: a Pilgrimage through Isaiah 6* (Nashville: Upper Room Books, 1996), p. 83.

2. James Dickey, "The Calling of Isaiah," *God's Images* (Birmingham: Oxmore House, 1977), *non pag.*

3. Waters, p. 84.

4. Br. Rick Curry, S.J., "Life's Bread," *The Santa Clara Lectures*, Vol. 7, No. 3 April 8, 2001, available online at http://scu.edu/bannancenter/eventsandconferences/lectures/archives/curry.cfm [Accessed September 1, 2005].

5. "Standing Ovation for Brother Rick Curry, S.J." at 50th Commencement, Fairfield, CT (May 21, 2000), available online at http://www.fairfield.edu/x6750.html [Accessed September 1, 2005].

# Like A Tree Planted

You have probably never thought seriously about tiptoeing through the treetops, but there is a place where you can do that very thing. A lush Brazilian rainforest is home to a spectacular "canopy walk." Tiptoeing through the tops of several hundred different kinds of trees, you will observe creation from an entirely different perspective.

You can look a golden-headed lion tamarin in the eye as it jumps from tree to tree. You will see termite nests the size of pumpkins, hanging from rubber trees that are dripping with natural latex.[1] Tree frogs and a type of lizard known as the flying dragon glide from tree to tree on wing-like skin flaps.

Rainforests were unimaginable to the prophet Jeremiah and the people of Judah, who lived in a land where water and rainfall were scarce. Jeremiah used vivid imagery in his witness to God's work and word, looking to trees for inspirational symbolism in his proclamation. Trees represent growth, life, and a means of physical sustenance for all of God's creation by providing security, shelter, food, and rest.

From the book of Genesis onward, tree imagery is woven throughout scripture. Beginning with the tree of the knowledge of good and evil in the Garden of Eden, we move toward the tree turned into a cross on Calvary Hill, and culminate in the tree of life in Revelation.

In God's plan, the tree of life is more than a metaphor. It also describes the physical branching out of families, a plan by which God's Word and teachings are passed on. God cares deeply about physical life as well as the spiritual. You are the branches that sustain the blossoming of new life. The Apostle Paul reminds us that, "It is not the spiritual which is first, but the physical, and then the spiritual" (1 Corinthians 15:46).

The root system is a vital part of the tree, even though it is almost totally invisible. Roots serve to anchor the tree and absorb water and minerals from the soil. Healthy trees bear fruit in season. Jesus urged his followers to bear fruit and to expect life experiences that would help them bear even more fruit (John 15:1-2, 4-8).

The tree depends on its leaves as well as its roots. You and I can be compared to the leaves on trees, presenting ourselves in an infinite variety of shapes, sizes, and colors. Oak, pine needle, weeping willow, or maple leaf, we are each unique. Even the same tree can have great variations in its individual leaves, adding to its appeal and interest. We can celebrate the diversity found throughout God's good creation.

Regardless of their differences, leaves share a common purpose, one of using water, sunlight, and carbon dioxide to provide nourishment for the entire tree.[2] Without those three elements, the tree is unable to survive; much less grow. Like the leaves of a tree, you are a source of food, shelter, and inspiration for the needs of others in this world.

A tree grows toward light, reaching toward the heavens. We also flourish in the light, abandoning the shadows of fear and doubt. The tree provides both shelter and shade to its furry and feathered friends. We, likewise, aid and assist those who are small and weak by the world's standards.

The tree sends its roots deep into good earth to be nourished by creation. When we are firmly rooted in the love of God, we are sustained by God's grace. When the tree dies and decays, it provides nourishment for new growth, and gives its place in the sun to others in need of light to flourish.

One afternoon, a neighbor phoned Jeff to see if his family could use some firewood. He took Jeff a truckload of short logs, which sat on the woodpile for several weeks. One afternoon, Jeff was in his yard when he noticed something unusual. One of the logs was sprouting several small green branches, even though it was sawed off at both ends. There is life in supposed "deadwood."

Obviously those sprouting branches could not continue to grow. Being cut off from their root system, they were doomed to die like cut flowers. We must be well-rooted in our faith to survive. Roots can supply an ongoing wellspring of moisture and nutrients. It is important for us to stay connected to God, the source of our life. God provides stability, nourishment, and life. Christ died that we might have new life in abundance. The God-centered persons who trust in God constantly renew their spiritual life energies. Abundant life is a result of being connected to God, the source of life.

In recent years, there has been an increasing interest in exploring family ancestry. Many of us wish we knew more about our own family trees, but tracing our roots back many generations can become difficult. It has been eons since God drew back the curtains on life's eternal drama. God is in charge of lighting, scenery, and cued us when time came for our entrances.

We have made our entrances onto life's grand stage after the play is already well underway, and would appreciate an opportunity to rewind into the past and review earlier scenes. Our lives have begun with the never-ending story of salvation well in progress.

Water shortages wreak havoc with flora and fauna alike. We have all seen the telltale signs of drought: brown lawns, cracked ground, dying crops, withered trees, parched wildlife. All these are signs that life is slowly being drained from creation. Sometimes not even sprinklers or irrigation systems can alleviate the damage of dry weather, with its scorching, blistering sun.

But where rivers run through the land, life abounds. Grass is green, the earth is firm, crops are thriving, the animal kingdom is frolicking, and unlike the fragile state of its drought-stricken counterpart, the tree by the river flourishes in the moist, rich soil along the riverbank.

We ourselves move through seasons of drought. Financial difficulties, family problems, illnesses, and tension at work all take their toll on us, leading to emotional drought. And, when we trust only in ourselves and leave out God, we find ourselves in a spiritual drought. These times leave us shriveled to the roots.

How can we find encouragement and revitalization when we feel that our energy is being sapped from us? By entrusting our lives to God. Like a tree planted by the waters, we can be nourished from underground streams of living water. Our lives can yield fruit, and our foliage is ever green and healthy.

Jeremiah may have associated himself with the weeping willow since he is referred to as the "Weeping Prophet." American artist, John Singer Sargent's, *Frieze of the Prophets* depicts several prophets in the moment of their inspiration. Each one is hearing something. More specifically, each is hearing the voice of God as God gives them words to speak to their people.

Jeremiah is conscious only of God. Sargent sees Jeremiah draped in a white garment that touches the ground. A veil covers his head, and his eyes are looking toward the ground. He is weeping, for he hears God tell him of the destruction of the nation with a long march toward enslavement in Babylon (Jeremiah 27:12-15).

Today's scripture lesson comes from Jeremiah's "Book of Consolation," where he is giving hope and encouragement to the people. Jeremiah's message for us today is quite simple and clear: Trust in God rather than in humans. Those who place their trust in humanity will exist merely as shrubs in the desert, a less than desirable environment undeniably.

Jeremiah compares a withered shrub with a watered tree to explain the concept of trust. The scrubby "shrubs" represent those who place their trust in themselves and other individuals when adversity strikes, and it will strike all of us at some time or other. The green, flourishing "trees" are those who place their trust in God.

God's Word says that when we trust in God we are as trees planted by the river. We flourish through the waters of our baptism as well, and are reborn and filled with new life. We no longer need to fear seasons of drought in our lives. God's sustaining and life-giving waters are forever with us.

When we gather together for worship, we are, in essence, transplanted to streams of living water. We send out our own deep roots, absorbing sustenance, growing strong, and becoming fruitful. Our fruit produces abundant seeds, ripe to be spread throughout the land.

In the early nineteenth century, John Chapman, better known as Johnny Appleseed, wandered the American frontier with a Bible in one hand and a bag of seeds in the other, planting trees wherever he went. Never carrying any weaponry, he lived by the Golden Rule. He bartered his seeds and seedlings for food and ill-fitting clothing,[3] which probably landed him, along with Jeremiah, at the top of Mr. Blackwell's "Worst Dressed List."

John Chapman was a visionary thinker well before it became trendy, leaving the beginnings of lush orchards throughout the Northwest Territory. We still benefit today from the fruits of his labors.

Jesus planted seeds, too, seeds of hope, joy, and faithfulness. To be fruitful, seeds must be nurtured, so please do water and feed those seeds. Then God takes over, doing what we cannot do, providing a way for redemption.

There is a wonderful story that touches the hearts of both young and old. Three young trees on a hill share the dreams of what each wants to be when it "grows up" — a beautiful treasure chest, a great sailing ship, and the tallest tree in the world, pointing people toward God.

Each wish is fulfilled, but in a surprising way those young trees could never have imagined. The desires of your own heart may also come to fruition in a very different way from what is expected.

Years pass, the three trees have grown to maturity, and woodcutters come. The tree that aspires to be a treasure chest is transformed into the manger that holds the treasure of the Christ Child. The tree that wants to be a ship becomes the sailboat tossed by the winds when Jesus commands the sea to be still. The last tree becomes the cross on which Jesus is crucified, and which points all people to God. All three trees are transformed through God's love.[4]

When we are rooted in the gospel of Jesus Christ, we live in God's abundance. We reach out to new people and new mission opportunities, and develop ways to be a public witness to the gospel. We are also rooted in the traditions of those faithful ones who have traveled this road before us, planting and nurturing the seeds that bear fruit in our lives. May the seeds of that trust find in each of you rich, moist soil and grow abundantly. God will do the rest.

1. Thomas L. Friedman, *The Lexus and the Olive Tree: Understanding Globalization* (New York: Farrar Straus Giroux, 1999), p. 226.

2. "Leaves," *Stewardship* (New Canaan, Connecticut: Parish Publishing, 2004), p. 3.

3. "The Story of Johnny Appleseed," online at http://www.millville.org/Workshops_f/Dich_FOLKLORE/WACKED/story.html [Accessed August 1, 2005].

4. Angela Elwell Hunt, *The Tale of Three Trees* (Scarsdale: Lion, 1989), *non pag.*

# The Possible Dream

Sibling rivalry. It's the pits. It has been around as long as there have been siblings around. Beginning with Cain and Abel, we see one brother disgruntled because God likes the other brother's sacrificial offering better. We remember, too, Isaac and Ishmael, Jacob and Esau, Rachel and Leah, the prodigal son and his older brother. Life is not fair.

Sibling rivalry, and there's a fight. For every kid who is doing a lot of hitting, there is usually a kid who is doing a lot of provoking. There's no such thing as an innocent sibling. A parent intervenes, only to discover that there are two contradictory stories about what brought on the disagreement. Where does the truth lie? There is probably truth in each story. Where is the sibling who never even secretly wishes that a brother or sister would disappear off the face of the earth?

In the book of Genesis, Joseph's brothers almost cause that very thing to happen. Nothing would make them happier than to be rid of that braggart Joseph. The powers of favoritism and jealousy are a deadly combination. When parents play favorites, they wreak havoc within the family bonds.

Father Jacob has favorite sons, largely because he had a favorite wife, Rachel. Joseph and Benjamin are the children of Rachel, and that makes them special. Joseph was the baby of the bunch, only to be replaced later by baby Benjamin. Children who are the last, and the least in birth order, are often granted special privileges. They are deemed too little to do for themselves what their older siblings recall doing for themselves at that very same age. Life is not fair.

Father Jacob had been jealous of his own twin brother, Esau, and had stolen Esau's blessing from their father Isaac by trickery, and then ran away from home. Later, when Jacob had to face Esau again, he had been terrified of the retribution he thought lay ahead for him. Now that he's a parent, Jacob seems to have developed a full-blown case of amnesia where sibling relationships are concerned. He is clueless about the rivalry among his own sons, and the part he has played in encouraging their jealousy and discontent.

Joseph is the eleventh son of twelve born to Jacob. And, Jacob's favorite. Jacob makes Joseph an expensive coat with long sleeves, which sets him far above his brothers in the wardrobe department. It's difficult to do any real work in a fine coat, so Joseph is off the hook when it comes to most chores. Joseph is also a tattletale. He would keep an eye on his brothers who were keeping an eye on the sheep in the fields and report back to his father.

To make matters worse, Joseph is a dreamer. He had dreams in which he saw his brothers and even the heavens bowing down to him. He could hardly wait to get to the breakfast table in the mornings to tell all his brothers about those outrageous dreams.

One day, Jacob sends Joseph on a journey to check on his brothers, who are a good distance away grazing the sheep. The brothers spot that tacky coat a mile away and make plans to do away with Joseph. Reuben argues against killing Joseph, so the brothers choose instead to throw him into a cistern. Reuben is secretly planning to return later to rescue Joseph from the cistern.

Imagine an enormous bud vase with a narrow neck and larger, more expansive bottom for collecting water, and that is what cisterns were like in the ancient world. Joseph would not be able to climb out through the narrow neck. The cistern is dry, so there is no chance of drowning, but it would have been a slow and tortuous death.

Then, brother Judah proposes another idea. Why not sell Joseph into slavery and make a little profit to boot? A caravan bound for Egypt happens to pass through the region at just the right time, and Joseph is history, or so the brothers think.

Joseph is then transported from some unimpressive little country town to a magnificent city, the capital of Egypt, a formidable world power in the tenth century B.C.E. God is with Joseph and he prospers (Genesis 39:2-3, 21, 23). In Egypt, Joseph's intelligence and leadership skills are recognized immediately by the powers that be.

Evidently, all those dreams are not a bunch of baloney after all. He becomes major domo at the home of Potiphar, one of Pharaoh's officials. Unfortunately, Mrs. Potiphar takes a liking to him and tries unsuccessfully to seduce Joseph. She does succeed in having him thrown into jail with her false accusations against him. Joseph languishes in jail for several years, interpreting dreams for fellow prisoners.

Pharaoh gets the word about Joseph's ability to interpret dreams and solicits his help. Pharaoh has dreamt there will be seven bountiful years in the crop department, followed by a seven-year famine, only he doesn't know that until Joseph tells him. As a reward, Pharaoh then appoints Joseph his Secretary of Agriculture. It isn't long before Joseph finds himself to be Pharaoh's right-hand man.

Years later, Joseph's ten big brothers travel to Egypt to grocery shop. There's a famine back home, so Dad sends them a little farther this time. They approach Joseph, Egypt's head grain grocer, who recognizes them right away. They had written him off a long time ago and have no idea who he is, dressed in that fancy military uniform and speaking a foreign language.

Joseph can't resist messing with his brothers a little, and pretends they are foreign spies up to no good. He questions the brothers about the family and discovers his father is still alive, he, Joseph, is dead, and there is a little brother at home who is now the favored son. Joseph runs into the next room and cries a little, blows his nose, and runs back to his brothers. His men load the brothers up with grain and secretly replace their money inside the sacks. Joseph sends them back home to bring Benjamin to him, while keeping Brother Simeon as a security deposit.

His brothers return, bringing Benjamin, gifts from Canaan, and double the money to finance their food. Joseph plans to share a meal with them at noon. He enters the dining hall, sees Benjamin, and hears that his dad is still alive. He runs into the next room again and cries a little, blows his nose, wipes his eyes, composes himself, and runs back to his brothers.

Again Joseph's men fill the sacks with grain and return the brothers' money. This time around, they also plant Joseph's favorite silver cup in Benjamin's sack. The brothers head back toward Canaan, but this time Joseph sends a man after them, to question them about his missing cup. Sacks are searched, and the silver cup is discovered in Benjamin's possession.

All the brothers return to Joseph and beg for Benjamin to be spared. It would kill their elderly father to lose Benjamin. Then Joseph cries again, and he doesn't run into the next room to hide. Pharaoh's household and all the Egyptians hear him sobbing. He tells his brothers that he is their long-lost Joseph, whom they sold into slavery so many years ago.

The brothers once had Joseph's life in their hands, only now they find the roles reversed. The sons of Jacob thought they had rid themselves of Brother Joseph permanently. When they recognize and realize that this powerful Egyptian is really a Hebrew, and their brother to boot, they see their lives passing before them. This is the end of the road. It's payback time. They will be in front of a firing squad before another day dawns.

But, that is not the case. Joseph moves quickly to comfort and reassure them. Joseph hugs them and cries over the lot of them. He tells them to hurry home and fetch his dad, and to tell Dad how successful he has become as a ruler in Egypt. The family will be his guests in Egypt for the next five years of the famine. They will be given land in Goshen. He realizes that his brothers meant their actions to be evil, but God has used the circumstances to bring good to the forefront, and to save the House of Jacob from starvation. And, they all live happily everafter.

So, we have the saga of another dysfunctional family. Very human, indeed. Every family is dysfunctional in one way or another. Joseph's comments to his brothers remind us of the truth that all things work together for good in the lives of those who love God. In every family, there is envy, competition, and unfairness. The family is a place of dark secrets and love mixed with hatred.

The very people we love are the ones who hurt us the most, and the ones we hurt. Life is not fair, but maybe we can look at life through the eyes of Joseph. A story that began with jealousy and deception turns out to be a story about preserving God's people. God's plan triumphs.

Jesus tells us to love our enemies (Luke 6:27). He died for them as well as for us. That is a tall order for humans. It is not easy to love siblings who plan your demise, but instead decide to sell you into slavery in a foreign land. Joseph doesn't blame or punish his older brothers, even though he has the power to do so. He puts the past into perspective and looks at how God has used the situation. Joseph has prospered greatly as governor of a world power, and has saved his family, who will become the nation of Israel, from starvation.

God does not cause evil things to happen but can and does work in and through those events to accomplish good. "Love your enemies." Miraculously, Joseph loves the jealous brothers, whose hatred deprived him of father and homeland, changing his life forever.

"Do good to those who hate you" (Luke 6:27b). Surprisingly, Joseph greets the frightened brothers, not with swift justice, but with joyful reconciliation and careful plans for their welfare. Jesus' words turn the world around and they can turn us around, too. Jesus' words, when we put them into action, can turn sadness into joy, anger into forgiveness, estrangement into community, and defeat into victory. The dream is possible, with God on our side.

# Sowing Eternal Seeds

Who among us has not been stunned by the splendor of a summer sunset, the sparkling spring waters of a mountain stream, brilliantly striking contrasts of autumn leaves twirling and spinning, or winter trees swaying gracefully against a cool, crisp sky?

I believe the Native American population has much to teach us when it comes to care of and respect for God's majestic creation. Chief Seattle declares that even the dust under his feet responds lovingly to his footsteps because it is the ashes of his ancestors. His bare feet are conscious of the soil's sympathetic touch. The soil is indeed rich with life.[1]

Iroquois Chief, Oren Lyons, is an author and tenured professor of American studies at the State University of New York. He explains how the Iroquois make decisions, always keeping in mind the Seventh Generation yet to come. They feel it is their responsibility to ensure that their progeny, the yet unborn generations, will have a world no worse than this, and hopefully better.[2] The future is in our hands.

The stewardship of creation is not a new idea. It is as old as the first chapter of the Bible, where we are given dominion over creation. Recycling cans, glass, and paper on an earth that is becoming an extensive pile of waste matter is one expression of that responsibility. Driving less and purchasing more gas-efficient automobiles is another. Supporting legislation that leads to clean air and fresh water is still another.

Protecting and enhancing this earth may require changes in our lifestyles. When we plow our fields, fill our gas tanks, set our thermostats, and choose between paper or plastic, we are making decisions that affect future generations. Those of you who live in areas where your recyclable materials are picked up at the curb may be very surprised to walk through your neighborhood on garbage collection day and notice the lack of recycle bins. These same households without the recycle bins frequently have multiple garbage cans that are literally overflowing with the spoils of humanity's creations.

No words can adequately describe the dignity of God's created order. The dawning of each new day calls forth adoration and praise. Every mountain, every hillside, every valley, is revered. Creation is a sacred place, leaving us awestruck by its beauty. The prophet Isaiah lauds creation as he speaks words of encouragement to his people in exile.

Two generations earlier, the Hebrew people had been scattered to the four winds by invading enemies. They had forgotten God's mighty acts, those very acts that had brought about their exodus from slavery in Egypt. They had strayed again from keeping the Law of Moses. Their story is our story, too.

The people and places may have changed, but the scenario is the same. God's people forget God, and rebel against God. We forget to set aside a time to read scripture and to talk with God. We forget to care for the poor, the marginalized, and the disenfranchised.

We rebel by not being good stewards of God's creation, by living beyond our means, by accumulating much more worldly wealth than is necessary for sustaining life, and by wasting our excesses. In spite of humanity's shortfalls, God's saving hand is always ready to intervene anew in our lives.

Our psalm for today recounts God's faithfulness in the past, sings praises to God in the present, and proclaims that God will always rule with justice and integrity in the future (Psalm 92:1-4, 12-15).

Isaiah is addressing those who are in exile in the faraway country of Babylon, offering comfort and consolation. A new exodus is close at hand, Isaiah explains, and salvation is on the horizon. Again, God will provide redemption from captivity and restoration in a land flowing with milk and honey.

Fertile fields and prolific vineyards were a part of God's promise to a landless people. Issues of faithfulness to God and possession of the land were interrelated in ancient times. In an earlier time and place, God had entered into an everlasting covenant with the people, and God honored that promise because God loves humanity with an everlasting love.

God's Word is the bread of life, our strength and sustenance. In the cycle of planting and harvesting, everything in its season will be provided. You may be the one chosen to cultivate the soil and plant your seeds, while another is destined to harvest what you have sown. In the Gospel of John, Jesus tells us that, "One sows and another reaps. I sent you to reap that for which you did not labor. Others have labored, and you have entered into their labor" (John 4:37-38).

We all know folks who have exiled themselves from corporate worship, claiming they can commune better with creation by walking in the woods or walking on the golf course than they can in this room. Still others claim that it's their only day to "sleep in," and they prefer to spend Sunday mornings at "St. Mattress-by-the-Springs." I do believe that God wants us here in this very room on Sunday mornings. Church is the place where we learn more about God's Word and how it speaks to us today. The most reliable place to find God is within the fellowship of other believers.

Isaiah compares God's Word to the rains and snow that come down from heaven to refresh and replenish the earth. God's Word inspires us to go out in joy and be led back in peace. Even the mountains are jubilant, the hills are alive with the sound of music, and the trees clap their limbs in response.

The painful, punishing thorns and briers of exile will be replaced by myrtle and cypress trees back in the homeland. The myrtle tree is first mentioned in scripture during the Babylonian captivity. As a fragrant evergreen, the myrtle is an appropriate symbol of the recovery and establishment of God's promises in Judah. Cypress trees were used for shipbuilding. Cypress was Noah's wood of choice when it came to building the ark. These trees will join all of creation in proclaiming new life for God's people.

You are an invaluable part of the very creation that proclaims the love and grace of God. You also proclaim God's message by the way you treat others, the kind and uplifting words you speak, your stewardship of possessions, and your actions, which speak loudest of all.

Twelve-year-old Allison really enjoyed youth choir, participating in rhythmic speech ensembles, and singing the contemporary songs she loved. She already knew most of the words from listening to the radio. The words of scripture came alive to her when set to the music that pulsed through her veins. On Wednesday afternoons, she began inviting another girl, who was a good friend and neighbor, to accompany her.

Allison's friend was a little skeptical about going to church at first, but Tom, the choir director, quickly won her over. It may have been his winsome personality, or the microwave popcorn and hot chocolate the group shared in the youth room after rehearsals. Whatever it was, she was having fun.

Although her family did not belong to a church, this visitor began to attend Sunday morning worship once a month when the youth choir provided special music. She also accompanied Allison to youth group on Sunday evenings, and before long, Pastor Cindy had signed her up for Allison's confirmation class. She joined the church along with Allison's class and remained a faithful, active youth member of the congregation.

Years later, Tom, who had been director of music at Allison's church, was teaching a seminary class in church music. Tom's class sang the hymns as they studied and learned hymnology. One afternoon they sang "What Wondrous Love Is This," the story of Christ's gracious life given for us. The final stanza ends with the words,

> *And when from death I'm free, I'll sing on, I'll sing on,*
> *And when from death I'm free, I'll sing on, and when*
> *    from death I'm free,*
> *I'll sing on and joyful be, and through eternity I'll sing*
> *    on,*
> *I'll sing on, and through eternity I'll sing on.*[3]

Tom then related the story of Allison's friend, and how we never know fully the impact on eternity of the seeds we plant. Allison's friend became an active member of her church, graduated from high school, and then went on to seminary. Tom astounded the class by saying, "That friend Allison brought to youth choir so many years ago is sitting in this very room with us today."

Class members looked around at one another, wondering, "Who could it be?" After a lengthy pause, Tom revealed her identity. She was a professor of biblical studies at that very seminary, and sitting in on the class at Tom's request that afternoon, all because of seeds a young girl named Allison had planted nearly a quarter century earlier. There was hardly a dry eye in the classroom.

Think of the lives this professor will touch as she prepares future pastors and lay professionals who, in turn, will equip others to plant seeds and spread God's Word. Through eternity, they will sing on because the voice of Allison has set the song into motion. Their influence will never end.

Toss a stone into a pond and long after that stone has settled into the silt on the bottom, you will continue to see the circles on the pond's surface ever-expanding, widening, disturbing, encompassing more and more of the once-placid surface. That's how it is with God's Word, once it has touched your life.

The prophet Isaiah has proclaimed that God's Word never returns empty. The ripple effect from Allison's invitation is eternal in nature, singing on and on. Because of the power of God's Word, Allison's influence will never end.

Take heart when you share your own faith stories of how God has touched your lives. They, as well, are timeless and eternal. Invite your friends to worship, to Bible studies, even to social events at church. You will never know all the lives you influence, the lives God has placed into your capable hands. May your voices also sing on, throughout eternity, or in the words of the prophet Isaiah, "It shall be to the Lord for a memorial, for an everlasting sign that shall not be cut off."

1. Chief Seattle, "Wilderness Quotes," *Outward Bound*, available online at http://www.wilderdom.com/QuotesWilderness.htm [Accessed September 1, 2005].

2. Oren Lyons, "The Faithkeeper," interview with Bill Moyers, Public Television, July 3, 1991, available online at http://www.ratical.org/many_worlds/6Nations/OL070391.html [Accessed September 1, 2005].

3. American folk hymn. Both words and tune are in the public domain.

## The Transfiguration Of Our Lord
## (Last Sunday After The Epiphany)
## Exodus 34:29-35

# Shine, Moses, Shine

Have you ever had a "mountaintop" experience? We use that term to describe various circumstances — a brilliant sunrise, a special time shared with friends or loved ones, a quiet moment of deep reflection. Such events are meaningful and important, but they are human experiences and have their place in the realm of the ordinary.

There are also glorious worship experiences, when we feel on top of the world. Momentous mountaintop experiences are exhilarating, causing us to want to preserve them indefinitely. We long to sustain spiritual and emotional moments and highs. High places are traditionally believed to be closer to heaven, therefore closer to God. The majesty of a mountain itself is a powerful presence. Mountains are a symbol of eternal endurance and stability, portraying the creator's might and majesty.

Throughout scripture, mountaintops have been places where humanity meets and communes with God. In the pre-scientific world, mountains were thought to be the dwelling places of the gods. It is on Mount Moriah that Abraham takes the giant leap of faith in laying his son, Isaac, on the altar of sacrifice. On Mount Carmel, Elijah sees the magnificent power of God in a triumph over the prophets of Baal.

Moses ascends Mount Sinai to be in the presence of God and to receive the Ten Commandments. After a lengthy stay on Mount Sinai, Moses comes down to his people at the foot of the mountain, unaware that his face is aglow with a godly radiance. His shining face is so full of the glory of God that he is a frightful sight to the Israelites, and must veil his face.

Moses had mountaintop experiences unlike any others, close encounters of the divine kind. On another mountain Moses meets God and Elijah, then Jesus along with James, Peter, and John. The voice of God makes clear the purpose of this extraordinary encounter: "This is my Son, my chosen, listen to him." Listen to Jesus, for in his words and actions you will hear and see God among us.

Both Moses and Elijah are strengthened in faith through their mountaintop encounters with God. When they join Jesus and his disciples on the Mount of Transfiguration, they are representatives of the law and the prophets. Moses knows firsthand the radiance streaming from Jesus because of Moses' own shining face when experiencing God's presence on Mount Sinai.

Moses has led an exciting life, full of drama and intrigue. In his earliest years, he sets sail in a life-saving basket, only to be plucked from the Nile River by Pharaoh's daughter. Moses, this child of slaves, is raised by royalty as the prince of Egypt, but is reminded of his roots in Hebrew slavery. After being raised in the royal palace, he throws away a dazzling career by killing an Egyptian taskmaster. He then becomes a fugitive fleeing for his life from the Egyptian police, and ends up in the desert wilderness.

Sitting by a well in the wilderness, he meets Zipporah, and later they marry. While employed as his father-in-law's shepherd, he grazes the sheep too close to Mount Horeb, also called Sinai, and notices a burning bush. Very curious about this phenomenon, Moses approaches the bush.

Suddenly a voice booms from the burning bush, "Moses, Moses!"

Realizing that this is the voice of God, Moses manages to stammer, "Here I am."

"Take off your sandals, you are standing on holy ground," the voice responds. A barefooted Moses beholds the bush, the voice, and the glory of God. A talking, burning bush is a truly hair-raising experience, but suddenly Moses is enveloped with a sense of peace that passes all understanding.

Moses and God converse, while God explains a plan to free God's people from their subservience in Egypt. Moses, in a worshipful mood, suddenly realizes that he is about to undergo another career change in midlife. He doesn't feel up to the challenge, but God promises to provide Moses with a spokesperson, and anything else he may need for the journey.

We marvel in the vulnerability of God, to be present in a simple earthly vessel — a plain old bush — to a sinner who is hiding from the law. God has a dream that God's people will be free from the abusive Egyptian rulers, and has a plan to bring it about. God descends into our world to become one of us as Moses embodies the presence of God for the people of Israel.

Moses seems to spend a great deal of time on the mountain with God, leaving the people in ordinary time below. Communing with God on Mount Sinai is the high point of Moses' life.[1] While Moses and God are having a mountaintop experience, the troops waiting below are getting restless, wondering when shiny-faced Moses will come down from that mountain and put on his silly veil.

They had hoped to stay at the Sinai Sheraton with its expansive menu, but found instead that they were enrolled in a forty-year outward bound school. They had to sleep on the ground, making their necks stiff, and eat ambrosia off the ground every single day. The people remaining in the valley are not happy campers, and turn their eyes from God's glory to idol worship. The back-to-Egypt committee convinces Aaron to make a golden calf, and that makes God and Moses mad.

In fact, Moses is so mad that he breaks every one of the Ten Commandments when he comes back down to the people. He breaks the tablets they are written on, that is. Then it's back up the mountain for a consultation with God, and to get the Ten Commandments replaced.

Exodus is sometimes referred to as "the first book of salvation." Exodus is the story of God's rescuing the people of Israel from slavery in Egypt and bringing them, over a period of many years, to the promised land. In Exodus, the Israelites are saved from Egypt and delivered to Sinai, where they receive the law, and the covenant relationship is renewed. The law is given so the people might freely serve both God and their neighbor better. Under the leadership of Moses, the Israelites move from oppressive slavery toward service to humanity.

Anthropologist and novelist, Zora Neale Hurston, relates that her own mama exhorted her children at every opportunity to "jump at de sun." They might not land on the sun, but at least they would get off the ground. Life is a myriad of experiences, Hurston explains. From the valley to the mountaintop, "I have been in sorrow's kitchen and licked out all the pots. Then I have stood on the peaky mountain wrapped in rainbows with a harp and a sword in my hands."[2] We can all identify with both the low and the high points in Hurston's life, because they mirror our life's journey.

We live in a society where "feeling good" is a high priority. Countless Christians want to make the church a forum for mountaintop highs in the form of emotional intensity. If they don't "feel" on top of the world during a worship service, then something is missing, and it must be the Holy Spirit. Yet, we know the Spirit of God permeates all of life. I am reminded of a bumper sticker that reads, "If God seems far away, guess who moved."

The Holy Spirit has been referred to as the "shy" member of the Trinity. Throughout the centuries, artists have portrayed all facets of the life of Christ: his birth, his travels and ministry, transfiguration, crucifixion, resurrection, and ascension. We have numerous paintings and sculptures of Moses and even artists' renditions of God, who is, by the way, created in our own image. But, there is not a museum or library or palace on earth that houses a portrait of the Holy Spirit.

It is in the valleys of life that we are stretched to our greatest potential. Martin Luther warns us about the bondage of emotionalism and the idolatry of feelings in our faith walks. We don't have to feel God's presence to know that God is present. God has given us intelligence and the ability to reason far beyond the effects of an emotional power surge.

As our faith matures, we know that God is faithful to the promises in scripture. There comes a time when we must put away the warm, fuzzy "flannel board Jesus" of our childhood. When the Bible

114

study facilitator asked if the class knew anything about Moses, one woman exclaimed, "Moses! Of course! The one who was found in the bulrushes. I always think of him as a baby in a basket." But, it is not as a baby that Moses climbs Mount Sinai to receive the Ten Commandments. It is not as a baby that he leads his people through the wilderness toward the promised land.

The same woman remarked, "Jesus! I love to think of Jesus lying helpless in a manger. That little child, so sweet." But, time marches on, and we can't keep Moses in a basket or Jesus in a manger. We must come out of the bulrushes and up from the river.

A journey awaits each of us in this life, a journey through the waters, across the wilderness, and up the mountainside. There is a life to be lived, in quiet places, on stormy seas, beyond betrayal and mistrust to Easter morning. Our journey is filled with study, marriage, parenthood, divorce, work, travel, success, and failure. All of this and much more are part of the journey.[3]

God's glory becomes your own when you are chosen to be sons and daughters of God. And you *are* chosen. You have been chosen by God and baptized into the glory of the death and resurrection of Jesus. You are marked with the cross of Christ forever, a mark that cannot be destroyed.

Your face will glow, too, as the love of Christ fills your being. This glow works its way into the world as you serve God and your neighbor, as you shine like stars in the world. The world's glory pales when compared with being a son or daughter of the risen Christ.

---

1. Consider sharing some of the words to the contemporary song, "Shine, Jesus, Shine" with the congregation. If it is not in your hymnal supplement, the words are available at http://www.grahamkendrick.co.uk/insight_story.htm [Accessed September 1, 2005].

2. Zora Neale Hurston, *Dust Tracks on a Road* (New York: Harper Perennial, 1991), p. 209.

3. Helen R. Ferguson, "The Journey," *Listen with Love* (Cincinnati: Forward Movement Publications, 1992), p. 5.

# Sermons On The First Readings

## For Sundays In
## Lent And Easter

## *The City Of Justice*

## Frank Ramirez

*Dedicated to Willis Hershberger, wise historian, teacher, and biblical scholar, in honor of the fair hearing he gave my sermons, and the helpful comments he shared afterward, and to the memory of Dora Hershberger, whose wry observations cut to the heart of biblical and personal truth.*

# Introduction

During Lent we get our house in order, spiritually and physically. On Shrove Tuesday, the day before Ash Wednesday, some of us use up all the fat in the kitchen to get ready for a season of fasting. Of course, this is usually just a good excuse to eat fatty treats like Paczki (pronounced poonchkee) while ignoring the possibility of fasting when the next lunchtime arises.

Some of us are not very good at this Lent thing, but our hearts are in the right place. We're headed in the right direction. Perhaps that's the essence of Lent. Even though it looks like nothing is happening, things are moving at a very swift speed toward something dark, then something very, very good.

Where I live, bulbs planted last autumn are still hidden, but already the stem is pushing through the cold, hard earth toward the light of the sun. Flowers are on the way. The hills are barren, but bare trees are just about to burst into bloom. The landscape looks calm, unmoving, but the planet is spinning while careening around the sun which is flying across space around a ravenous black hole at the center of the galaxy which is circling other galaxies in a mad dash away from everything. All is well.

That's because once more we relive this most important church season. Jesus comes down from the Mount of the Transfiguration the week before Lent, and we take a long breath. Everyone wonders why Jesus appears to be doing nothing but the die is already cast. There will be a sudden, mad plunge past the feetwashing in the upper room toward the cross, the grave, and beyond to an empty tomb and a risen Lord.

Our Redeemer lives. It was just as true when Job said it while mired in the depths of mystery and despair (Job 19:25). It's just as true now. Our Redeemer lives.

Politics change, and so do policies. Empires come and go. But these three things are sure — Christ Has Died. Christ Is Risen. Christ Will Come Again.

Jesus lives not only as a risen Lord, but in a risen people who are living the life of a resurrected people, speaking the truth to power, sharing the life of the upside down kingdom of Jesus Christ. Our Redeemer lives in the faithfulness of God's people, in our shared past. And our Redeemer lives in those historians, writers, and artists who still bless us as a people.

Lent comes from the verb for lengthen in old Anglo-Saxon, referring to the days that are growing longer. The word was also used for the season of Spring. Lent is forty days long (not counting Sundays) and calls to mind the forty years God's people wandered in the desert, as well as the forty days Moses spent on Mount Sinai and Jesus spent fasting in the wilderness. This is meant to be a time for repentance and renewal for both individuals and the community of faith.

We do Lent and Easter every year. Is there anything really new about it? Maybe not. But then, is there anything new about spring, about children, about gardens? It's all the same. But in that sameness we find endless variety and the constant renewal of hope and restoration of our faith in God's love.

I have called this collection of sermons "The City Of Justice." Justice is the theme of the prophets, including Isaiah and Joel, who provide texts for this season. The call of these prophets, like the mission of Jesus and his disciples, was for justice now, not just in the world to come. Living in the kingdom and by the rules of the kingdom begins long before we take our place before that throne that is surrounded by the glassy sea.

The Acts of the Apostles mostly takes place in cities. That's not surprising. Some people think of Christianity as a country faith, and picture little brown churches in the vale. But Christianity was a city religion from the beginning, and especially during the first three centuries of the Christian era.

The movement of the Bible is from the Garden of Eden through justice to the city of God as portrayed in Revelation. The city is where the people are. The city is where justice can be missing. The city was where Jesus was murdered, and where Jesus was raised. The city is where the apostles waited for the Spirit, and the cities of the Roman Empire are where the gospel first took root and grew. Welcome to the City Of Justice. Welcome to the journey through Lent to Easter and beyond. Welcome.

The story of Cain Lackey comes from my own book, *The Meanest Man in Patrick County and Other Unlikely Brethren Heroes*, published in 2004 by Brethren Press. Poems that are quoted are in the public domain.

Frank Ramirez

PS: In the introduction I mention Paczki, which is a Polish treat I became familiar with when I lived the South Bend, Indiana, area. I'm including the recipe for your pre-Lenten enjoyment.

# Recipe For Paczki
## (pronounced poonchkee)

| | |
|---|---|
| 2 c. flour | 1/2 c. sugar |
| 2 c. boiling milk | 1 tsp. vanilla |
| 3 1/2 oz. yeast | 1-2 tsp. grated orange rind |
| 1/4 c. lukewarm milk | 1/4 lb. butter, melted |
| 6 egg yolks | |

Flour
Jam or preserves
Oil for deep-fat frying
Confectioner's sugar (powdered sugar)

Sift 1 cup flour into boiling milk; remove from heat and beat until smooth. Cool. Dissolve yeast in the 1/4 cup lukewarm milk. Add to flour mixture; stir and let stand 1/2 hour. Cream egg yolks and sugar. Add vanilla and orange rind and add to the dough when it begins to rise. Add remaining 1 cup flour and the butter; work with fingers until dough begins to stand away from the hands. Let stand until it has risen to about twice its bulk. Roll out on a floured board to 5/8 inch thickness and cut out circles with pastry cutter. Place a teaspoon of jam in center of half the circles, using only the chunks of fruit, not the syrup. Cover with remaining circles. Press edges together and let stand in warm place to rise again. Fry a few at a time in deep fat, taking care not to heat the oil so much that the dough will burn. Drain on paper towels and serve dusted with confectioners' sugar.

Thanks to Nancy Glon, Goshen, Indiana, for this recipe.

## Ash Wednesday
## Joel 2:1-2, 12-17

# Ashes And Bugs

Ah, spring! The days are getting longer, and hopefully warmer. There are so many things to anticipate: the first robin, snowdrop flowers, and that garden perennial — asparagus. People are looking forward to their first chance to bring pictures from their well-worn seed catalogs to life.

There is one thing we don't look forward to — the appearance of the first grasshopper. Descending on us like an army, they are ready to eat the best of what we planted, just when our gardens are starting to show promise! They are voracious and relentless.

When the prophet Joel spoke to God's people, the memory of a plague of insects was still fresh; precious crops had been destroyed and hunger reigned. But God promised the people joy beyond disaster, and full gardens despite devastation. God's Word brings hope. In our own struggles, despite heartbreaking setbacks, there is the promise of hope, as well. And it all begins on this day, Ash Wednesday, that some of us will just plain forget about.

Ash Wednesday comes in the middle of nowhere. Our worship cycle is built around Sundays. The four Sundays of Advent, the Sundays in Lent, and the Sundays of Easter — the big holiday, Easter Sunday itself — all are on Sundays!

But Ash Wednesday sneaks up on you. People ask: Is that today? Oops, I forgot. It's not very convenient. It is an interruption. It doesn't even fall on the same date every year. At least Christmas, which falls on every day of the week at one time or another, at least has the good sense to fall on the same date — December 25. You can't say to yourself, "Ah, it's February 19, or March 5," or whatever, and know by the date that it is Ash Wednesday.

And there's another good reason to try to forget. Ash Wednesday is an unwelcome reminder. A *memento mori*, the Latin phrase that means, "reminder of my death." You are dust and to dust you will return. Or rather, I am dust, and to dust I must return. I, too, will die.

One of the scripture passages we examine on this day is the one from the prophet Joel that tells us terrible things have been happening in the land. There were environmental ravages — a plague of locusts has devastated the crops, bad weather, bad luck, bad politics. In the midst of all this, the people found they couldn't bring their offerings to the temple. If only, they cry, the Day of the Lord would come. Then everything would be all right.

It's hard to figure out exactly when, and to whom, Joel was preaching. The circumstances he described could have fit a couple different periods. But it doesn't matter, because economic and political disasters strike all ages, and his words speak to all people.

Joel reminds the people that there's a better offering than the one they brought to the temple. Fasting, lamentation, mourning — repentance. Especially the latter.

The problems of the people are real. Insects bring economic ruin. Try to stop them. Sometimes you simply can't. The people see them like an army of the Lord bringing judgment for past sins. Farming is tough enough in the best of times, but when something like this happens, all of society might fall apart.

Joel makes things worse by describing what these implacable foes are like. "They have the appearance of horses, and like warhorses they charge. As with the rumbling of chariots, they leap on the tops of the mountains, like the crackling of a flame of fire devouring the stubble, like a powerful army drawn up for battle" (2:4-5). Thanks, Joel. Like the people couldn't see that already!

Then he suggests that something worse is coming. The Day of the Lord! A day of judgment, darkness and not light.

Now that must have caught the people off guard. They assumed that since they are God's people, the Day of the Lord is good news! The Day of the Lord is supposed to be glorious. Like the oldies song: "My boyfriend's back and you're gonna be in trouble...." or the chant we might hear at football games: "We're number one! We're number one!"

But Joel describes it as a day of judgment. One in which we may be found wanting, even though we consider ourselves one of God's own.

That's the way we Americans tend to consider ourselves — automatically God's people. As a matter of fact, we tend to assume God is leaning on our side just because we're Americans. We never think about the fact that we buy more, consume more, waste more, sin more, and ignore God more than others. Christian sociologists have been saying for decades if you want to find the cutting edge of Christianity, it's not in the Western world any more — it's in Africa and Latin America.

The prophet Joel isn't just speaking to his time. He's talking to us, too. The Day of the Lord is more than automobiles crashing out of control or airliners falling out of the sky, but is it a call to ask ourselves if we are ready? It is a day of harrowing gloom. Who can stand in the face of such a day?

The poet, John Donne, thought about the end of the world and what it might mean to us personally in one of his Holy Sonnets (1633), when he wrote:

> At the round earth's imagined corners, blow
> Your trumpets, Angels, and arise, arise
> From death, you numberless infinities
> Of souls, and to your scattered bodies go,
> All whom the flood did, and fire shall o'erthrow,
> All whom war, dearth, age, agues, tyrannies,
> Despair, law, chance, hath slain, and you whose eyes
> Shall behold God, and never taste death's woe.
> But let them sleep, Lord, and me mourn a space
> For, if above all these my sins abound
> 'Tis late to ask abundance of thy grace
> When we are there; here on this lowly ground
> Teach me how to repent, for that's as good
> As if thou hadst seal'd my pardon, with thy blood.

The poet recognized that the Day of the Lord is not good news if you are not ready. He asks for just a little more time to repent. That time is now.

And that's Joel's message to his time and to our time: Rend your hearts and not your clothing. Return to the Lord. Joel wrote in a time when people did not have large wardrobes. Rending your clothes as a sign of repentance and grief is not just a dramatic thing to do, it is a true sacrifice. And Joel wants us to go even farther. He wants us to rend our hearts, change our ways — repent!

While there's still time.

If we do, God will have pity. Things will change. Joel orders that the trumpet be blown again, to summon everyone to repentance. He wants us to know that our God may even now turn back, turn away, if we turn back, and turn away.

Joel says later in his book, "I will repay you for the years that the swarming locust has eaten, the hopper, the destroyer, and the cutter, my great army, which I sent against you" (Joel 2:25). Now that is a promise that streches the imagination. How can we get lost time back?

We live in difficult times. Even though years have gone by, many people are still reeling, not only from the terrible events of September 11, but the evil we have brought upon ourselves, through domestic terrorism such as the Oklahoma City bombing, or the economic terrorism when corporate executives gut pension plans or destroy the lives of workers while fashioning themselves million-dollar parachutes. This is the kind of thing that draws God's wrath, that reminds us that the Day of the Lord is at hand.

How do we deal with such an overwhelming evil? We begin by repenting — trusting, as Joel said, that "... the Lord became jealous for his land, and had pity on his people" (Joel 2:18).

We take matters into our own hands as well. Joel's prophecy also reminds me that the food we plant is desired not only by the insects who share our creation, but by humankind as well. As you make plans for a garden, whether it's a flower box in a city window or a truck patch on half an acre, picture ways you can bless others in your community, perhaps through a local food bank or by giving produce to people you know.

Now what do ashes have to do with all this? It's not magic. There is nothing special about the ashes themselves. Ashes are a symbol of the repentance Job expressed after calling out God and God calling back. Take Job. He repents from dust and ashes, he accepts a new life, he lives like there's no tomorrow, because he now knows there really is a God and it really matters!

It is never too late for us to repent as individuals, as the church, as a nation, as a world. In their name we rend our hearts and not our clothing. We return to the Lord, our God, for he is gracious and merciful, slow to anger, and abounding in steadfast love.

God hasn't given up on us. That's why this day is about more than just ashes and bugs. God is sending Jesus to die for us, to live for us. Will we accept the blessing that is coming our way? Will we show to others the same grace God has shown to us?

When the biblical prophets talk about the coming end, they're not only reminding God's people that the Day of the Lord is bad news for sinners, they also talk about a delay — a delay just long enough for us to repent, and to go forward in God's mission.

That's certainly what the prophet Joel is telling us. While God's people look forward to the end as a day when their enemies will get what's coming to them, Joel challenges them to look within their own hearts, to repent, and restore justice and righteousness in the land.

This is the heart of Ash Wednesday. What matters is that today you begin a journey for Jesus and with Jesus, through death and beyond to resurrection.

While there's still time. Amen.

# What's In A Name?

What's in a name? Does a name matter? Does it really matter if you're named Tom, Dick, or Harry — or Sharon, Sue, or Maggie? Hard to say.

Consider the case of Gerald Ford, a former president of the United States. He was sixteen years old when a strange man sat down next to him at a soda fountain, introduced himself as his father, and told Gerald his name was really Leslie King, Jr. President Ford sounds very American, but in our democratic society, would we really want a person named King to be president?

The noted Christian writer, C. S. Lewis, was born Clive Stapes, but when he was four years old he walked into the family room, thumped his chest with his thumb, and said, "He is Jacksie!" And for the rest of his life his friends called him Jack, which seemed to suit the man much better.

Names can say things about our ancestry. In some places, like Sweden or Norway, to be named Johnson means that your father was named John. Your child might well have a different last name if your first name is different from your parents. In Russia it is the middle name that includes the father's first name. Ivanovich and Ivanovna mean that the son or daughter's father was named Ivan.

Names can be used against us. A poll watcher observed a presidential election in El Salvador and discovered that one went to vote not according to address but according to last name. However, a last name is taken from the mother, and that means that a husband, a wife, and a child might have three different last names, meaning they had to go to three different polling stations. That is not a problem for rich people who can drive around town, but for poor people it can become next to impossible for everyone in the family to vote.

Some names tell a story about the person. In the novel, *The Lord of the Rings*, by the Christian writer J.R.R. Tolkien there is a particular creature called Treebeard who is one of the Ents, a tree-like race that lives for centuries. Treebeard makes it clear that his real name would take a long time to recite because in his long, slow language a person's name has to tell the person's story, and those who have lived a long time have very long names indeed.

It's not just individuals, but groups that have names as well, and ideally their name should say something about them. Many of us are proud to call ourselves Americans, for instance, but I wonder how many of us really know that much about Amerigo Vespucci. He was the map maker who named a continent after himself. In the end, I suspect it is not Amerigo in whom we take great pride, but the story of the people who have inhabited that continent that makes us proud of who we are. It is our understanding of ourselves as a people, our particular view of our story, that makes us happy.

For instance, we tend to think of ourselves as a nation of immigrants, of people who came at one generation or another to seek a better life for themselves and for their descendants, who endured great hardships and worked long hours to carve out a niche in the new land. Whether it is our distant ancestors, or we ourselves, who made the crossing, it's a story we share in common with most people who live here.

But not all. Others can claim that their ancestors were here thousands of years before others arrived, and these people might tell the story of European immigration much differently. They might talk about slaughter, genocide, the deliberate and accidental spread of disease, the destruction of species like bison or buffalo, when telling the story of this nation. How we name things makes a big difference.

In today's scripture passage, Moses is giving the people a name and identity, as well as a name to call upon, as they prepare to cross over to the promised land. Now he could have simply reminded them that they had called aloud to God in their slavery and had been found, redeemed, and freed, sent across the desert while all the time observing miracles and wonders, a people who had seen God speak on Mount Sinai, and who had followed their prophet and lawgiver, Moses himself.

Or Moses could have reminded them of all their whining, of their distrust, of their determination to return to slavery rather than trust in the God who freed them, of their lack of faith that God would feed them, give them water, sustain them. He could have called them "idol builders" after what they did while he was up on the mountain receiving the Ten Commandments.

Instead, Moses invited them to continue in a close relationship with God, to give an offering of their firstfruits in thankfulness after they had entered into their land, and to say simply, "A wandering Aramean was my ancestor." He invited the people to call to mind the wandering of Abraham and Sarah, and their eventual faithfulness.

The people who would now own their land, who would worship God in a fixed place, the temple, instead of a movable tent like the tabernacle, the people who would define their families geographically as well as genetically, were reminded by Moses that they were wanderers once and might wander again.

They were also told that in the wake of the tremendous story of the liberation and exodus, they were also known as a *thankful* people, an *offering* people, a people who gave back to God and to God's people a portion of their own. The very fact that they — and we — are to call to mind our days as wanderers is to prevent us from taking too much credit for what we have and what we've done, and to give glory to God. As Abraham was a wanderer, so we too must be ready to wander, when God calls us and sends us forth to preach the gospel.

It's a different way of looking at things. Some of us are mobile, but others are tied to a patch of earth and have been that way for generations. But, our father was a wandering Aramean. And because we are wanderers, and the descendants of wanderers, we must never forget to give thanks — in profound gratitude — for what we have and what we have been given.

Throughout this passage Moses uses the name of God. Usually translated Lord and presented in all capitals in our Bible translations, this name on the one hand tells us nothing about God except that God exists. It is a form of the verb *to be*, and partly tells us that God is unknowable. Beyond the fact that God exists, there is nothing we can know about God.

And yet God is very knowable — through the relationship God has with the people. This God says to Moses in Exodus, "I am the God of your father, the God of Abraham, the God of Isaac, and the God of Jacob" (Exodus 3:6). On the one hand, that tells us nothing. It doesn't tell us what God looks like or sounds like, and the Hebrew Scriptures have no intention of telling us anything of the sort.

But it does tell us what God *acts* like — by calling to mind our ancestors, the name *I Am* suggests that the way we know God is to call to mind by long memory what God has accomplished with the people in all generations. It's what God does, not what God says about God, that matters.

As the people prepare to enter into the promised land to give thanks, they are reminded that theirs is the God of Abraham, and that means a lot.

As we enter the season of Lent, we, too, are reminded of our spiritual ancestry, of the God who has a track record with us, and what that record means. Just as the father of all of us was a wandering Aramean, so, too, the Son of Man complained that, "Foxes have holes, and birds of the air have nests; but the Son of Man has nowhere to lay his head" (Matthew 8:20).

And the Apostle Paul once shared his glittering resume. As he put it, he was "... a member of the people of Israel, of the tribe of Benjamin, a Hebrew born of Hebrews; as to the law, a Pharisee; as to zeal, a persecutor of the church; as to righteousness under the law, blameless" (Philippians 3:5-6).

Paul's resume is fairly impressive. It outlines his relationships to his family and his faith. It is full of meaning and depth. It's worth something. Paul puts it all in perspective. There is one relationship that is key, that is crucial, that illuminates and preserves all the other relationships. This is what is important.

As he hastens to add: "Yet whatever gains I had, these I have come to regard as loss because of Christ" (Philippians 3:7).

It is our relationship to God, the way we take the name of Jesus, that matters more than our ancestry, our family name, our genealogies, our nationalities, our ethnic background, as the hymn writer puts it, "... the vain things that charm me most, I sacrifice them through his blood."

If we are known as a disciple of Jesus, as one who is ready to suffer and die for the name that we claim above all others, we are a member of the family of God. If we allow other things — pride over nationality or name or economic status, the team we root for, the school we attended — if we allow these other things to matter more, we have nothing. And we understand the value of nothing.

That's why it is so important for the people to give of their abundance, and that is why Moses wants to remind them it is their identity, as descendants of a wandering Aramean. It's because they are God's people.

Some people think when the gospel quotes Jesus as saying that we will always have the poor among us that suggests that there is no use in trying to work against poverty, since we will never solve the problem. But that ignores what Jesus was saying.

Jesus was actually quoting Deuteronomy 15:11, where Moses while talking about the year of jubilee said, "Since there will never cease to be some in need on the earth, I therefore command you, 'Open your hand to the poor and needy neighbor in your land.' " This verse was quoted by Jesus when the woman washed his feet and some criticized her for wasting the gift. Jesus said in reply that the poor would always be with us and some have taken that to mean we'll always have the poor so there's nothing you can do about it. You can see, however, that Jesus was quoting the law to say that since we will always have the poor we must never cease giving. The people who were criticizing the woman for what she did needed to mind their own business and set about helping the poor with their own cash instead of worrying about hers!

We are a people of abundance. Even though there are those of us who struggle to pay our bills, and often go without, we are measuring ourselves by the standards of a society that is too rich for its

133

own good. We are all rich by the standards of the rest of the world. Certainly even the richest who lived in Jesus' day would have thought that with our heat and air conditioning and microwaves and satellite television and cell phones that we were the richest people who ever lived. And so we are. And, if we want to be named and known by our wealth, we will die by our wealth.

What's in a name? If we name ourselves descendants of Abraham, brothers and sisters of Jesus, children of God, we will see true abundance by knowing only Christ. And we know Christ in the poor. As Jesus says in Matthew 25:40, "... just as you did it to one of the least of these who are members of my family, you did it to me."

You will know Christ in the poor. You will know Christ in your giving. You will know Christ in your relationships. You must have Christ at the center. It is what makes all other things possible and gives them meaning.

Lent is known as a season of giving *up*, but it is far more important to simply give, and to resist the temptation to give *in*. Give to the work of the church. Give to others. Give *up* because you want to be able to give *more*, and because you refuse to give in to our culture of wealth, power, acquisitiveness, envy, and greed. You bear great names — the names of Abraham and Jesus, and the God who *is*, and the promise of what is to come. These names make life worth living, and other lives worth saving. Amen.

## Abraham Believed God

If you've traveled with small children in a car, you've probably heard this conversation more than once. Sooner or later, whether the journey is half an hour or half a day, someone asks, "When do we get there?"

"Soon."

"How much longer?"

"A few minutes."

How long do we have to wait? It is an essential question asked in scripture. Job, the psalmist, and God's people wonder over time how long they will have to wait until God's will is done on earth as it is in heaven. We pray that phrase in the Lord's Prayer as our way of recognizing that things still aren't as they ought to be.

Some worry whether asking God how long it will be smacks of backtalk and impertinance. Oddly enough, God seems to respect backtalkers. God is different from earthly rulers who surround themselves with yes-men. Unlike the Wicked Witch Of The West who, in the musical, *The Wiz*, sings, "Don't nobody tell me no bad news." God seems to want to hear our complaints.

In today's scripture, God reminds Abram of the wonderful plans he has for him. Instead of saying, "Thanks, Lord," Abram replies, "O Lord God, what will you give me, for I continue childless, and the heir of my house is Eliezer of Damascus? ... You have given me no offspring, and so a slave born in my house is to be my heir" (Genesis 15:2-3).

One would expect a pagan god on his high throne to react to such uppityness with a little thunder bolt therapy, but one element

135

of our faith is that God is secure on the throne. There are no rivals, no other claimants to the title. God is one. And God, from a powerful position, replies like a secure ruler. A polite ruler. A mannered ruler.

The advice columnist known as Miss Manners once pointed out that manners are not, as some people might describe them, arbitrary rules designed to shackle ordinary folks. Just the opposite. The purpose of manners is to protect the powerless from the powerful by linking everyone in a network of responsibility and accountability. God sets the example by being polite to Abram. God makes an enormous promise to Abram even though Abram has impolitely bemoaned his current state of affairs and is impatient for change.

Abram believes the promise, and he believes it before God catalogs the rewards that will be given him; all the lands that will belong to his descendants. Abram's response brings yet another blessing ("and it was reckoned to him as righteousness"). Abram receives an embarrassment of riches. He will not complain anymore about delays.

This is the essence of faith — to stare into the void and jump, to know that knowledge can carry you so far and no farther. The Old Testament rarely speaks in the positive sense of the word *belief*. On most occasions, it speaks of those who don't believe in God. Some suggest that it is because belief is presupposed in everyday life. It is in crisis situations, however, that we know whether we actually believe.

This scene of blessing takes place after a crisis situation. It was necessary for Abram to rescue his nephew Lot after he was caught up in battles between a confusing array of kings. Abram is caught up in larger politics on the world scene, and the blessing he received earlier from God proves to be powerful. "I will bless those who bless you, and the one who curses you I will curse ..." (Genesis 12:3).

This scene is followed by a strange and awe-inspiring ceremony, in which God takes upon himself the weight of the covenant. Abram is directed to split a sacrifice in half. Buzzards come, a sign of foreboding, but a mysterious flame appears in the dark and crosses between the pieces. A human who would make a covenant of this sort would be saying, "May this tearing a body in half happen to me if I let you down." This is what God is saying, as well. It is a solemn pledge from the Creator to the created. Both covenant and pledge are instigated and guaranteed by God. Like the hymn says, "What wondrous love is this that caused the Lord of bliss to bear the dreadful curse for my soul?"

This is a staggering promise — that a man and a woman in their old age could and would still have a child and, more importantly, a future with hope. Is this what we show to our seniors? Think of the people we know in nursing homes. These are caring places with dedicated workers. Nevertheless, many who live in these places are confined to wheelchairs or have very limited mobility. Their struggle with despair can be very difficult. What share in the ministry of the church, what place in the prayer ministry, do we encourage in our nursing home residents?

When we visit our loved ones and friends there, we should bring them hope — not a vague everything-will-be-okay sort of hope — but a practical hope built upon possibilities around us. We must remember that God isn't through with us no matter how old we are. We may have more limitations depending on our circumstances, but God is still calling us to pray and to minister to and for each other. There are practical ways to serve each other, even within the confines of a nursing home.

Finding meaning is important at all stages of our lives, and redefining it based on our circumstances can be just as important. The scripture assures us that Abram believes God, and this is credited to him as righteousness. However, both Abram and Sarai see the basic absurdity of the situation and both laugh at different times. It is one more example of the way God accepts our reactions as part of a full relationship. There is not some sacred way to approach God that precludes everything else. We need not always restrict ourselves to pious mouthings. We can argue with God, we can express anger, we can laugh.

Because we love.

In the same way, our understanding of salvation through the cross, dying to live, losing to gain, may seem absurd to the world.

We can laugh along with the joke because we know that despite its absurdity, it is true. Laughter is as essential as awe when it comes to our good news, our gospel. Laughter is perspective. We see clearly, while the world barely sees at all.

Some might be content to accept the fact that, as Genesis 15:6 says, "And he believed the Lord; and the Lord reckoned it to him as righteousness" and not worry about how exactly the thing works. Is Abraham's belief a reflection of his faith or a reflection of his works?

You see, both the Apostle Paul and James, the brother of Jesus, quote this verse, yet they seem to quote it in quite different contexts. In Galatians 3:5-7 we read: "Well then, does God supply you with the Spirit and work miracles among you by your doing the works of the law, or by your believing what you heard? Just as Abraham 'believed God, and it was reckoned to him as righteousness,' ... those who believe are the descendants of Abraham."

But James writes: "Thus the scripture was fulfilled that says, 'Abraham believed God, and it was reckoned to him as righteousness,' and he was called the friend of God. You see that a person is justified by works and not by faith alone" (James 2:23-24).

The controversy between faith and works was not settled by the Apostle Paul 2,000 years ago — it is an essential tension and a constant contradiction that is not settled within our heart of hearts.

If our salvation is by faith alone, can't we all just profess our faith in Jesus as our Lord and Savior and just be done with it? We could stay home on Sunday mornings and put our feet up and read the paper and maybe eat leftovers and get some real rest on the sabbath.

If our salvation is by works alone, then does it really matter what we profess as long as we're doing the work of Jesus Christ? Do we even have to know about Jesus to do his work?

When Paul wrote his letter to Galatian Christians, faith in Jesus was still centered in Jerusalem, and many assumed a new Christian had to adopt Jewish cultural practices.

But in the Roman Empire there were many different cultural practices. People didn't think the same way. To some, circumcision was not the mark of a covenant but a disfigurement of a body they considered beautiful. While worship of one God was attractive, the complex food laws made no sense when consumption of meat was a social practice that involved, at least technically, the worship of a pagan god.

Paul was advocating for the acceptance of new converts who would follow Jesus but not shed their own cultural and ethnic backgrounds. In today's terms, it was as if everyone had to become Irish or Italian or Ukrainian in order to become a follower of Jesus. Yet, anyone who has lived in a multicultural setting knows that worship takes delightfully different forms in the African churches, in the many Hispanic traditions, among Asians of various sorts, as well as all the different European varieties.

At the Jerusalem Council described in Acts 15:1-35, James, the brother of Jesus, and the other Jerusalem leaders met with Paul, Barnabas, and others to discuss the matter. The result, described both in Acts and in Galatians, seems to indicate that Paul "won." Salvation was by faith in Jesus, not in the acts of a believer.

Central to Paul's arguments was his interpretation of the Hebrew Scriptures. According to Paul, Abraham acted by faith. There was no Hebrew Law for him to obey. Paul quoted Genesis 15:6 to show that Abraham "believed God, and it was reckoned to him as righteousness" (Galatians 3:6).

If Paul won, James doesn't seem to know it. In his letter, James also refers to Abraham when he writes, "Was not our ancestor Abraham justified by works when he offered his son Isaac on the altar? You see that faith was active along with his works, and faith was brought to completion by the works. Thus the scripture was fulfilled that says, 'Abraham believed God, and it was reckoned to him as righteousness,' and he was called the friend of God. You see that a person is justified by works and not by faith alone" (James 2:21-24).

James went on to say, "If a brother or sister is naked and lacks daily food, and one of you says to them, 'Go in peace; keep warm and eat your fill,' and yet you do not supply their bodily needs, what is the good of that? So faith by itself, if it has no works, is dead" (James 2:15-17).

139

In the same letter he also wrote: "Religion that is pure and undefiled before God, the Father, is this: to care for orphans and widows in their distress, and to keep oneself unstained by the world" (James 1:27).

In examining this contradiction, I would first remind us all that neither Paul nor James were twenty-first-century North Americans. They were both Jewish, both citizens of an empire that spanned the western world, and both struggled with cultural assumptions that divided genders, races, and social and economic classes as a matter of course. Both were martyred for their faith.

As Jews, they believed there were two ways, a *yetzer ha'tov*, a good way, and a *yetzer ha'ra*, a bad way. They believed we were able to make choices between those two ways. But in one of those "Same Planet, Different Worlds" kind of things they took those same building blocks and came to look at the world in different, complementary ways.

Remember Paul, who insists that we are saved by faith and not works, nevertheless is constantly promoting good works. At the Jerusalem conference, Paul agrees to take up a collection for the poor in Jerusalem. He speaks of that collection's importance in 2 Corinthians 8 and 9. On another trip to Jerusalem one of his good deeds was to pay the fees to release four Christians from a Nazarite vow (Acts 21:24).

Faith in Jesus seems essential, but Jesus himself doesn't seem to care much about it. I do not recall a single verse in which he says of himself, "Proclaim my name and be saved." He is always pointing to his Heavenly Father. The Sermon on the Mount seems very works-oriented. In Matthew 25:31-46, Jesus describes an end-time judgment scenario based totally on good works.

It seems to me that most Christians give lip service to Paul's formulation about grace over law, they also believe in their hearts, as it is stated in Matthew 25 and James 1:27, that our works save us.

Does either extreme, faith or works, have much to do with faith in Jesus Christ? Haven't we all met Christians who insist that since they have "come forward" and expressed their faith in Jesus they can no longer sin? They claim whatever they do is not a sin, whether it's ignoring a parent's medical condition, looking down with contempt on people of other races, or simply living in callous disregard of the sufferings of others around the world, they cannot be touched by reason or argument. They are never wrong.

On the other hand, haven't we met those who are so dedicated to the work of Jesus yet would be hard pressed to quote a single verse of a gospel outside the Sermon on the Mount? Jesus becomes a convenient hat rack on which to hang their arguments.

If there is any conundrum associated with scripture, any apparent contradiction for which we should give thanks, it may be that the tension between faith and works is essential to building the real body of Christ. Every denomination, every small Bible study group, each race and ethnic enclave, all the Christians spread across every continent, should be pulling each other back and forth, challenging, teaching, and most of all, loving each other.

Life is messy. It's never fully resolved. Things don't always have to work out. When it comes to the great questions, do we have to have an answer today, or can it wait until next Tuesday? Most of all, can we give ourselves time to work on these problems together?

Remember the thief on the cross? Was he saved by faith or works? Faith in what? There was no risen Lord — or even a fully crucified Jesus. Then was he saved by works? But he didn't do anything. He didn't rescue Jesus, or alleviate his physical sufferings. The thief spoke.

I'm not going to try to settle whether the thief was saved by works or faith. I just know he's home free. And when it comes to the millions who serve Jesus by declarations of faith or words or actions or simply good intentions, I'm not going to try to settle exactly how the mechanism works that saves them.

I'm just going to praise God. Amen.

# He Will Abundantly Pardon

Perhaps you have taken a vacation with the intention of seeking out some historical or national monument. Some of the favorites are probably Mount Rushmore, the Liberty Bell, the Gettysburg Battlefield, or Valley Forge. Indeed, this may have been the point of the whole vacation, to take in an important site that ties the past to the present, and on into the future.

Certainly, if you have been to Valley Forge, for instance, even on a warm summer's day, it is hard not to shiver as you consider the horrific winter conditions that tested the valiant few whose faithfulness preserved the liberties we enjoy today. Or, perhaps, you have watched the pattern of the shadows change on the four presidents memorialized on Mount Rushmore, and wondered if in the future some fifth face will prove worthy of being carved in stone.

Other times, however, you may have had another goal as you drove across this great country, moving swiftly along some highway on the great plains or in the midst of giant forests beneath the face of immense mountains, when you noticed a battered historical marker ahead. There may have been a warning — "Historical Marker Ahead." Or, perhaps, you spotted it as you are drove down the highway. Did you wonder, "Should I stop? What is being memorialized out here in the middle of nowhere? What great and significant event occurred that later generations wished to preserve for the memory of humankind?"

If you have ever stopped for such memorials, you quickly discovered that while some are for famous events that many people have heard of, some commemorate obscure happenings. At one point, perhaps, these were famous things and are now forgotten. We have to ask: How long is human memory? How soon do we forget? That's one reason we need memorials. The things we think we will know forever slip our minds.

But there's another reason for memorials, and that is to influence how we look back on an event, how we interpret it. The Monocacy Battlefield, near the Monocacy River in Maryland, is a good illustration of this. There are two sets of contradictory monuments scattered throughout the Civil War battlefield. Both are right but only one is correct.

One set, erected about fifty years after the fighting ended by the Daughters of the Confederacy, celebrates a Confederate victory on Northern soil. The other set, erected by the Park Service, celebrates a Union victory. The truth is that veteran Southern troops did defeat raw Union troops, but the battle itself delayed the Confederate advance by a day and prevented them from reaching an undefended Washington, D.C. before it was reinforced with battle-hardened soldiers.

In today's scripture passage, Isaiah is trying to do two things when it comes to memorials — he is trying to draw the memory of the people back to an important and forgotten historical perspective, and he is trying to influence that perspective, as well.

Isaiah is calling the people back to the memory of the good things God has done, is doing, and will do. One key word is *berit*, covenant. Isaiah wants to talk about the covenant God has made with the people, which is the source of the good things God has shared in the past and will share in the future. He is writing to a shell-shocked people who have suffered great trauma and after the manner of a road sign designed to catch our attention, Isaiah uses an image which can't help but cause them to take notice.

Isaiah phrases his memorial as an invitation. Just as Wisdom in the book of Proverbs cries aloud to get the attention of the people, so Isaiah hollers out an invitation, much like one would do in the marketplace to attract customers.

I'm reminded of the county fair, where vendors try to get our attention. What will you eat while you're there? Homemade donuts, fried bread, a cheese-steak sandwich, onions rings, a corn dog, or maybe just a giant pretzel! There are so many choices. Now, imagine that while we're salivating over all the choices and trying to figure out what it'll cost, a single voice rises above the din and offers it all for free!

Concrete gifts of water, wine, milk, and bread are offered, good things, necessary things, the staff of life. Come here and eat and drink, Isaiah shouts in the marketplace, and just when he has our attention, he tells us the most amazing thing of all.

What Isaiah is really talking about is the covenant God has made with his servant King David, but now God extends that covenant, that gift, that promise, with all the people — and all of us!

This is God's plan. It's God's way of thinking. God is more aware than we of the king's failings, the people's failings, our failings, yet the promise is not only renewed, it is extended to cover a greater number of people.

What should our response be? It should be immediate. "Seek the Lord while he may be found, call upon him while he is near; let the wicked forsake their way and the unrighteous their thoughts; let them return to the Lord, that he may have mercy on them, and to our God, for he will abundantly pardon" (vv. 6-7).

In a way this makes no sense. We're used to insurance firms restricting coverage, companies reducing their liability, fine print on all those marvelous medical ads on television making it clear the offer is not quite as breathtaking as we thought.

This is more than manna, which sustains us for our day's work, even in the desert, and which is generous enough. This is food for eternity. We may not fully realize its value, any more than did the people who received the bread from Jesus and who followed him until he talked about the living bread. So generous and breathtaking is this offer that we may simply fail to understand it, and fall back on our old mainstays.

That's why Isaiah is doing his best to get our attention. God is preparing to abundantly pardon. Not grudgingly, stingily, but abundantly. God's Word will "not return to me empty, but it shall accomplish that which I purpose ..." (v. 11). And we indeed "shall go out in joy, and be led back in peace" (v. 12).

145

All of nature will join in this celebration. Just as we celebrate God's breathtaking wonders in our national parks, so too these wonders celebrate with us, according to Isaiah, in response to God's promises. All "the trees of the field shall clap their hands" (v. 12).

God doesn't think like us. God's ways are not our ways, and you cannot receive this gift if you insist on clinging to the old ways. Time and again this is what God's people did, in response to the Old Covenant and the New Covenant. We are afraid to take a risk, to try something new, to stop and listen, truly listen, to what God has to offer. Instead, we fall back on the old ways and forget.

The sin of forgetting what God has done for us as individuals and as people, that's something we see with God's people in the desert, and ourselves in our own desert. We cling to the ways of violence instead of redemption, of hatred instead of risking love, of fear instead of overwhelming joy. It's not that the world is not dangerous. Of course it is. But we are the people of God's peace. We were not given a spirit of fear, but of joy.

There are plenty of things to fear in today's world, but they should not dominate our thinking. Most of us make it through the day. Most of us are not shot, punched, diced, clipped, bent, folded, or mutilated. Most of us don't have to be survivors. We can be team players. We can work together for all, rather than striving to eliminate all others.

As for those who do suffer, who have suffered, who are victims — that's where we are called as God's people, as messengers like Isaiah, to spread the good news. We do not apply Band-Aids. We do not make things well with a word. But, we walk with those who are hurting in order to bring hope.

Isaiah didn't turn to a people who were shell-shocked from invasion and captivity and say there was nothing wrong. He didn't say that as God's people we don't grieve. There is plenty wrong, and we do grieve, but he told us that in a broken world where sorrowful things happen, God intends always to be a part of our future, a future filled with hope and purpose. His presence was a reminder that in sorrow, God is present. The historical markers that proclaim the exile and return are hope and peace.

146

It's not a message the world is ready for. We want to hold on to the old hatreds, the old grudges. We want to respond to hate with hate, to violence with violence. But God will abundantly pardon. Not just pardon, not grudgingly pardon, but abundantly pardon. Can we do less, with each other, and with those around the world? We must tell them of this abundant joy, in the midst of all of life's travails and beyond.

Jesus was criticized because he and his disciples didn't fast, didn't wear ashes, but ate, drank, and displayed the marks of life and living. The cross lay ahead for Jesus and many of his disciples, and for us as well, but as today's scripture tells us, as the heavens are higher than the earth, so are God's ways higher than our ways.

Stop. In the midst of our technological marketplace, listen to the voice that rises above the others. On the journey of life in which we hurry, often without purpose or joy, slow down, stop, read the memorializing marker. Remember God's history, God's promises, and adopt a different way of looking at the world.

Things aren't what you think — they're much, much better. Amen.

# Gateway To Grace

When you visit a church camp you're aware that you're separated from civilization. When you take a walk late at night, for whatever reason, and it's usually for whatever reason, you can't help but wonder what that rustling in the darkness might be. It's probably a raccoon, or a smaller animal, as frightened of you as you are pretending that you're not frightened of it.

But it could be a bear. It's an unnerving experience to see a bear close up. Bears in the wild are the epitome of untamed nature. They don't fit into neat categories. They're certainly not sympathetic to humans, like dogs, or tolerant, like cats. People are not safe around bears. Bears have their own agenda. They act according to their own reason, with their own internal logic. You can't control a bear, but if your luck holds, you get to walk away.

Sometimes.

There's an old poem by Hillaire Belloc that goes like this:

*B stands for Bear.*
*When bears are seen approaching in the distance*
*Make up your mind at once between retreat and armed*
*    resistance.*
*One gentleman remained to fight, with what result for*
*    him?*
*The bear, with ill-concealed delight, devoured him limb*
*    from limb.*
*Another fellow turned and ran. He ran extremely hard.*
*The bear was faster than the man and beat him by a*
*    yard.*

Or maybe it's like that old joke: What's the most important thing to remember when you and a friend encounter a bear in the forest? Simply this — you don't have to be faster than the bear, just faster than your friend.

What do bears have to do with Joshua? After all, this day's text seems to be about a river crossing, the building of a monument, and the cessation of heavenly welfare as the manna stops falling. But there is a connection. So I want to jump ahead to the next few verses, before coming back to our starting point. Open your Bibles to Joshua 5:13-16.

Forty years of wandering are over for Joshua. Now God's promises are about to be fulfilled. Ahead lies the battle of Jericho, and many trials. Behind lies the passing of a leader, Moses, who can never be replaced.

And on the nervous night before a battle, Joshua finds himself in the dark — literally — without a clue as to what might happen.

There is a literal rustle in the woods. Who goes there? A bear?

In my mind, what follows is one of the spookiest passages in scripture, worthy of being shared around the campfire on a moonless night under a dark dish of stars.

Someone is standing before Joshua, a man with a sword. He quickly tries to categorize this intruder. Friend or foe — *my* friend or *my* foe.

"Joshua walked toward him and said to him, 'Are you on our side or on that of our enemies?' He replied, 'On neither side. I have come now as the captain of the army of Yahweh' " (Joshua 5:13-14 NJB).

Joshua falls on his face in terror, for the captain of the army of Yahweh can be none other than God. Then the captain speaks to Joshua as he had spoken to Moses a generation before. "Take your sandals off your feet, for the place where you are standing is holy" (Joshua 5:15 NJB).

And knowing the identity of the captain, Joshua must have known instantly that the question "*My* friend or foe?" was the wrong question. This is not Joshua's battle. It is the captain's battle.

Joshua is standing face-to-face with God.

Whoa, get your facts straight, some might say. Joshua is talking to an angel, not directly to God. However, we sometimes forget that in the Old Testament the line is not sharply drawn between God and angels. We tend to think of angels as people. They are not people. They are something different. They are to some extent more than just messengers, which is the literal meaning of their title. They are the present Word of God.

When we speak, sound comes out. When God speaks, something happens. When God speaks, we hear, see, and feel it. The heart palpitates, the eyes bulge, the skin crackles, and we mistake wonder for fear, as the children of Israel found when the Shekinah descended on Mount Sinai. Also consider the second chapter of Judges when an angel appears, causing great fright in Israel, and speaks as Almighty God. We may conclude that when God speaks, he "breathes" angels.

Some may say that God doesn't do things like this. But one thing we can be sure of — just as bears do pretty much what they want in camp, so God can do pretty much what he wants. After all, it's God's world. We just live in it.

Joshua stands before God and lives. He is becoming God's servant. He's getting the priorities straight that we need as well. It's not a question of whether God is on our side, but whether we're on God's side. It's time to get rid of the things that encumber us, the attachments to this earth that may be attractive, but which bind us fast to the earth. The idolatry of racism, the illusion of nationalism, the temptation of materialism — get rid of them. Recognize who is the captain of the army of the Lord.

It's a little scary. As the scripture text tells us (5:12), it means no more manna! The manna fed the children of Israel in the wilderness, but evidently it could be pretty tiresome fare. It was free for the taking, and it was a sign of God's blessing and goodness, but I wonder if it could really compare to that first tomato of the spring, the red, ripe, juicy tomato that some of us dream about when we look over the seed catalogs in the dead of winter. A tomato that is partly the result of our own labor, but is also the result of the deep majestic wonder that is God's Holy Spirit, moving in our midst, drawing life from the ground and from our lives as well.

Once we are free of the manna, once we are free of the law, once we boldly enter into the territory of grace, we come to a place where both success and failure are possible, where there are no guarantees, where anything can happen. It's a little scary. Okay, it's a lot scary. But so is forgiveness and transformation.

We've looked at the verses that follow today's scripture passage. Now let's jump backward and see what happened before. It's all part of the crossing over at the River Jordan, and how God's people rededicated themselves to what their ancestors had promised many years before. The people of God had seen great things — the plagues that struck Egypt, the brooding mystery of the passing over, and the simple grace of the Passover. They had watched the waters of the Red Sea part and had crossed over, and had seen the chariots of the Egyptians, the mightiest high-tech army of the ancient world, swallowed up in the waters that closed behind them.

Yet, they had also rebelled again and again. They forgot the horrors of slavery and pined for their old condition, an affront to the God who had rescued them. When there was trouble there were also troublemakers who painted a rosy picture of a past that never was, and led the people astray.

That can happen nowadays as people pretend that the past was simpler and better. Life was not simpler. It was full of tremendous drudgery, of hard work from dawn to dusk just to scrabble out survival. If historical dramas and books show us the glittering world of the very rich in ages past, we forget that most people were bitterly poor. They did not live long lives. The slightest infection could cast them into eternity. They were subject to the whims of rulers who believed they were descended from gods but whose personal morals suggested they were more likely descended from demons.

Those who look back with fondness to a century ago might conveniently forget that blacks were oppressed in our country and subject to horrific lynchings, often hung from trees and burned alive for crimes they had not committed.

People certainly forget that disease and illness killed many people long before their time, and others grew prematurely old. A century ago, only four percent of the people were over the age of eighty. Now the number is closer to twelve percent!

But we forget the past. We romanticize it. And those things we should really remember, such as the blessings of God in all ages, we ignore. So when the faithless generation had died in the desert, Joshua turns to their children and grandchildren and reacquaints them with their history, and invites the men to be circumcised, something that had been neglected. He invited them to reclaim their heritage; to enter into the gateway toward freedom.

Because they were ready to walk through that gateway, to cross Jordan and claim God's promises, the scripture tells us: "The Lord said to Joshua, 'Today I have rolled away from you the disgrace of Egypt.' And so that place is called Gilgal to this day" (Joshua 5:9).

The disgrace of Egypt was still on them, despite their escape from that land, because they were still slaves to their past. Crossing Jordan, entering the gateway, they put away the disgrace and prepared to enter a mature relationship with God.

And the manna ceased.

In today's scripture text nothing really happens. And yet everything happens. Because a believer and a people are now ready to claim God's blessings.

In Lent we are given the chance to reclaim who we are as a people, to prepare to enter into glory land, and to meet God face-to-face in the person of the risen Jesus. In a sense nothing happens. We go to church and behave as if nothing happened. But everything is happening: in the quiet prayer warriors who hold destruction at bay because of the power of their prayers, among the children who wriggle and bring life to our congregation by their refusal to "behave" which seems to mean do anything but express joy in living, through the active mission people who see every day as an opportunity to praise God through active ministry to others. Every thing is happening in the planners and the sweepers and the bakers and the singers, in all the people and everyone — everything is happening here. We are called to prepare ourselves once more to be God's people, to put aside the constraints of the laws that worked for us in the desert of our lives, and run through the gateway to Grace, and our real home.

Come, let us reclaim our past as Christians, recall the glorious story of how we were lost in the slavery of sin, and how we were reclaimed, renamed, and restored to our heritage. The manna of the law, the belief that everything can be divided into a clear right and wrong without our having to make any mature decisions as believers, will cease. Instead we will claim the grace that saves us, and allows us to view others whose faults are no worse than our own, to be seen with the eyes of grace as well.

We'll understand that our God is in charge, not us. That there's no telling what God will do, but that we can rest assured that what God does is good. The shame of the past will roll away, and we will become God's partners, God's mature people, ready to live by the rules of a kingdom not yet recognized by this world, but which will, in God's time, become apparent to all. In the meantime, we will cross over our own Jordan, and say with the psalmist:

> *Make a joyful noise to the Lord, all the earth. Worship the Lord with gladness; come into his presence with singing. Know that the Lord is God. It is he that made us, and we are his; we are his people, and the sheep of his pasture. Enter his gates with thanksgiving, and his courts with praise. Give thanks to him, bless his name. For the Lord is good; his steadfast love endures forever, and his faithfulness to all generations.*
>
> — Psalm 100

And there's no shame in that at all. Who goes there? Someone good. And who goes with that someone good? Us. Praise God. Amen.

154

# Past, Present, Future

We have a great history as a nation, but many of us are content with the pious stories we learned as children and shy away from learning more about the great events that shaped America. For instance, most people would prefer the story that, as a child, George Washington said, "I cannot tell a lie," in admitting he had cut down a cherry tree with his axe. The true story, according to Henry Wiencek in his book, *An Imperfect God*, is that Washington admitted to his mother that he had ridden a favorite horse of hers to death.

Wiencek's book is one of three recent volumes that invite us to learn more about the man who was the father of our country. Wiekncek's book explores Washington's uncomfortable relationship with slaves and slavery, and chronicles how this very imperfect man grew until he became very uncomfortable indeed with the institution that marred our nation's founding.

The book, *His Excellency George Washington*, by Joseph J. Ellis, examines how the defeats he suffered as a young officer taught him the lessons he needed for victory in the Revolution, and how this one person held the country together, both in war and in peace.

David McCullough's *1776* reminds us how precariously the whole Revolution hung in that fateful year, and how the victories at Christmastime insured that the Revolution would remain viable even after terrible defeats, allowing the French to recognize the new nation and get involved in the war for independence.

As important as these books are, teaching us about the past, we can become so focused on the past that we lose a vision for the

155

future and indeed, can come to resent modern prophets who point the way. Dr. Martin Luther King, Jr., lived a couple of centuries after Washington, but his nonviolent struggle against racism, and his famous "I Have A Dream" speech were really fulfillments of the path toward freedom and equality imperfectly begun at our nation's founding. An understanding of both past and present events is necessary to know who we are.

In the same way, Isaiah begins this passage by inviting his people to look back at their founding father, Moses, and the great events of the Exodus that set them free as a people. When he speaks of the Lord "who makes a way in the sea, a path in the mighty waters, who brings out chariot and horse, army and warrior; they lie down, they cannot rise, they are extinguished, quenched like a wick ..." (Isaiah 43:16-17), he is unmistakably pointing to the events that shaped God's people as a nation. Just as surely as most of us would recognize a painting of George Washington crossing the Delaware, the people of Israel had a mental picture of the parting of the waters of the Red Sea, and the moment when they closed back on Pharaoh's chariots!

But just as quickly, Isaiah tells us the words of the Lord: "Do not remember the former things, or consider the things of old. I am about to do a new thing; now it springs forth, do you not perceive it? I will make a way in the wilderness and rivers in the desert" (Isaiah 43:18-19). This is his "I Have A Dream" speech.

There was no danger of the people forgetting the Exodus. They celebrated it every year in the Passover. That festival brought families together to recall the past, and tie it to the present, so they could envision God's future with them. But if they are so focused on the past they cannot look to that future, they will not see that God is doing something new, something that will bring freedom from sin as surely as the Exodus brought freedom from slavery.

This will be an event so great that it will tie all of humanity and nature together. The images of creation having a part in the great redemption to come that is mentioned in this scripture is nothing new. The righteousness of God outlined in the Old and New Testaments is not limited to humanity, but includes all of creation. That's one of the reasons we should care for creation now. If Jesus is the heir of all things, then we must recognize that the heir will return and expect to receive that inheritance from the stewards. We are the stewards of creation, and if we do not care for what is put in our charge, and which does not belong to us but is entrusted to us, then we will prove to be poor stewards indeed.

Isaiah is looking forward to that heir of all things, none other than Jesus himself. And at this point in Lent, so should we. During the Advent and Christmas season we grew to love the child in the manger. Now we are challenged by the adult that infant has become — challenged to become God's new people, the people God wants us to become. Looking back should inspire us to look forward rather than freezing the past.

We began by talking about American history, but there's an even more ancient American history that can be instructive as well. That's the history of the Anasazi, the Native Americans who built one of the greatest civilizations of any age. They built structures such as Pueblo Bonito in Chaco Canyon, five stories high in places, and containing over 600 rooms for crop storage and religious purposes. Pueblo Bonito was bigger than anything ever built in America or Europe until the late nineteenth century. The Anasazi created one of the great civilizations — and then walked away from it.

In his book, *Anasazi America*, author, David E. Stuart, charts the course of the amazing people who inhabited the Four Corners area of the American Southwest. Over the course of hundreds of years, these people developed an amazing lifestyle, thriving despite an average rainfall of eight to ten inches a year by changing with the times. Turkeys provided eggs, dogs protected crops, plants provided medicinals as well as food, and always, corn was planted on every available plot in the hope that some of it would thrive.

Eventually, the great houses, with their hundreds of rooms, were built as storage and religious centers. The Anasazi did not observe a difference between the sacred and secular as we do in our society. About a millennium ago, a complex system of hundreds of miles of roads linked distant settlements in a web of trade and worship. During this time, some of the greatest buildings ever constructed rose while Europe foundered in the Dark Ages; a time some call "the thousand years without a bath."

But at one point, the Anasazi system failed. There were periods of catastrophic drought and their precious resources dwindled. It no longer made sense to build great houses and construct royal roads. What happened? According to Stuart, the Anasazi walked away from this way of life, rejected power, and changed to a more egalitarian system that emphasized one's place in the community, conformity to a peculiar way of life, and the necessity of putting others first. The Pueblo Indians, who exist today despite efforts to wipe them out through war and disease, are the descendants of that great system.

"A durable community is one that balances growth with efficiency and refuses to be seduced by greed and power." Stuart writes, and adds that greed "is not a badge of honor. It is the signature of a dying society."

Isaiah wanted his people to walk away from greed and power. So did Jesus whose Sermon on the Mount invites us to an even more perfect system, if we are willing to become a peculiar people who reject power, the trappings of the culture, and the temptation to excuse ourselves because "everyone else acts that way."

It means walking away from a culture that values power and prestige over the community of faith, which chooses death over life.

It seems to me that the wave of so-called "reality television," while entertaining to some, is built upon the idea that there's only one winner, and everyone else is a loser. By contrast, the Sermon on the Mount invites us to live with all people by rules that promote life and salvation rather than death and destruction.

These sayings, which may seem counterintuitive at first are, in the end, the only way to live — if we want to live like Jesus.

Historically, the church of Jesus Christ has tried to find a way to get out of doing what Jesus mandated. One of the most popular "outs" given by church leaders is that this Sermon on the Mount is delivered to the disciples, not the crowds. It doesn't count for us. Only those specially chosen by Jesus should turn the other cheek.

This way of thinking became necessary when Emperor Constantine made Christianity legal around the year 315 A.D. Once the church and state became one, then it was important for rulers to be able to authorize the torture, mutilation, and slaying of enemies and friends alike, and still be able to show up for worship on Sunday. Churches prized their relationship with the state, and those who professed suspicion about this relationship were often branded heretics.

Eventually, it was simply assumed that you couldn't have a church unless it was supported by the state, and supported the state in turn. Even the reformers, who did great work by challenging an established church by creating churches of their own, assumed that the church and state needed to work in concert, that their aims and goals were one.

By contrast, the radical reformers, typified by the Anabaptists of the sixteenth century and the Pietists of the seventeenth and eighteenth century, and represented in the modern world by the Amish, Mennonites, and Brethren, insisted that the Sermon on the Mount was the norm, rather than the exception, and that it was possible to live this way of life — assuming you weren't bothered by the fact that you'd be persecuted, shunned, slandered, driven away, arrested, tortured, and murdered.

Assuming you didn't mind standing with Jesus and suffering the same fate.

Are you prepared to walk away from the lures of power and wealth? Are you really and truly willing to take up your cross and follow Jesus? Are you prepared to look back into biblical history not as a literary exercise but because you intend to live forward, into the future, as the stewards of God's earth and disciples of Jesus Christ?

It means being willing to change. And it means you might be misunderstood, reviled, and persecuted by those in authority.

The Roman historian, Tacitus, writing around the year 115 A.D., calls to mind that in order to get rid of rumors that he himself had set fire to Rome, the Emperor Nero attempted to pin the blame on Christians and to persecute them. He felt he could get away with it because Christians were "a class hated for their abominations."

Tacitus referred to our faith as "a most mischievous superstition" which should have been squelched when Pontius Pilate crucified Christ, but which had, by then, spread throughout the entire Roman Empire and found a home in the capital city itself.

Tacitus believed that all Christians hated the rest of humanity and practiced cannibalism and were disloyal to the state. These things weren't true, but it didn't prevent them from being tortured and killed.

What do people think about us? Do they think we are self-righteous hypocrites who look down on others, judgmental, impossible to please, closed minded? Do they have reason to believe that way?

What is true? Have we looked to our past, our Old and New Testament roots, so that we claim our glorious future, not to hoard it to ourselves but to share it with all humanity? Will we practice the same selfless love that Jesus outlined in the Sermon on the Mount and which he himself practiced, loving and forgiving his executioners even as they nailed him to a cross? Are we ready to change the world by following his nonviolent path?

Martin Luther King, Jr., said that one reason he practiced nonviolence was that he hoped not only to free his people, but to save his enemies. Jesus called us to love our enemies, and to work for their salvation, not their eradication. That is our real heritage. Claiming the past, present, and future of our faith is expressed best in this simple phrase: Christ Has Died, Christ Is Risen, Christ Will Come Again! Die with Christ, rise as a new person, secure in the knowledge that Jesus is coming back, work for the kingdom by the rules of the kingdom! God is doing a new thing! Walk away from the old and claim our shared eternal reward. Amen.

# Essentials

D. L. Miller of Mount Morris, Illinois, was a world traveler among a people who didn't travel much. He was a Dunker, one of the Plain People, who lived in the late nineteenth century. He wore a dark coat and dark pants and a long beard without a mustache. When others bought cars, the Dunkers kept their horses and buggies. If you were a believer, then you dressed like everyone else in your church, and acted like everyone in your church, and made a point of never standing out. His people made a point of keeping themselves separate and unstained from the world — and that meant no missionaries.

The rest of the Christian world was getting caught up with missionary zeal but the Dunkers were a little cautious. What if their young people went out on missions and came back different? Maybe the women wouldn't want to wear plain clothes and prayer veils. Maybe the young men would want to wear bow ties and bowlers. Better to stay at home and preach the gospel in comfortable surroundings.

But D. L. Miller took it into his head to go on a trip around the world. Not only that, he brought a new-fangled camera with him. He traveled to the Holy Land, and to Egypt, and to the seven cities of Revelation. He went to Africa and India and China.

When he got back, he traveled from one Dunker church to another, showing his glass slides with another new-fangled invention — the magic lantern. This primitive slide projection machine made the rest of the world come alive. Suddenly those people in other countries became real, as he showed their faces and told stories

161

about them. They saw real suffering and anguish, a need for teachers, doctors, nurses, evangelists — caring for people of all stripes. They saw a need, a hunger for the gospel. The young people grew excited. A few bearded elders cautioned the rest, but soon Dunker youths were traveling to India, Africa, and China, baptizing people in the name of the Father, the Son, and the Holy Spirit.

And they realized that people in these hot climates were not going to wear prayer coverings and Dunker beards and dark clothing. It made sense. The plain garb didn't matter. Horses and buggies didn't matter. Instead, like others in the mission fields, the missionaries preached a simple gospel.

It was the same for other missionaries of other faiths, they discovered. Back home in the states, their priests and ministers might argue about points of theology, about the means and method of baptism and communion, about songs and hymns and choruses and chants, but in the mission fields it was all about the *essentials*. It was all about Jesus!

What do we believe? What do we confess? Are we angry and against things that do not matter? Or are we talking about nothing but Jesus and the mission of Jesus?

This Isaiah passage is written to a people who may have forgotten about what is essential. They need someone to show them the heart of the faith. They need a teacher to make suffering real to them, so they will put aside all distractions and focus on what is needed now.

This passage is known as the third of the great servant songs in scripture. The speaker is quite aware there is suffering. Using the title and name of God, he says, "The Lord God has given me the tongue of a teacher, that I may know how to sustain the weary with a word ..." (Isaiah 50:4). This commission comes from God. It is God's work that this ancient missionary must accomplish.

These words speak to Isaiah's time, but they also point to the mission and ministry of Jesus. Indeed Jesus says: "Come to me, all you that are weary and are carrying heavy burdens, and I will give you rest" (Matthew 11:28). We are so weary, we bear such burdens, we are in such pain, but we ignore the teacher, the one who comes to show us the way.

It is not a way around pain, or without pain, but through pain. We see clearly the images of the trial and torture of Jesus in the words of Isaiah: "I gave my back to those who struck me, and my cheeks to those who pulled out the beard; I did not hide my face from insult and spitting" (Isaiah 50:6).

But these are not words of defeat. Isaiah says, "He who vindicates me is near ..." (Isaiah 50:8). This is the same thing Jesus proclaims from the cross. We are familiar with his words of despair: "My God, my God, why have you forsaken me? Why are you so far from helping me, from the words of my groaning?" What most of us don't seem to know is that these are the opening words of Psalm 22. In Jesus' day one had only to quote the first verse of a psalm for all to call to mind the rest of it as well. The psalm catalogs the many horrors endured by God's servant, but also contains the promise of vindication and restoration, of being heard by God in agony, of being delivered!

Jesus speaks from pain to us in pain. We are emptied but are filled once more by God. It is the Lord God who hears us, rescues us, redeems us.

No one seeks pain. No one wants pain, but our culture treats pain like an outrage, like an affront, as if God and society have let us down. Our lives can never be pain free. We should work for the elimination of pain in the lives of the living and the dying, but on this, Passion Sunday, we must also recognize pain as an invitation — to minister and to serve. Missionaries were quick to recognize the pain across the ocean and to answer it, focusing on the essentials of the gospel and ignoring all the distractions of denomination and sect.

In addition to the invitation that comes from the pain of others, we must see in our own pain the brokenness that allows God to shine through, and for others to minister to us as well.

Isaiah's servant issues a challenge to us. He also provides meaning to what would otherwise be meaningless. Jesus accepted the significance of these words, and his actions are what make this coming Friday *good* and not just painful, harsh, and cruel. Obedience leads to righteousness and victory.

When Paul wrote to the Christians in Philippi he used language that would have shocked some of his fellow believers. He borrowed the language of the pagan altars when he spoke, in chapter 2, of Jesus being poured out like an offering, and he then made it clear that in the emptying came the elevation. Jesus, equal with God, took on the form of a slave, washing the feet of his disciples, and enduring the execution reserved for slaves. That is why every knee will bow and every tongue confess that he is Lord.

From the beginning, Christians have recognized what the death and resurrection of Jesus really means. In his obedience, he was highly exalted. It was in Isaiah's passage. It happened in real life, after a real trial and a real execution.

Our own obedience will exalt us, but it will also expose us to ridicule and even danger.

On this Sunday we call to mind that the people hailed Jesus, confessed him as Savior, when he entered into Jerusalem. They called him a prophet, the son of David, the one who comes in the name of the Lord. The one before whom every knee should bow. With what enthusiasm do they greet him? How nervous Pilate and the Roman troops must have been. Pilate was in the Fortress Antonia, right next to the temple, watching and wondering, what does this mean? Is this another peasant rebel ready to lead people to their doom? Why do they greet him in a manner befitting royalty? And this man acts royal, accepting their acclamations. Yet, there is something different about him, this carpenter king....

There's irony aplenty here because we know everything they're saying and thinking is true and then some. But it's not what they think. Jesus is even more than they imagine. He's not just their king. He's Lord of the universe, creator of all that is seen and unseen. Yet he has made himself accessible. He can be touched — and killed.

We who know the story remember that the crowd quickly turned, calling for his death — watching, mocking, reviling him.

If we had been there, what would we have done? Are we fair-weather Christians? Are we Christians only when it's easy, and not when it involves pain or danger?

When our faith makes us too comfortable, when it seems as if all of society is in agreement with us, when it gets too easy, we should be wary. If we stand up for the homeless or dispossessed, if we take the side of the oppressed, against the wealthy and powerful, we should expect resistance from the world.

Sister Helen Prejean, who works for victims' rights and also against the death penalty, noted in her book, *Dead Man Walking*, that if you "... get involved with poor people ... controversy follows you like a hungry dog" and went on to note ironically, "If you work for social change, you're *political*, but if you acquiesce and go along with the status quo, you're *above* politics" (p. 111).

So expect it. Because Peter spoke like a Galilean, he was accused of being one of the followers of Jesus. If we speak in the language of love for God's poor people, they will accuse us as well. We can deny it like Peter, or we can stand by the cross, like the women of the gospels. We can confess Jesus when it's hard to do so, or wait for the time when at the name of Jesus every knee will bow.

We can't always be popular and be a Christian. There are times when we can fit into American society well enough, but there are times when we are more than Americans. We are Christians first. There will not be a separate door into heaven for different nationalities, any more than there will be separate doors for racial or ethnic categories.

Paul asks us to "let the same mind be in you that was in Christ Jesus" (Philippians 2:5), and Isaiah encourages us to remember that "it is the Lord God who helps me" (Isaiah 50:9) when others bring accusations. Let us put on our game faces and stand up for Jesus.

Is this possible? Can we do such a thing? We can. We do. We have. Isaiah said: "The Lord God helps me; therefore I have not been disgraced; therefore I have set my face like flint, and I know that I shall not be put to shame ..." (Isaiah 50:7). Time and again Christian disciples, faced with the choice of standing by Jesus or standing for the world, have set their faces like flint and have not been put to shame.

On a February day in the year 156, Polycarp, the overseer of the church in Smyrna, was arrested on the charge of practicing the

Christian faith. In his youth he had known the Apostle John and others who had known the Lord in the flesh. In the *Martyrdom of Polycarp* we read:

> *Therefore he was brought forward to the Proconsul, who asked him if he were Polycarp. When he said he was one and the same, he tried to dissuade him, saying, "Remember your age ... Swear allegiance (to Caesar) and I'll release you." Polycarp answered, "I have been his slave 86 years and he has never treated me unjustly. How is it possible I should blaspheme my king who saved me?"* — *Martyrdom of Polycarp* (9:2-3)

He was burned at the stake and did not die until he was pierced through the heart with a dagger. His example encouraged other Christians to endure, even unto death.

This is, after all, the Christian week. Experience it all. Push your comfort level. Jesus is headed on a collision course with established religious and political authorities. Are you? Ahead of us lies the empty tomb and the resurrection, but to get there we must meditate on the Last Supper, which is part of Maundy Thursday. We must stand by the cross on Good Friday. We must experience the long, dark melancholy of Holy Saturday. Then and only then can we legitimately stand with all the disciples who have suffered for the sake of the gospel and proclaim, "He is risen! He is risen, indeed!" Amen.

# Priceless

---

The Island of Rodriguez in the Pacific Ocean, not that far from Zanzibar, has mainly managed to stay out of the notice of history, if history is the record of slaughter and disease. But thanks to extraordinary events far, far away it managed to impinge itself on human history on at least one occasion.

On August 27 of 1883, James Wallis, chief of police on Rodriguez Island, not far from Zanzibar, wrote: "Several times during the night (26-27) reports were heard coming from the eastward, like the distant roar of heavy guns. These reports continued at intervals of between three and four hours, until 3 p.m. on August 27, and the last two were heard in the directions of Oyster Bay and Port Mathurie." What Wallis was hearing were the distant eruptions of the Volcano Krakatoa, 2,968 miles away. There is no recorded instance in human history of a sound being heard from further away.

Except, of course, the echoes of that hammer driving in the nails on a hill far away, on Golgotha.

The sound is not only heard among Christians 2,000 years later, but it was heard hundreds of years earlier, by the prophet Isaiah, who was looking at a people who had lost sight of their salvation, who mistook prices for real values.

Isaiah was one who knew suffering firsthand. He had endured ridicule, persecution, physical punishment, and if we are to believe tradition, he would eventually be murdered for his faith. His task — to proclaim God's news for his time and for all time — was not

167

a task he took lightly. Certainly, if we read his commissioning correctly, it was in the presence of God himself and the heavenly throne room that he took upon himself the task of being God's messenger.

In the present passage, Isaiah can only express surprise — a surprise he expects we will share. Who would believe what he has to report — that someone would be willing to innocently endure not just physical pain, but abuse, misunderstanding, shame? How could it be that the servant God intends to lift up, to honor, to exalt, should achieve this status by suffering? We expect just the opposite.

Isaiah is seeing clearly, not through a glass darkly, but more clearly than we see, that stark X-marks-the-spot that stares in *this* face on *this* day of all days. He was seeing the cross.

The cross is the central symbol of our faith. We can be very casual about wearing the cross around the neck or on the lapel. We sometimes forget, however, that the cross is a symbol of terror, despair, horror, degradation, agony, and humiliation. It was a form of execution reserved for the lowest of the low, for those outside the pale of humanity, whose bodies would be dumped in the garbage heaps afterward to be torn apart by wild dogs. Indeed, Paul's listeners must have cringed every time he used the word "cross." It was obscene.

So shameful was the image of the cross to our ancestors in the faith, so obscene the method of execution, that for over four centuries the church chose not to use that symbol in its art.

Well, there is one example of the cross used in a drawing from early Christian history, but it is drawn by an opponent of the faith. You can see it in *Ante Pacem*, by Graydon F. Snyder. It's a piece of graffiti in the slave quarters, a crude drawing that shows the crucifixion of a man with the head of a donkey. At his feet is an individual engaged in adoration. There's a single line written beneath it: "Alexamenos worships his god."

This anti-Christian drawing makes it clear how shameful the cross could be. Yet this Alexamenos was not ashamed to claim Jesus as Lord, even though it led to ridicule. It helps us realize why Christians did not wear the cross as a symbol for centuries.

More important than whether we wear the cross is whether we bear the cross. Anna Mow was a missionary, mother, writer, and teacher, an active speaker, and much loved disciple of Jesus Christ. She seemed willing to endure anything for the sake of her Savior. Perhaps that's why it seemed so ironic that one who was such a great communicator should suffer an affliction that made it nearly impossible for her to communicate.

Despite having suffered a debilitating stroke that limited her ability to write and speak, she dictated a final book to demonstrate that one may not only wear, but also bear the cross.

Published as *Two or Ninety-Two* by Brethren Press, Anna's book is sparkling, bright as a running brook in spring, yet filled with the same brooding depth of a pond deep from the melting snows. In a helpless condition she describes as "a world of suffering," Anna writes, "I can't even choose what kind of suffering I'll have. But I can choose what my attitude is going to be toward suffering."

Calling upon the example of Job, Anna differentiates between a God who sends suffering and one who permits it. "No matter what happens to us, we are within his loving care. Our Lord suffered. Paul's thorn in the flesh was never taken away. We may suffer. If we trust him, the suffering will never be useless."

And then there's this: "No one is ever useless to God. No one who can pray is ever useless. There are many people to perform the needed activities, but too few to take the time for prayer."

The cross as an instrument of torture also represents the intersection of two roads. It is the place where heaven and earth come together. It is the spot where we meet Jesus.

So Paul wrote about Jesus that "... though he was in the form of God, did not regard equality with God as something to be exploited, but emptied himself, taking the form of a slave, being born in human likeness. And being found in human form, he humbled himself and became obedient to the point of death — even death on a cross" (Philippians 2:5-8).

This is where we come together. At our broken points. This is where we have something in common.

How do we come to this intersection? One way is through our suffering. Much of our suffering is unsought, but it finds us anyway. There is no place in that dark valley we travel where we will not find Jesus waiting.

For others, we arrive at this spot by taking upon ourselves the name of Jesus. To do so is to invite the world to crush you as well.

Yet our lives are not spent in suffering. No one is called to intentionally seek out the experience. For those who are currently blessed with health in the midst of faithful living, there are other ways to join Jesus at the cross.

In the Roman Empire many paid with suffering and death when they were baptized as Christians. But the Celts seem to have accepted the faith without fighting it. The Celtic Christians spoke of Red Martyrdom, White Martyrdom, and Green Martyrdom. The first obviously refers to those who died for their faith, but the other two categories denoted those who gave up home and homeland to follow where God led. We who are convinced that our future is in our own hands are probably ready to stand up for Jesus with our lives — but not our livelihoods. How many of us would really be willing to give up home and homeland for the call of the gospel?

This is the holy day which forces us to focus on the cross. The mistake would be to act as if the cross was all there was. As a symbol of suffering, of sacrifice, of pure love, it is unequalled. But that's not all there is. There's more. There's triumph.

The trouble is, we know the ending. We have read the end of the book. We know that Jesus didn't stay safely dead. This is what the powers would like us to believe.

We do not need to obsess on the cross. It is the intersection between heaven and earth. It is the key that unlocks heaven's gate.

Now we must pass through heaven's gate. We must walk beyond and live in the kingdom now. God's kingdom is not fully realized in this world. It's dangerous to try to live by the rules of the kingdom right now. It got Jesus killed, and many other martyrs besides.

But there's not only a cross, there's an empty tomb, and trust me, the powers that be would love to keep Jesus on that cross. It's safer that way.

The cross was supposed to eradicate the carpenter and all he stood for. It was supposed to end the problem. Just as the death of Stephen, of John, and the other martyrs, was supposed to put an end to Christianity. Just tear it up by the roots and it will die.

It doesn't work that way. This calls to mind a scene from a book about Jesus, where the writer noted: "I watched my neighbor down the road pull up the dandelions to prevent their spread. Meanwhile, just a few yards away my son Jacob was reciting what he had learned about dandelions at school the previous day — while blowing on the puffy heads to spread the seeds. Each one caught the wind and was lost to sight as it sailed into the sun. No problem. There were going to be plenty more dandelions next spring. That's the way it works. There's a stiff breeze blowing and you can't put the seeds back on the stem. You can't put Jesus back in the tomb" (Frank Ramirez, *The Gospel of Mark* [Nashville: faithQuest, 1996], p. 60.)

The powers, the governments, the principalities, want to stuff Jesus in the box. If they can keep him on the cross, your attention will be diverted from the real work. Yes, "when I survey the wondrous cross, on which the prince of glory died, my richest gain I count but loss, and pour contempt on all my pride."

Yes, Paul said, "For I decided to know nothing among you except Jesus Christ, and him crucified" (1 Corinthians 2:2). But more importantly, we know he is risen. The angels at the ascension asked the apostles why they were looking up in the air. There was work to do. Pick up your cross? You've already got it, but start walking toward your resurrection, now and in the life to come.

We began by talking about the noise that Krakatoa, that great volcano made, a noise so great it was heard nearly 3,000 miles away. But it also left a lasting mark for two years and more, on the horizons of most places in the world, creating fantastic sunsets.

On the day before Thanksgiving, 1883, the fire department of Poughkeepsie rushed out to fight a fire that was clearly only a few blocks away. It was a tremendous fire, lighting up the entire sky. They rushed up one street and down another until they came to the river, and realized the fire had to be on the other side of the river. They finally had to stop and let the fire burn.

171

Only later did someone explain to them that the fire they observed was 93 million miles away, and it was the sun shining through the dust still settling from the volcano three months before.

Nevertheless, the fire company was content it had answered the call. We, ourselves, can still answer the call, even if the task seems bigger than we can imagine, or farther away that we suppose. The call is out there, the call of Christ's cross, his suffering, death, and resurrection. God has a plan for your life. The question is whether we will respond or not.

It matters. It matters because nothing is more valuable to us than this cross. How valuable? Consider the following price list:

- Two wooden beams, a four-by-four post fourteen feet high and a two-by-four crossbar — total $9.
- Three spikes — 24 cents.
- Hemp Rope — $5.99 for a fifty-foot coil.
- Dice to roll for castoff clothing — 99 cents.
- Real life in Christ — Priceless.

For most of what life offers us there is cash and credit.
For everything that really matters there's the cross of Jesus.

# The Easter Era

Most of us probably enjoy taking part in Easter rituals both here at church and at home. There are things we have done since we were children, and we're glad to pass them on to the next generation.

Some of these practices are deeply religious. We may have taken part in solemn Maundy Thursday and Good Friday services, or greeted the Easter Sunrise with song and celebration! Some of the practices may be a little secular, but we practice them religiously as well — breaking our Lenten fasts with a special treat, plundering the Easter basket for favorite goodies, a dinner centering around ham — you name it, we do it.

But at the heart of all these practices is one basic assumption — we know about Easter. We know why we celebrate. We know that Jesus is risen!

Today is Easter. The Christian writer, C. S. Lewis, referred to our faith as one unashamedly based on miracles, and called the resurrection the central miracle. His friend and fellow writer, J.R.R. Tolkien, referred to Easter as a "eucatastrophe," or good catastrophe, a radical and miraculous turn in human history.

There's no way around the resurrection in Christianity. If this were not true, it would be up to us to abandon Christianity and seek some other way to serve God. If this central fact were not the core of our confession, we would be wasting our time. Paul says pretty much the same thing, then comforts us with these words: "But in fact Christ has been raised from the dead, the first fruits of those who have died" (1 Corinthians 15:20).

173

That's why we're here. The most incredible thing in the world happened, and we are witnesses to it. People were willing to die horribly in the early years of the faith to uphold that witness, and others, having seen the sincerity of their deaths, were willing to die as well. That tradition continues today. Some believe that more Christians have been martyred the world over in the past century than in all the Christian centuries before. Like the unlikely Apostle Paul, we all need to be ready to witness to the good news, no matter what the cost.

But in order to celebrate this day of days, we have to know about it. Some people don't even know who Jesus is. Some people in the world today have never heard the good news about Jesus Christ. They don't know about the manger, about the baptism, the temptation, the Sermon on the Mount, the triumphant entry, the upsetting of the moneychangers, the contentions in the temple, and the breaking of the bread. They know nothing of the plotting, the conniving, the betraying, the arresting, the railroading, the condemning, the torturing, the murdering, the burying — and the raising, hallelujah, the raising. And they live in our neighborhoods!

Someone has to tell them. Someone has to get out of their tracks, get so far beyond their comfort zone that comfort takes on a whole new meaning and it has nothing to do with comfortable chairs and water beading up on the outside of a glass of iced tea and falling asleep in front of the ball game. Someone has to go and someone has to support them.

Our customs and practices are so much fun that we hate to get out of that comfort zone. We like to stay put, until someone — usually the Holy Spirit — makes it impossible for us to rest until we help in some great or small measure for the Word to get out there.

The resurrection of Jesus Christ is not exactly ancient history in today's passage from the book of Acts, but it's common knowledge — to those who know about it. Still, God's people are quite comfortable within their own ethnic boundaries and only reluctantly push the envelope to include others from the Roman Empire. The Roman Empire stretched in those days from the western edge of Asia to the British Isles, from Northern Africa to Northern

Europe. It included a large number of nationalities, languages, ethnic and racial groups, people of all economic classes — and almost none of them knew anything about Jesus. There were no 24-hour news channels to report about the events of Judea. There was almost no news as we know it — just stories, just rumors run rampant.

And the Holy Spirit sent Peter to preach to a centurion, a member of the hated occupying army, a sarge. Centurions were non-commissioned officers. They were in charge of around a hundred people — hence the name. They were not nobles who were appointed on the basis of their family connections and hence higher in rank. They were commoners who worked their way up the ranks.

Chapter 10 of Acts is one of those crucial chapters where a door opens up and God's people, people of every stripe, flood through it.

This is a story about outsiders. It begins with an angelic appearance at the home of the aforementioned Cornelius, the centurion. Talk about outsiders, Cornelius was not only a Gentile; he was an officer in the hated army of occupation. He was also, however, a God-fearer, one of those Gentiles who believed in the God of Israel but either could not join the faith of God's people, or was not welcome.

The angel told him that God had heard his prayers. Salvation was about to come to his house. He was to send for Peter, who was staying with Simon, the tanner. A barrier was broken with these very words. The profession of tanner, though necessary, was considered unclean by folks who got their hands dirty in other professions. Many folks avoided associating with tanners. Perhaps this unorthodox association put Peter in a receptive mind for the marvelous vision that followed.

The same Spirit that spoke to Cornelius gave Peter a vision of food that was considered off limits to his people, according to Jewish dietary laws. He was told to eat the forbidden food anyway. When he awoke still puzzling over what he had seen in the vision, he was told by the Spirit that he would find emissaries from Cornelius at his door, and that he was to travel to the house of the centurion. And it happened!

175

First he invited the Gentile emissaries to stay at his home, another step toward interracial acceptance. Peter then traveled with an entourage to Cornelius. There Peter told all about his vision and proclaimed that God plays no favorites. The Spirit filled the Gentiles who heard the message. All who were present realized that there was nothing to prevent them from being baptized. Furthermore there was no requirement that these people must be circumcised first. They became Christians without having to become Jews first. The faith was cracked wide open!

In the same way, it took a long time — centuries really — before people realized that a person can become a Christian without first becoming European. Africans, Native Americans, Hispanics, Asians, all of humanity, can become Christian and retain their native background and outlook.

The late missionary, Chalmer Faw, who in 1943 was serving in Garkida, Nigeria, received an invitation to preach in a town many miles away in an isolated village. He was also asked to lead a Love Feast, a three-part communion service that included feetwashing, the agape meal, along with the bread and cup. Faw agreed. Everything went as planned.

Then he wrote: "At the close of the meeting, I went around and greeted the old chief, the village elders, and many local citizens, all on hand to witness this grand occasion. The chief murmured something to me in Whona that was translated as: 'The next time that you and your people come out and hold this service, I want to be in it and I want all my village to have a part in it!' "

He continued, "I was too astounded at the time to ask what he meant by that, but on the way back to Garkida I had ample time to talk it over with my Bura Christians. What they explained to me was essentially as follows: 'The Whona chief is an old man. He can remember when the first white men came in (the British colonial officers) and sent his young men to work on the roads or forced them to fight in their wars. But this is the first time in his long life that he has seen a white man get down on his knees in the dark and wash a black man's feet! And if that is what this new religion (Christianity) means, he wants it and he wants all his people to have a part in it!' "

The old chief didn't understand a word of what was read or said in the service, but he saw all that was done and the action spoke for itself, a message he would never forget.

Acts 10 has to be one of our favorite passages in the Bible. It's all true. Even though we think of Paul as the apostle to the Gentiles, it was Peter who made the first move. No. That's wrong. It was the Spirit. The Spirit who spoke to Cornelius. The Spirit who spoke to Peter. The living Spirit.

Acts 10 is still happening. Every time you read a missionary magazine and see a photograph of a missionary standing next to newly baptized converts, people who had never known there was such a thing as gospel, much less made a choice for Jesus, you are looking at the Apostle Peter, the centurion Cornelius, and the action of the Holy Spirit. You are looking at people living in the age of Acts! Which means you and I are living in the age of Acts as well.

This is the age of miracles. Though our American churches may be asleep, the African and Latin American church is alive and thriving, battling persecution, standing strong in the faith, and demonstrating, as Peter said, "... God shows no partiality, but in every nation anyone who fears him and does what is right is acceptable to him" (Acts 10:34-35).

Remember that. God is not American. God is not British. God is not Canadian or German or Italian or Irish or Nigerian or Costa Rican or Mexican or Chinese or Russian or Indian. God is God!

This is the era of the Spirit's triumph. It's important we get on board as well, and to do so we have to be prepared to get beyond that comfort zone.

When you go to the ancient Indian cliff dwellings at Mesa Verde, you are warned that in order to visit one of the sites you have to be able to get down on your hands and knees and crawl through a tunnel. If you can't squeeze through the hole, you can't go. If you are too claustrophobic to try, you can't go.

On the first Easter Day, Peter and the beloved disciple had to be able to run into the tomb, an unclean place, in order to understand at last that Jesus is risen. It is not something they can discover by standing at a safe distance. You may run and come to a stop like Peter, or sprint past like John, you may puzzle over it like one, or get it immediately like the other, but the witnesses who have seen the light include all of these. There is not one safe, comfortable, ordinary category into which we can squeeze all the witnesses. Like the ruins at Mesa Verde, if you are too fastidious to squeeze through the path God has chosen for you — you can't go to heaven.

Peter had to go to a place that was very uncomfortable to him at first — the home of a Gentile. Before you can go into the mission field abroad, or because you can with good conscience support a missionary who is already abroad, you had better start looking at the mission field in our midst. You had better start visiting nursing homes and hospitals, and calling on people in our midst without looking down your nose at them because they don't meet your standards, standards that God knows nothing about. In our nation, the church hour remains the most segregated hour in American society — racially, economically, philosophically. We put up all sorts of barriers to keep others out, unseen gates and doors to separate ourselves from the world, and all the time God is hollering at us to get out there, get into the ball game, and bring people in. If you don't want to bring people into the church, at least have the good grace to get out.

The resurrection is not just a trick or a wonder. It's an alteration — to the world, to society, to us. It's either the most important thing that has ever happened, or it is time to be honest about things and do something else on Sundays.

It happened. There are witnesses.

We are transformed by God. There is no place we cannot go, no place we dare not go, to take this overwhelmingly important message. It is not something to be kept safe within these four walls. It is imperative that we get the word out! He is risen.

Witnesses are martyrs. Are you a witness? Amen.

# Who?

My guess is that unless you're a fan of Elizabethan theater you've never heard of Robert Greene (1560?-1592). In his day, however, he was a well-known and respected poet and essayist. His best-known play, "Friar Bacon and Friar Bungay," remained popular for decades. Yet, for the most part, he is remembered solely for one phrase in a pamphlet written on his deathbed, in which he lashed out at everybody and everything. In that one passage he characterized the young William Shakespeare as "an upstart crow" for supposing he could write without a college education. As it turns out, Will could.

For better or worse, many people who were extraordinarily famous in their day are all but forgotten now, except for their connection to someone famous. What do we really know about Stephen A. Douglas except that he debated Abraham Lincoln? How about Thomas Dewey? He was a major political figure of the middle part of the twentieth century, but the main reason he is remembered is because of a photograph of Harry S. Truman, the newly re-elected president of the United States, gleefully holding up the incorrect headline that read: "Dewey Defeats Truman."

The same might be said for Gamaliel, a first-century rabbi and teacher. In the Mishnah, a second-century Jewish commentary on scripture, he is especially revered. There it is said that "when he died the glory of the Torah ended."

However, for most Christians his fame rests only upon his oft-quoted remark in the book of Acts. At the time, the apostles were warned by religious authorities that they were to stop teaching about

Jesus, or face dire consequences. Perhaps this command came because the authorities feared that the disciples of Jesus would draw the ire of the Roman authorities who would interpret their plan to turn the world upside down as open rebellion against the Empire. More likely, however, it was jealousy for the power these disciples brought to their preaching. The apostles disobeyed this command, saying, "We must obey God rather than any human authority" (Acts 5:29).

The Rabbi Gamaliel cites two instances in which false teachers were eventually discredited and their followers scattered. "So in the present case," Gamaliel says, "I tell you, keep away from these men and let them alone; because if this plan or this undertaking is of human origin, it will fail; but if it is of God, you will not be able to overthrow them — in that case you may even be found fighting against God" (Acts 5:38-39).

There's a little mystery involved in this scene. Luke is a careful historian. For much of the latter part of his book he himself was present. For other scenes it is easy to guess which of the apostles or participants might have been his source. But Gamaliel's famous saying was part of a closed court session. Gamaliel seems to have wanted to slow down the Sanhedrin before they did something rash, so he spoke to them in private. Who might have heard this scene so that Luke could report it? Perhaps, and this is just a guess on the part of some Bible readers, it was one of Gamaliel's pupils — none other than Saul, who would later have his life changed on the road to Damascus! (cf. Acts 22:3).

Put simply, Gamaliel suggests that when it comes to innovations in the practice of faith, time will tell. The perspective of the present moment is a lot like a large plain, so flat that it's difficult to get a good look at things. Let enough time go by and it's as if we have climbed a mountain. Suddenly we can see everything laid out before us and things make sense.

Prophets come among us and challenge our comfortable assumptions. Most of us want to be let alone. The tendency is to attempt to discredit these prophets instead of listening to them. Take the Reverend Martin Luther King, Jr., a Christian minister who preached nonviolent resistance to the racism that was accepted in his day. Even people who thought racism was a bad thing assumed there was nothing to be done about it.

Along came King, and some political and religious leaders tried to discredit him as a person, rather than consider his message. The FBI tried to destroy his reputation. Racists, preachers, and politicians, screamed and hollered.

But in Birmingham, Alabama, some religious leaders who were not racists simply encouraged him to go away and not disturb things, much like the religious leaders of Jerusalem who did not want the apostles upsetting the apple cart. Martin Luther King's famed "Letter from a Birmingham Jail" is addressed to these people. Folks probably a lot like us.

There are many examples of people who stood up to the authorities, and were proven right, even though at the time everyone thought they were wrong. Take the case of Ralph and Mary Smeltzer, teachers who lived in Southern California in the middle of the twentieth century. They are good examples of those who suffered dishonor for the name of Jesus and yet were vindicated in the end. The two stood up for the victims of Japanese American internment during World War II, receiving death threats because they spoke out against the internment, quit their jobs in the public school systems so they could teach in the internment camps, and later helped relocate many of those interned to other parts of the country.

Later, they worked with such major Christian civil rights leaders as Martin Luther King, Jr., and Andrew Young. They were criticized by the church's mainstream for defending the rights of outsiders and minorities. Yet, history shows they were on the right side, while those who counseled against helping Japanese Americans and African Americans have been proven wrong, wrong, wrong.

Another good example of a Christian with a great idea who found opposition at first was Dan West (1893-1971), from the state of Indiana. He was a Christian aid worker in Spain in 1936 during their Civil War. West agonized over the life and death decisions involving the cups of powdered milk he gave to starving children. There was never enough milk, and infants that received no milk died. He realized: "These children don't need a cup, they need a cow." If only, he thought to himself, he could bring some of the cows from his native Indiana to hungry people then they could produce their own milk. And then he wondered — why not do exactly that?

Then he got another idea — why not send impregnated cows so those who received the gift of life in the name of Jesus Christ could pass it along to another and become part of the chain? When he first approached Christian aid groups in England with the idea there was some enthusiasm, until he explained that he intended to feed people on both sides of the coming World War. Christians refused to help.

West returned home to Indiana in 1938. He told dairy farmers who belonged to his denomination, the Church of the Brethren, about his idea. Some were frightened by his idea, and called him a Communist. In those days that word could destroy a person's reputation. But others thought the idea so good, and so obvious, they wondered why no one had thought of it earlier. Cows were quickly donated by the Indiana farmers. The first three were named Faith, Hope, and Charity. It took a while for the program to get off the ground, and the first cows actually went to Puerto Rico, rather than Europe where they were intended. But when World War II ended, West and the others began to wage peace. Animals were shipped to people on both sides of the conflict. The idea grew, and many churches were invited to join in the ecumenical organization known today as Heifer International.

Millions of animals of all sorts have been given to people in 128 different countries, but the mission — providing a future with hope by working in partnership with the hungry to help provide a long-term source of food in the name of Jesus — has remained unchanged.

The fact is, every idea goes through three basic stages. Stage 1 is "It will never work." Stage 2 is "It might work, but it's not worth doing." Stage 3 is "I'm glad I thought of it."

We see this not only in the groundbreaking work of the prophets, but even in advances in the way we worship. This is especially true when it comes to music, where people are always ready to circle the wagons to protect the church from heresy!

182

Thomas Ken (1637-1711) lived in a time when the established English churches believed the only songs that might be sung in church were metrical arrangements of the psalms and other scriptures. What we know as hymns were considered blasphemous, because it was thought people were trying to write new scriptures.

In 1672, he wrote *Manual of Prayers for the Use of the Scholars of Winchester College.* Included was a twelve-stanza song called "Awake My Soul And With The Sun." Ken insisted that the boys who learned these songs sing them only in their rooms and not in church, in order to avoid giving offense.

This song, which was forbidden to be sung in church, is now perhaps sung in church more than any other song in the English language — at least the last stanza is! You know it better as the Doxology:

> *Praise God from whom all blessings flow;*
> *Praise him all creatures here below;*
> *Praise him above ye heavenly hosts;*
> *Praise Father, Son, and Holy Ghost.*

In the past some churches have taken stands against pianos and organs. There was a time when familiar hymns such as "I Love To Tell The Story" or "The Old Rugged Cross" were considered new hymns. No doubt people stood four-square against them, pleading with others to sing "the old hymns of the church"! Now these are the old hymns, and we find that some speak out against praise choruses, drums and guitars, or what are truly the old hymns of the church — chants, Gregorian or otherwise!

Despite Gamaliel's warning, the apostles were beaten before they were released with the warning that they were to stop preaching about Jesus. But the followers of Jesus had no intention of following this order. As Luke tells us, "As they left the council, they rejoiced that they were considered worthy to suffer dishonor for the sake of the name. And every day in the temple and at home they did not cease to teach and proclaim Jesus as the Messiah" (Acts 5:41-42).

So where will you stand with regard to the prophets in our midst? Will you criticize every idea simply because it is new? Will you stand against people who call us to social and economic justice, hallmarks of the ministry of Jesus? Remember, it was Jesus who, when he came home to Nazareth, unrolled the Isaiah scroll, and read: "The Spirit of the Lord is upon me, because he has anointed me to bring good news to the poor. He has sent me to proclaim release to the captives and recovery of sight to the blind, to let the oppressed go free, to proclaim the year of the Lord's favor" (Luke 4:18-19).

Those who do follow Jesus can expect opposition, suffering, and even death. Some of the apostles who stood up to the authorities were themselves killed for their faith. Many of the reformers who tried to help lead the church back to our roots were themselves killed.

Certainly the apostles themselves suffered. Gamaliel seems to have counseled a nonviolent course — but though the religious authorities did not kill the apostles, as they had planned, they did have them lashed 39 times. Still, as Luke notes, "As they left the council, they rejoiced that they were considered worthy to suffer dishonor for the sake of the name" (Acts 5:41).

Now, as then, believers have to expect some opposition when they preach the gospel. And now, as then, believers should show some tolerance and patience for unusual witness. If we are not ready to accept the honor of being persecuted for God's good news of justice, peace, and salvation, then can we at least, as Gamaliel counsels, stand to the side while new innovations are brought to worship and praise. Can we stand to the side while others forget trials in the mission field, and still others serve in the name of Jesus by defending death row inmates, pleading for the poor, and accompanying the outcasts who seek redress from civil authorities?

As Gamaliel warned, if something is not of God, it will fail in time. But do you really want to be found standing in the way of God's will? Amen.

# Fruit With Feet

There has rarely been a transformation from sinner to saint as dramatic as that of Paul, former persecutor of Christians, who became the apostle to the Gentiles. However, the story of Cain Lackey from Patrick County, Virginia, comes close.

Cain Lackey was known as the Meanest Man in Patrick County. He was rough and tough. The year was 1892 and Patrick County, Virginia, was a place of dirt fields and mud roads. There wasn't always enough food. People died because there were no doctors. Some places were almost impossible to get to because of the roads.

For all that, it was still very beautiful. There were the majestic Blue Ridge Mountains, and the music of winding rivers racing over the boulders in their streambeds. In the western part of the county were rich fields and long grasses. There were dairy farms, and orchards so plentiful that the smell of the fruit was like perfume.

Two ministers, Brother Dove and Brother Elgin, were standing at the edge of a swamp. Down below, a tough, wiry man was digging a ditch. Brother Dove was a revival preacher, new in town, and Brother Elgin warned him about the man who was digging: Cain Lackey, the Meanest Man.

Brother Elgin proceeded to tell Brother Dove about Cain Lackey, how he could carry a railroad tie the way most men carried a two-by-four, how he could out-wrestle and out-fight anyone else who'd ever passed through these parts. And he told him about the famous fight against a man known as Champion Ben, who he'd laid low with a single blow, and how it had required twelve men with mule spurs to pull Cain Lackey off the former champion.

Brother Elgin also told him about the man's father, who kept him from school, worked him from dawn to dusk, made him sleep outdoors all summer long, and how Cain had built a working mill by himself at the age of ten.

No one could level another man with his fist like Cain. No one was stronger or meaner.

"Well, he certainly looks like the strongest man in the county," Brother Dove said, watching the way Cain Lackey thrust his shovel into the swamp, and sent great clouds of mud into the air behind him.

"I'm going to invite him to the revival," Brother Dove said suddenly.

"He'll never come," Brother Elgin said.

"He'll definitely never come if we don't ask him," Brother Dove replied.

Brother Elgin watched as the Brethren minister descended into the swamp. Brother Elgin could see Brother Dove step first ankle deep, then knee deep into the swamp, getting mud and gunk all over him. He watched as Brother Dove stuck out his hand to Cain Lackey. After a moment, Cain took the hand.

A few moments later Brother Dove was walking back to Brother Elgin. Mud clung to his boots and pants.

"What did he say?" Brother Elgin asked. Cain Lackey had already returned to digging. Not much seemed to keep him from work.

"He said he'd come. Is he as good as his word?"

"Yes," came the reply. "If he tells you he'll come he'll be there. He's just that way. He'll do what he tells you. But if he tells you he'll give you a whipping, he'll do that, too."

That night at the revival, the church was full. People had come from miles around to hear Brother Dove. There were young people and old people. There were children and mothers and fathers and aunts and uncles, grandmothers and grandfathers, and plenty of babies. All the windows were open, and still it was hot, very hot inside, yet no one left. No one wanted to leave, because when someone like Brother Dove came to preach it was something special, very special.

186

The songs were the sorts of songs that everyone already knew. A sweaty man in the front of the church moved his arms up and down, right and left, to direct the singing, but everyone already knew the songs. They didn't need songbooks which was a good thing, as there weren't enough for everyone. Brother Dove looked out over the congregation, and then he saw, in the doorway of the church, a big man standing. It was Cain Lackey, all right, and he had a child in his arms. He hadn't thought about it, but he now knew that Cain Lackey was married, and had children. There was a darling child in his arms. There was no room for anyone else in the church, but when Cain came in the door, people were afraid of him and made room for him to sit down.

Opening his Bible, Brother Dove began to read, and to talk. It got hotter and hotter in the building, and Brother Dove was dripping with sweat, and so was everyone else. It had gotten dark outside, and it was getting dark in the church as well. He could barely see into the back row, and he wondered, what did Cain Lackey, the Meanest Man in Patrick County, think about what he was saying?

The song went on and on, louder and louder. Some were crying in the church, and some were squeezing forward so that Brother Dove and Brother Elgin and all the other Brethren ministers could pray for them. Sometimes they were so weak they could hardly stand. Many people were coming forward.

Brother Dove could see a dark shadow, a silhouette of a man, standing at the back of the church. Cain Lackey was standing, but he could see there was no way Cain Lackey could come forward, even if he wanted to. The church was too packed.

And then he saw something that surprised him. Cain Lackey was standing on top of a church bench. He was holding a little girl in his arms, and she was fast asleep. This person who was supposed to be the worst person in Patrick County had a little girl asleep in his arms, and he was coming forward by walking on top of the church benches.

The other ministers stood back as if they were shocked, but Brother Dove welcomed Cain Lackey, and hugged him very tightly, him and his daughter. Then Brother Dove invited Cain Lackey to kneel while they prayed together. All along, the singing continued.

Then a cool breeze blew in the window, a breeze that brought relief and comfort.

When he was through praying, Brother Dove raised his hands and suddenly everyone was quiet. No one was singing. No one was crying. Everyone was listening.

"Today you have seen a miracle of grace," he said. "God has called this man to do great things. You will be the ones who will see these things. Welcome this man into our church!"

Cain Lackey went on to learn to read and write. He became a minister and built many churches. He was elected to public office and spent tax money to build roads to improve access to rural areas even though it made him unpopular. He worked to provide social services for poor people who had been ignored by other politicians. He smashed stills where he found them. He changed lives. He stayed extraordinarily strong to the end of his days, once lifting a sack full of anvils over his head when he was told — erroneously — that another man had done the same. Most of all, he lived a life of grace and service to Jesus Christ.

One of his descendents went on to become a college president. Another became the head of a denominational pension plan. His many descendents proudly told stories of the fellow who was known as the Meanest Man in Patrick County.

Our faith is all about transformation. There's an old saying, "The fruit doesn't fall far from the tree." It's a way of saying that people can't change. But that's not the Christian belief. We believe that fruit can sprout legs and run to Jesus! When Luke wrote his history that we call "The Acts of the Apostles," he lived in a time when biographies were written to show you could never change. If you were great you were born great, grew up great, and stayed great. If you were rotten, you were born rotten, grew up rotten, and stayed rotten.

But Luke's Gospel showed that people could be transformed. The stories of the good Samaritan and the prodigal son demonstrated how love could change attitudes and lives. Jesus invited people to a new relationship with God. And Saul's conversion is the greatest act of transformation — and kindness — in the New

Testament. It's one of those "if he can change I guess I can change" stories that we need to prove that our gospel truly transforms lives.

Paul must have seemed an unlikely apostle. Luke reminds us that though Paul was not an active participant in the execution of Stephen, he approved of his death. Paul himself recalls elsewhere how he was fervent in persecution, determined to eradicate the Jesus movement by any means possible. In Galatians 1:13 he says that he "violently" laid hands on Christians. Perhaps Luke was reluctant to talk about Paul helping to get Christians executed, but Paul knew what he had done.

In a sense, Paul represents all those people, Christians, Jews, and Muslims, and other faiths as well, who kill in the name of God. There have been such people in all times who believe that God is pleased with their killing. In the past, Christians killed other Christians, along with Jews and Muslims, who did not profess the same beliefs, often over minor points of theology that today would seem ridiculous to us.

On the one hand, it's sad to think 2,000 years later, people of faith are killing others in the name of God — but perhaps Paul's example can give us hope as well — he was changed by a living Jesus. Others can as well.

That's another part of this scripture that is important. Jesus, who ascended into heaven, is shown to be still risen, still alive, and still active, able to change lives and direct history. Jesus is able to use the same fire that drove Saul to fanatically preserve the purity of his faith to open the doors of that faith to include others. Saul believed that Christians were contaminating the faith he grew up with. Jesus showed him that the circle was going to be widened until the promise given to Abraham — that all nations would be blessed in his name — would finally come true.

An encounter with the risen Jesus changed Saul. This personal experience resulted in his loss of sight, then its restoration, and finally a lifelong commitment to the gospel. Surely John Newton was thinking of this when he wrote in his famous hymn, "I once was lost, but now am found, was blind, but now I see."

Paul went on to become the prime interpreter of Christianity to the Roman Empire and by extension to all of Christendom even to the present day. Although we know him as Paul, he remained Saul to the end of his days as well. There is a misconception that when Saul was converted, his name was changed to Paul, but he lived in both worlds, had a Jewish and a Greek name, and was comfortable in cosmopolitan settings. After his conversion, he continued to use his Hebrew name Saul until he became active in the larger Roman Empire. And he continued to worship using Jewish practices because they were comfortable for him, even while standing up for others so they could be allowed to retain their ethnic heritage when they became Christian.

That's because there is no one ethnic heritage that is Christian. People of all nationalities, races, and ethnic backgrounds are welcomed into the faith and can retain these backgrounds when they become Christian. Our faith is not an American faith, for instance. It is a faith in Jesus.

Initially, believers were skeptical of this former persecutor. When Paul recovered from his experience with the risen Jesus he began to preach the gospel. The skepticism expressed about Paul's conversion is understandable. Even today, people are suspicious of jailhouse and celebrity conversions. They want to see if they will last.

Fortunately Barnabas, himself a respected Christian leader, stood up for Paul when others were skeptical, even though his own reputation might have been at stake in so doing. As a result, Paul preached until people got angry enough to want to kill him, a sure sign of his effectiveness!

In the same way, people were skeptical of Cain Lackey when he accepted Jesus as Lord and Savior, and at first they were not sure they wanted to accept him in their church. But he was patient, attended worship faithfully, learned to read and write, and eventually impressed people so much he was called into the ministry.

When others join our fellowship, we must be ready to stand up for them — and to give them a little space to grow. We don't welcome a person one week and force them onto the stewards committee the next! But we must be open for the time when new people are ready to join us in the work for Jesus, because if we don't demonstrate to the world that Jesus changes lives, who will?

In the end, this isn't about Saul or Cain Lackey or Barnabas or Brother Dove. Or you. Or me. The real news in the book of Acts always centers on the action of the Spirit. Luke tells us: "Meanwhile the church throughout Judea, Galilee, and Samaria had peace and was built up. Living in the fear of the Lord and in the comfort of the Holy Spirit, it increased in numbers" (Acts 9:31). The Spirit of God is alive and active in our midst. The only thing holding the Spirit back is our own skepticism, our own reluctance to accept people, our hardened hearts and closed minds.

After all, if Saul could accept Jesus, if Jesus could use Saul, then perhaps God can even use us. Amen.

# God's Call For All

A church in Pennsylvania reported the death of one of their members recently. Though this woman and her husband, who had died a few years before, had been immensely wealthy, people spoke not of their wealth, although they were very generous, but of what this woman did.

They talked about the cookies she would bake for church functions, the in-home visiting she did, the leadership she provided for the youth, and the soapsuds that lathered her arms as she did dishes after every church dinner. People felt the need to share these memories because this is what they knew they would really miss — the selfless service that came naturally and easily.

And they also talked about how much they were going to miss her cinnamon rolls.

Paul might have recognized this woman, when he wrote 1 Timothy 6:17-19: "As for those who in the present age are rich, command them not to be haughty, or to set their hopes on the uncertainty of riches, but rather on God who richly provides us with everything for our enjoyment. They are to do good, to be rich in good works, generous, and ready to share, thus storing up for themselves the treasure of a good foundation for the future, so that they may take hold of the life that really is life."

Tabitha was a very similar sort of person, one known to be "devoted to good works and acts of charity" (Acts 9:36). When Tabitha died, her friends sent for the Apostle Peter. When he arrived, people were quick to show him the same sorts of things. As it says, "All the widows stood beside him, weeping and showing tunics and other clothing that Dorcas had made while she was with them" (Acts 9:39).

Remember that widows in the ancient world could not get jobs or take care of themselves. They were dependant upon living relatives, and if they had none, they were totally dependent on charity.

This doesn't mean the widows only thought of Tabitha in terms of what she had done for them. It means they realized the relationship of receiving and giving had ended. When Peter became an agent of healing, when the Holy Spirit brought her back to life, it was a symbol of the reunion we shall all enjoy when we are restored to each other.

The Apostle Paul says that none of us live to ourselves and none of us die to ourselves. There is a link, a tie that binds us together, and although it is a matter of faith, something that is unseen, that cannot be weighed or measured, it becomes visible in the ways we practice mutual aid.

What exactly is mutual aid? The definitions vary, but if experts can't agree what it is, they can certainly agree what mutual aid is not. For one thing, mutual aid is never having things work out evenly. Within the body of Christ there is giving and receiving between this person and that, and it never works out that one person gives or receives precisely what another person gives or gets. We pray, we bake, we clean, we teach, we cry, we spend, we rest, we lift, we tote, we glue little stars on the top of construction paper stables with tiny hands, and we wrap soap and toothpaste and headache capsules into towels to send overseas with wrinkled hands. We write checks with tired hands and we wrap energized hands around hymnals to sing all the louder for the benefit of those about to be baptized and we bend our knees as our trembling hands prepare to wash the feet of a brother or sister as we get about as close to Jesus as we're likely to get this side of the river and it never, never, never works out evenly. Mutual aid is about tangibles and intangibles. The spiritual giving and the material giving work out the same in the eyes we're granted through scripture. We're amphibians, half spirit and half body, as C. S. Lewis used to say, so making sure the survivors of a disaster are prayed for, and their stuff replaced, matters pretty much the same.

Within the body of Christ the rules are thrown out the window. We get more than we bargained for, we give more than we need. On the morning of the church potluck, you begin to count the platters and realize folks are bringing two or three dishes this day, instead of the one they were instructed.

That is grace. The conventional wisdom is that we're supposed to give value for value, and receive the same. A pound of potatoes should cost the same for everyone. Equal effort should lead to equal reward. That's precisely the way it should work in the secular world. We need that protection, because we're fallen creatures.

We should, however, be uncomfortable if that attitude seeps into our corporate life as a church. The fact that we drop off a pie at your house doesn't mean you need to send one back. You might drop off some extra brownies months later, if you're in the baking mood, or better yet, you might take those brownies over to someone who just began attending the church. If someone visits you in the hospital, you might visit a totally different person when it's their turn, or arrange the covered dishes to be taken by your Sunday school class to the family.

Mutual aid is an essential element of the Christian faith. It's one of the building blocks of the Christian community. It's found in the Old Testament and the New Testament.

Mutual aid is tricky. When scriptures mention having all things in common, for the most part there is some semblance of private ownership, but perhaps stewardship would be a better word. It is expected that in greater and lesser ways that we take care of each other and put our stuff at each others' disposal when the need is there.

This mutuality is designed to protect God's people as individuals and a community. It's found, for instance, in the Ten Commandments. The rules set up the framework for a just and equitable society, but Exodus 20:12 is especially helpful in understanding mutual aid. The verse reads: "Honor your father and your mother, so that your days may be long in the land that the Lord your God is giving you." Here is a call to the people of God to take care of older, perhaps less productive members. Although the commandment is written in the context of a male-oriented patriarchal society it guarantees protection for women as well as men. It is aimed at the protection of individuals (some of whom may be less deserving than others) but the rewards are promised to the entire body and not to individuals. Taking care of one's elders does not guarantee a long life to the individual caregiver. We all know that some parents outlive their children on many sad occasions, but this level of care to all guarantees long life and secure life for all, a higher quality of life for the people as a whole. In other words, an action taken by one member of the community benefits others besides that individual, and raises the quality of life for all. This mutuality is at the heart of the concept of mutual aid in the scriptures.

Consider an essential part of the Torah, the Law of Moses contained in the first five books of the Bible. "When you reap the harvest of your land, you shall not reap to the very edges of your field, or gather the gleanings of your harvest. You shall not strip your vineyard bare, or gather the fallen grapes of your vineyard; you shall leave them for the poor and the alien: I am the Lord your God" (Leviticus 19:9-10).

This is not an isolated verse. On several occasions, God's Word is directed toward the haves, with regard to the have nots. The message is clear. A way has to be found to take care of everyone. It's not a question of voluntary charity. It's mutual aid.

The community of God is commanded to find a way for individuals to take care of each other. In the case of these laws, the door was opened even for an outsider, Ruth the Moabite, a member of a nation despised by Israelites, to take part in the bounty of the land and ultimately to become a part of the faith story.

The impatience of the prophets at the people's inability to share God's justice and bounty is evident in all their pages. "I desire mercy and not sacrifice" (cf Hosea 6:6). Indeed, many report that when they read the Bible from cover to cover they are surprised to discover that the one consistent theme in scripture from first to last was God's call to justice, and that call had a definite economic edge.

The duty of the people of God to take care of each other is explored in a much more intentional way in the New Testament. From the beginning, there is the assumption in the ministry of Jesus that all are included in the circle of care. Lepers, ethnic outsiders, tax collectors, untouchables, women, all who might be marginalized, are touched and accepted by Jesus, and brought into the community. They can then choose to become followers, able to help in the caring for each other. Others marvel that these people can be accepted and protected, but Jesus defends their inclusion.

So it is not surprising that the early Christians assumed that they were responsible for the care of all who touched their community. Moreover, this included not just spiritual, but financial assistance on the part of the believers.

We see this reciprocity expressed first in the lives of those who cared for Jesus. The picture emerges during his ministry of a large body of believers who moved from place to place. In addition to Jesus and the twelve apostles, there are references to a sizable number of disciples, male and female. The fact is that all of these people needed to eat and drink, and a place to sleep. Mary of Magdala, after careful Bible study, emerges as a woman of means, possibly of the upper class, who helped support the ministry of Jesus along with several other women, including Joanna, the wife of Chuza, Herod's steward, and Susanna (Luke 8:1-3). The home of Martha, Mary, and Lazarus in Judea also provided for Jesus during his trips south toward Jerusalem. The disciples had every expectation that the community of faith would take care of their needs (Luke 10:1-9), and in addition they shared out of a common purse (John 12:6).

Mutual aid is different than charity. True charity expects nothing in return, especially because it is often directed toward those outside of the fellowship. But mutual aid within the fellowship of believers (the Greek word is *koinonia*) is more than an obligation. It is joy.

Jesus admonished the people to "Love your neighbor as yourself," which is drawn from Leviticus 19:18. Among the most famous passages which illustrate the intention of the group to practice mutual aid and assistance is this verse from Acts 4:32: "Now the whole group of those who believed were of one heart and soul, and no one claimed private ownership of any possessions, but everything they owned was held in common."

Several other scriptures speak to the necessity of mutual aid. These include:

*Bear one another's burdens, and in this way you will fulfill the law of Christ.*              — Galatians 6:2

*For the whole law is summed up in a single commandment, "You shall love your neighbor as yourself."*
                                        — Galatians 5:14

*You do well if you really fulfill the royal law according to the scripture, "You shall love your neighbor as yourself."*              — James 2:8

*I do not mean that there should be relief for others and pressure on you, but it is a question of a fair balance between your present abundance and their need, so that their abundance may be for your need, in order that there may be a fair balance. As it is written, "The one who had much did not have too much, and the one who had little did not have too little."*
                                        — 2 Corinthians 8:13-15

In today's passage, we see that Tabitha gave much but probably died poor. There is no mention of oils for anointing or other things that might indicate wealth. Her real wealth lay in the high regard in which she was held by others. And when Tabitha was healed she returned to her work, not because she had to, but because there was no way to stop her!

Tabitha played an important part in her church. How do you think you will be viewed when it is your turn to be eulogized? How would you like to be remembered? How do we practice mutual aid among ourselves? Are we truly blest by the ties that bind us? Are we ready to serve each other?

We are saved by our faith, and not by our works, but as James, the brother of Jesus, tells us that faith without works is dead, and to quote him directly, "Religion that is pure and undefiled before God, the Father, is this: to care for orphans and widows in their distress, and to keep oneself unstained by the world" (James 1:27).

198

There's a song that says, "They'll know we are Christians by our love." Let's hope so. Let's hope they know us by the mutual aid that we practice, by the caring we display for each other, by the words that we share and the lives that we live. And our living faith. Amen.

# Jumping Through Hoops

Lancaster County, Pennsylvania, is a place where the old ways matter. The Amish still ride their buggies up and down the green hills. Most churches have spires, and they frame the landscape with the proclaimed piety of their people. Change comes slowly. Sometimes that's good, especially when we're talking about the basics of the faith.

Sometimes that's bad. Like when people refuse to change the little things. A lot of the churches, especially the Plain People like the Amish, Brethren, and Mennonite, practice a three-part communion service that includes the feetwashing, a full meal called the love feast, along with the bread and cup. The story is told how a new pastor tried to lead an old, established church in the feetwashing. The men were seated around one set of tables and the women around other tables. The pastor gave the instruction for the person at the front left corner to wash the feet of the person to the left, and then to continue in a counter-clockwise fashion.

No one moved. There was absolute silence. The pastor wondered what he had done wrong. The silence stretched longer and longer and the situation got more and more uncomfortable.

It turned out that in that particular congregation the feetwashing took place in a clockwise, not a counter-clockwise fashion. For the people in the church this was close to heresy. Even next to impossible.

Finally one of the elders rescued the situation by standing up, clearing his throat, and saying, "All right. I guess we can do it this way just once." And the evening was saved.

Some churches resist change. And some do more than just resist it — they fight it, clawing, kicking, and screaming the whole way. Usually we're not talking about the Virgin Birth, the Divinity of Christ, and the Resurrection. It's about practices in the kitchen, where people sit, who controls the purse strings, who's allowed in women's fellowship, and things of that nature.

And, people do not always conduct their battles in public. The Holy Righteous Church of the Parking Lot is a recognizable feature of the American church landscape. Small groups of self-appointed guardians of the faith meet in parking lots, looking furtively over their shoulders should others approach, and protect the church from the invasion of, well, openness and good ideas.

A generation ago some churches fought the purchase of copiers by insisting that mimeographs were good enough for the apostles and prophets. Aging sound systems are preserved because they are a testimony to the previous hi-fi generation who purchased them, even though state of the art equipment could enable everyone to hear clearly. Some churches resisted the computer revolution, and others fought it by donating ancient computers that crashed frequently and were next to useless.

In movies, Christians are portrayed as difficult, inflexible, judgmental, solemn, killjoys. You think of films like *How Green Was My Valley* or *Pollyanna.* Sometimes it's true.

In today's scripture, the Holy Spirit has accomplished a great thing — the good news of Jesus Christ has been accepted by Cornelius the centurion and his whole household. The Apostle Peter has helped to break down barriers that separated people. As he would note later in a letter, "Once you were not a people, but now you are God's people; once you had not received mercy, but now you have received mercy" (1 Peter 2:10).

But word has gotten back to the church elders, and they call Peter in to account for what he has done. In point of fact, he hasn't done anything. The Holy Spirit has accomplished this impossible task of bringing people together, but these elders fear a church that is open to all people and they criticize Peter publicly.

In this case, it is because they are circumcised and they want all male believers to be circumcised. Nowadays this may not be a point of controversy, but there may be another hoop, or a whole series of hoops, that people need to jump through in order to fit in.

In Elkhart County, in the state of Indiana, there is a famous corner, the meeting of the rural two-lane highways known as County Roads 11 and 38. On three of the four corners there is a Mennonite church, but each one is different. All three share the same history of religious persecution that led them to seek America as a place of religious freedom. Each one believes in and practices simple living, peace, and service to all humanity in the name of Jesus. But one of them, the Beachy Amish congregation, refuses to use electricity in the homes. The members come in horse and buggies, and there is an outhouse and shelters for horses next to the simple, white meeting house. The people dress in the plain garb — and are pretty proud of it!

The folks across the street are popularly known as the Black Car Mennonites. Each one drives an American car, and each car is black. Their building is also plain and white, and the people dress in garb that is plainer than their neighbors, although they do not conform with the fashions of the church across the street.

The third church is very large, and accepts believers who dress in many different fashions. There are cars of all makes and models, and the congregation is very active in ministry to all ages, and to people around the world. Some of the women wear head coverings. This church probably has the fewest number of hoops for believers to jump through. Their influence is far greater in the community and in the world.

In the current scripture passage the Apostle Peter is patient, probably far more patient than most of us would be. As Acts says, "Then Peter began to explain it to them, step by step ..." (11:4). He tells the story of what God has done. It is not recorded if they were enthusiastic about it, but for the time being, they accepted what had occurred — although this same argument had to be settled again in Acts 15, and according to the letters of Paul it was revisited many times more.

How open are we to accepting others? How closed are our churches, whether we admit it or not? Lots of churches say, "We're a friendly church," but what they mean is that they are friendly to each other. If a newcomer arrives, that person may not be greeted and welcomed, nor invited to return. It is possible to go to some churches and never shake a single hand or share a single word with another believer.

And, it's not just because they are unfriendly at heart. Some people say, "I don't want to greet someone because I might have already met them and I don't want to make a mistake." Which is worse — to admit a mistake and laugh over it, giving time to get know a person better, or taking the chance on ignoring someone who is sincerely seeking Jesus, and who discovers that the church is every bit as unfriendly as they were told?

Once people are in the church, the question is whether we have the grace to allow them to become new creatures in Christ. People, especially in small towns, have long memories. In the Acts of the Apostles there is a reference to the "Synagogue of the Freedmen" (6:9). Freedmen were former slaves, and probably the descendents of former slaves as well. Roman society was class conscious, and the fact that one had been a slave, or that one's ancestors were slaves, was never forgotten. These believers had been marginalized into their own little ghetto, and could not escape the taint of their past.

The passage says that they argued with Stephen over the good news of Jesus Christ. Perhaps the fact that they had been categorized as Freedmen, recognized for their station in life instead of who they were, that made them resentful of others doing well, and of the lifegiving message Stephen had brought.

Christians sometimes have longer memories than God. While God forgives, some Christians never let people forget their past and don't hesitate to bring it up in public, early and often. Sayings such as, "The fruit never falls far from the tree," might be good for agriculture, but not for families of believers.

"If then God gave them the same gift that he gave us when we believed in the Lord Jesus Christ, who was I that I could hinder God?" (Acts 11:17). That's the question Peter asked of himself — and by extension the question asked for us as well. Yet the quest for the pure church — and by pure what the person usually means is exclusive — is not only fruitless, it is un-Christian. We hinder

God by creating barriers, not recognizing that we become a laughingstock when we do so.

In this story it seems as if Peter's opponent at least gave him an honest hearing. That is what we expect of each other in the Christian faith. However, in recent years Christians have taken up the manners of the larger, secular world. Instead of listening to each other, Christians have begun to shout at each other, as well as outshouting each other. Peter was inviting all to listen, to discern, to come to a consensus. He was willing to answer the questions given to him, even with their accusatory tone, because he expected to be treated with respect.

Talk shows and talking-head panels feature people who insist that their side has never done anything wrong, while the other side has done everything wrong. The members of these debates, if the word can be used, demonize other human beings and assign them the worst motives, even though people tend to come to their views honestly and sincerely. The level of conversation in our society has coarsened to the point where many are turned off from the discussion and from the important issues of our day.

Christians must never be afraid of talking, and more importantly, listening. People of good faith disagree in the Acts of the Apostles, but they learn from each other and they grow. At the best of times they treat each other with respect.

Remember that every person is made in the image of God. With the image of God before you, dare you do anything but treat others with respect and love?

Maybe it really doesn't matter. But it ought to. The fact is that American Christianity as well as European Christianity is no longer on the cutting edge. It is clear that the church in Africa, Asia, and Latin America is far more vibrant and alive. They grow with none of our constraints, none of our preconceived notions. They don't form study committees and worry about building construction, organization, and hymnals. They spread the gospel to all nations — and let the buildings and organization follow, rather than precede their work!

At a recent meeting of a national denomination, a representative of the mission churches in the Dominican Republic reported on the decision to start churches in Haiti. People from the DR are traditionally prejudiced against Haitians, but these new Christians realized that in Christ there is no east or west, and that as Peter discovered earlier, "I truly understand that God shows no partiality, but in every nation anyone who fears him and does what is right is acceptable to him" (Acts 10:34-35). So they broke down the racial barriers that separated them and took the gospel across the border.

At first, the denominational board responded by discussing which district should have administrative responsibilities, and before which meeting the proposal should be delivered in order to get permission for this mission work. But the representative from the DR spoke up and explained that the church was not asking for permission. The work had already begun! They were asking for a blessing!

Once that was clear, the blessing was given. Praise and prayer were raised, and the board realized they had been taught a lesson about how the gospel truly works.

I said earlier that the controversy about opening the church was settled only temporarily in this passage. The issue was raised again and again in Acts, and it continues to be raised to this day. The worship hour in America is still the most segregated hour in our society.

But there is a real church that is living and growing and breathing. The Spirit is present and the people are alive. Do we intend to be a part of that church, or do we want to be part of the group that thinks it is the church, that is more preoccupied with meetings and minutes and rules than the action of the Spirit and message of salvation for all? Are our doors open wide enough? If not, who intends to open them, and to tell our community and the world that we are church for everyone. Are you going to be a gatekeeper who would rather protect nothing in order to preserve our status, or are you going to be a part of the Spirit's work in this world?

That's the question for this morning. What is your answer? Amen.

# What Church Looks Like

There's the story of the man who was lost on a desert island for a decade. When he was finally rescued people were astounded to discover he had built an entire town out of palm branches. There was a movie theater — with no movies, of course — a grocery story with empty shelves, an apartment building, a department store, several houses, and at each end of the little town he had built a church.

Why had he done it, he was asked. "To keep sane," he replied. Why two churches?

"Well," the man said, "this church over here is the place where I worshiped my Creator. Though I was cast adrift, cut off from all human contact, I never felt alone because God is with me, and even though the pews were empty I felt that the communion of saints, believers both past and present, were never more than a breath away. I needed this church more than I needed life itself."

"So what about the other church?" he was asked.

"Oh, that," he replied curtly. "That's the church I wouldn't be caught dead in."

We all have different ideas about what makes a church. Christians disagree about what a church looks like. Is the small country church the benchmark, the little brown church in the vale? Is the megachurch the only true church? The seeker church. The suburban church? The urban church? The ethnic church? Is the house church the only real model? Do we need paid clergy or the free ministry? Is it the church where they sing praise choruses and perform dramas, or is the church with the full-time choir director and organist who produce the community's presentation of the *Messiah* each year?

The answer is probably all of the above. Each one has something to offer that the others can't provide. It's impossible to define church, because church is what it is. As long as two or three are present, then Jesus is present also, and that may be enough.

The house church was the basic model of first-century Christianity, though it would be difficult to give a generic description of house churches. Each one had its own characteristics and flavor. The Christian faith brought together individuals from different economic and ethnic backgrounds. Generally, a wealthier member supplied the home and sometimes the leadership, for the church. The church at Corinth, for instance, seems to have consisted of at least four house churches, the "Paul" church, the "Apollos" church, the "Peter" church, and the "Christ" church.

The first-century church was not only composed mostly of house churches, but it was also a city church. Many Christians are suspicious of the cities and see it as a place of sin and separation from God, yet pretty much all the letters of Paul are written to city churches. Christianity was a city religion for most of the first three centuries of its existence. Indeed the term "pagan" is taken from the Latin term for country folk. Pagans came from the country. Christians came from the city.

Certainly, the city is where all the people are. Although many Christians prefer the countryside and look on the city as the pagan place, the images of salvation in the New Testament are tied to the city. It is the New Jerusalem, not the New Eden that descends from heaven at the end of Revelation and the tree of life is transplanted from the old Garden of Eden into that new Jerusalem. The city is the center of salvation.

In the previous chapter of Acts (15), Luke paints a picture of triumph for the church (the Council of Jerusalem) followed by a disaster (the argument between Paul and Barnabas over Mark, leading to their separation). The trouble was, Mark had left a missionary journey before its completion and Paul no longer trusted him. Later the rift would be healed, for Paul mentions in 2 Timothy 4:11 how useful Mark had been for him.

In the passage for today, Paul and Silas, with their new traveling companion, Timothy, have arrived in Philippi, one of the great cities of the Roman Empire. Philippi was in Macedonia, north of the Grecian peninsula. It was a city of some 10,000 people on the Via Egnatia, a major east-west trade route, and it was a cosmopolitan city, with many different ethnic and racial groups.

More importantly, it was a Roman colony, and its citizens were also citizens of Rome. Even though Rome was over 800 miles away, the people there, many of them retirees from the Roman army who had never seen Rome but had served Rome all their lives, had all the privileges of Roman citizenship. They were used to serving a place they had never seen, living by the rules of a place they had never seen, and proclaiming themselves citizens of a place they had never seen.

The Apostle Paul was led to Philippi by a dream in which he saw a man from Macedonia begging him to bring the gospel to them. He found a people ready to serve a heaven they had never seen, to live by the rules of heaven though they had never seen it, and to become citizens of heaven though they had never seen it.

Paul's pattern when arriving at city was to go first to its synagogue to meet with those whose faith he shared. In Philippi there was no synagogue, perhaps because there weren't the ten men required as a minimum for worship. He had heard, however, that there was a prayer group that met by the river, and he went there instead.

Although we associate rivers with the countryside, cities depended on rivers for commerce, for beauty, for water, which is the stuff of life itself. There's something mysterious and beautiful about rivers, about the way they become the lifeblood of people, taking folks different places, providing food and recreation, providing water for the trees that line their banks.

Rivers run through scriptures. Water is life, after all. The rivers that define Eden, the river Jordan that runs through biblical narrative, the Tigris and Euphrates, the Nile, and of course the river that runs through the New Jerusalem. The rivers of Psalms, by the waters we wept as we lay down our harps. Namaan is cured in a river. Elijah takes flight near a river. John the Baptist calls people to repentance in a river. And Jesus is baptized in that river.

Psalm 46 says: "There is a river whose streams make glad the city of God, the holy habitation of the Most High" (Psalm 46:4). And where is that river? "... in the midst of the city," of course (46:5).

In the movie, *O Brother, Where Art Thou?* the Christians coming forward for baptism step into the river singing the old traditional folk song:

> *As I went down in the river to pray,*
> *Studying about that good old way*
> *And who shall wear the starry crown*
> *Good Lord, show me the way!*
> *Oh, children, let's go down, let's go down, come on down.*
> *Oh, children, let's go down, down in the river to pray.*

In this text Paul goes to the river to find believers because there is no synagogue in this town, and that's what he finds — believers who cannot form a church because they do not conform to the standards of that time. They are Gentiles, they are single women, they are believers whose belief is not accepted by others.

This prayer group consisted of that class of people known as God-fearers. These were Gentiles who believed in the God of Israel, but for one reason or another were not able to take the next step and become part of God's people. This could have been for one of several reasons. It was not easy to convert to Judaism in those days, and converts were actively discouraged. Some men would not have wanted to undergo circumcision, which they would have considered mutilation of a body whose beauty came from God. Women whose husbands were not also converts were probably not welcome to join on their own. But these individuals would have been fairly familiar with the scriptures and with the practices of the faith.

In this instance, the prayer group consisted entirely of women, and their worship leader was also a woman. Lydia, perhaps named after the region from which she came, was a wealthy individual with a business in purple cloth, a highly prized commodity in the ancient world. The purple dye might have been part of an imperial monopoly granted to Lydia's family because of service to Rome in times past. She would have had a great deal of social importance, for normally in that time women were not named in public, but what she seems to have craved more than anything else was acceptance into the family of God.

The original Greek text makes it clear that these women did not gather together by accident. They gathered together in a structured manner to worship. The women had active church lives, but their church could never meet under the strictures of Judaism.

There was nothing to stop them from becoming Christians, however. They did not need to be attached to a male to join. Lydia and her household, including servants, were baptized, and as the head of a house, she probably became the worship leader for the house church. This was evidently not unusual in early Christianity. Frescos illustrating the ancient practice of the love feast show women, presumably the homeowners, administering the rite.

Lydia's home becomes Paul's home. She wants to give back, and Paul has the good grace to receive. Her response to her baptism is to open her home as a church. Make no mistake. This is not a case of a lonely single woman who wants to have a couple of men share the house with her. On the contrary, as a head of household there would have been layers of relatives and servants who lived in her large-scale villa. Paul and Silas would have had quarters of their own, which would become the base of operations for Paul and his company as they began the evangelization of Macedonia.

Something that is easy to overlook in this passage is a very small word — "we." Starting in this chapter the author, Luke, makes it clear that at certain times he is part of the group that travels with Paul. He is the source for these parts of the book, an actual eyewitness of events.

He doesn't make a big deal and say, "Hey, look! I'm here." But he is definitely part of the picture.

Some wonder if Luke was a proud native of Philippi. Certainly he was referred to by Paul as "Luke, the beloved physician," (Colossians 4:14) and Philippi was famous for its medical school.

Luke, though a participant, is not as interested in what he is doing as what God is doing, and that is why he wants to tell us about Lydia, and the river, and the good things that come when we push ourselves beyond the comfort zone and reach out to those who others aren't interested in. Because when we act as God's ambassadors among the lost, there is no telling what will happen next.

And when we're finally in a place where there's no telling what will happen next. *That's* when we're *really* in a church. Amen.

## The Ascension Of Our Lord
## Acts 1:1-11

# What Are You Looking At?

One of the most obvious things about the night sky is the moon, especially the full moon. The full moon transforms not only the sky, but the earth, creating a dimmer, second kind of day, casting long shadows, and providing some guidance to those who find themselves outdoors.

Certainly, it is one of the things that children first notice about the sky. They can point to the moon, ask what it is, stare at it in wonder.

And then, a few days later, the child can wonder — where did it go?

The sun, after all, travels in a more orderly fashion. The sun rises and the sun sets. It begins and ends the day. It's not day without the sun. But it can be night without the moon. Sometimes it's the most obvious thing in the night sky and sometimes it's not there at all.

That's part of what Luke intends to address in this passage — Jesus is the most important person to ever live. He has turned the world upside down, fulfilled the scriptures, and changed the way we look at things. More than that, he had died and risen back to life. The risen Jesus is Lord of the church. How can there be a church without a visible Jesus?

So where is Jesus? Where did he go? These are the essential questions that Luke has for new converts, and especially for someone named Theophilus.

While no one is quite sure if Theophilus was a single person, or was a fictional person designed to represent all Christians, Luke opens the Acts of the Apostles with what sounds like the standard dedication of his time. Remember that one did not publish a book the same way then as now. Luke didn't submit sample chapters of a manuscript to a publisher who might have sent him a cash advance so he'd finish it, then publish it and send him royalties. Writing required a patron who supported the working artist until the work was completed.

It seems likely that Theophilus — whose name means "the one who loves God" — was a wealthy convert, a Christian who supported Luke while he worked on his two part history of Jesus and the action of the Holy Spirit. That first part of the work — the Gospel of Luke — told what Jesus did during his earthly ministry, and ended with the Ascension. The Acts of the Apostles, however, had no one central character. Neither Peter nor James nor Paul nor anyone else seems to be the hero of the story.

Actually, Luke was writing a history of the Holy Spirit, not of any one person, and that Holy Spirit is active among many different people, and the Holy Spirit is the one constant throughout the book.

As stated earlier, Luke has essential questions to answer for Theophilus and other new converts. If Jesus was raised from the dead, where did he go? Why is he not still among us?

In the gospel, Luke presents the resurrection appearances of Jesus as real events and intends to do the same with the ascension of Jesus, which occurs at the end of the gospel and is reviewed at the beginning of Acts. Jesus returns to life not as some vague sort of spirit, or a good feeling sharing by the surviving disciples. Luke is at pains to demonstrate that the risen Jesus could eat and drink with the disciples! He wants us to accept it as something extraordinary that happened in the ordinary world.

Jesus leaves the disciples with a task that they are to share — to spread the good news about the kingdom of God: "... you will be my witnesses in Jerusalem, in all Judea and Samaria, and to the ends of the earth" (Acts 1:8). This is in response to their desire to know when God's kingdom would be inaugurated. They wanted to be spectators. Jesus wants them to be participants in spreading the gospel.

Jesus inaugurated that good news when he opened the Isaiah scroll in his hometown and read aloud these words: "The Spirit of the Lord is upon me, because he has anointed me to bring good news to the poor. He has sent me to proclaim release to the captives and recovery of sight to the blind, to let the oppressed go free, to proclaim the year of the Lord's favor" (Luke 4:18-19).

Jesus promises the disciples they will receive that same Spirit to go about the same task. It is not a task that any one of us can accomplish by ourselves, but together we are expected to go about it anyway!

Perhaps that is the greatest reason Jesus ascended into heaven. Had he remained on earth, the disciples would have continued to crowd around him — and who can blame them? If we had access to the risen Lord, physically and in the flesh, wouldn't we be tempted to attempt to stand by his side?

But it's not allowed, not in this life anyway. We get glimpses, the Spirit sends us greetings, we feel the presence of God very strongly at times — and certainly God is always present wherever we go — but we're also sent out to work in the trenches, to do the difficult work of the kingdom, to get up and go even though we'd rather stay put.

The power and authority of Jesus is passed on to the disciples, even though not one of us measures up to Jesus. That doesn't matter. Elisha was no Elijah, but he saw his master ascend into heaven and the prophetic mantle fell on him.

Moreover, the manner of Jesus' ascent calls to mind the way he will descend some day. Luke uses language that deliberately calls to mind the prophet Daniel — "I saw in the night visions, and, behold, one like the Son of man came with the clouds of heaven, and came to the Ancient of days, and they brought him near before him" (Daniel 7:13 KJV).

This is the same Jesus who will return, the apostles are assured. So it is promised in Revelation: "Look! He is coming with the clouds; every eye will see him, even those who pierced him; and on his account all the tribes of the earth will wail. So it is to be. Amen" (Revelation 1:7).

What would we have seen had we been there at the ascension? I haven't a clue. Jesus appeared to ascend into heaven, but what does that mean? I don't know if there are any scientific instruments that could have measured or weighed what happened. But it happened. And the apostles stared into heaven, believers who had just seen the unbelievable.

When good friends and family leave us we sometimes stare after them long after they are gone, long after the car has gone around the bend, or the plane has disappeared into the clouds, or the train has become a speck on the horizon. Had we been standing there with the apostles we might have continued to stare as well.

But it's not allowed. Two men in white came to them and scolded them with words of hope — if the combination is possible: "Men of Galilee, why do you stand looking up toward heaven? This Jesus, who has been taken up from you into heaven, will come in the same way as you saw him go into heaven" (Acts 1:11). In other words — get to work — but don't forget that Jesus is coming back.

Our trust in the imminent return of Jesus is an essential belief. But we are not to stand slackjawed on the hillside staring at the sky waiting for his return. Nor are we to spend our time circling dates on the calendar, predicting his return in the face of his assurance that none of us could possibly know the date.

No, as Christians we know we are to be found at our post, sharing the cup of cold water, feeding the hungry, clothing the naked, kneeling to wash a brother's or sister's feet. When Jesus returns in glory, our eyes may be turned to the ground, but we'll feel the light of the ages at our back, and with slow but solid satisfaction we will turn to face he who we have always trusted and known.

There are two mistakes we could make in the wake of the ascension. One is to continue to stare into heaven, to be so focused on the return of Jesus, which is a central element of our faith, that we neglect the work of the kingdom. The other is to wait on the sidelines. We are expected to get into the ball game.

Speaking of ball games, only the oldest among of us will remember the glory days of the Green Bay Packers during the '60s, when they won championship after championship. The great Vince

Lombardi was their coach. During their last championship year one of the linemen, Jerry Kramer, kept a diary of the football season which was eventually published as the book, *Instant Replay*. Early in the book, Kramer reports a speech by legendary coach Vince Lombardi, who eulogized a player who had been taken from their midst by the expansion draft. Lombardi made it clear that the player could never be replaced and would always stand as an example to the rest of them. However, regarding another player who left the team to get more money, Lombardi said tersely, "We will replace the other fellow."

In this first chapter of Acts, the apostles suffer two losses. Jesus is irreplaceable, although in a sense, Jesus will always be with them. But Judas is gone, too. The apostles have to close ranks and move on, but one senses they won't forget him, either. All churches deal with the loss of members who leave in glorious circumstances, but there are also those who leave under difficult circumstances, and at which time we're not always sure what to say or do.

We never really replace those who leave us, whether for good reason or bad. But we are expected to continue. Losing a key member is not an excuse to stop discipling. It is an invitation for us all to try even harder.

After the ascension, Jesus is no longer accessible in the same way as during his earthly ministry, but Luke tells us Jesus is very present. This ascension into heaven shapes the way we look at the world. It causes us to look back to the ministry of Jesus so we may find a pattern for our own, but it also encourages us to look forward to the perfect kingdom God will institute. It opens the door for the Holy Spirit to enter the world more fully, to become the center of our lives, invisible, yet always moving among us, never seen, often felt, always known.

Thanks to the ascension we, like the disciples, must move away from our comfortable home territory and take that good news to the ends of the earth, stopping along the way to the Samaritans of our lives, those people who we might think of as our enemies, but who are really our partners in God's work. Remember that the inhabitants of Jerusalem and Judea were distrustful of the Samaritans, who were actually very much like them. I'm sure the average

Roman citizen couldn't tell one of God's people from a Samaritan. Our work begins with those who we feel uncomfortable with and goes on from there.

Most of all, Luke reminds us that Jesus will return, and while we are not to stare into space while waiting for him, this should affect everything we do, the way we look at the world, the way we treat others.

This passage is a transitional period. Jesus is gone and the Holy Spirit has not yet arrived. The apostles seem content to return to and remain in Jerusalem, remembering their irreplaceable leader and serving each other in the upper room.

One thing is certain. The church without the Holy Spirit is not about to spread the gospel throughout the world. The apostles gather in Jerusalem, but they do not proceed to kindle the new church. They wait for Pentecost. They will not have to wait very long. Amen.

# Jailhouse Rock

Do you remember the old folk tune that went something like this? *(sing or recite)*

> *The bear went over the mountain.*
> *The bear went over the mountain.*
> *The bear went over the mountain —*
> *To see what he could see.*
>
> *And all that he could see, and all that he could see,*
> *Was the other side of the mountain, the other side of*
>    *the mountain*
> *The other side of the mountain was all that he could*
>    *see!*

Maybe the only thing you can see from a high place is the other side of that high place, but still, the view can be worth it.

Take a moment to think of the highest spot you've stood on, and the farthest distance you've seen. Maybe you've taken a trip to Chicago and had a look from the top of the Sear's Tower. Maybe you've been to Mount Whitney, or Denali, or Pike's Peak, or just someplace local, and huffed and puffed to the top, and got a look around. Whatever that highest spot was, just take a moment, right now, close your eyes, and think about it. Think about what you saw. Just take a moment.

Have you thought about it? Then turn to your neighbor and tell that neighbor where that spot was and what you saw. *(pause for conversations)*

I hope you saw something worth seeing. Being high up can be a good thing, because we get a great perspective.

Perspective is something you can learn from looking over a great distance, but perspective is also something you learn from looking out over a great deal of time, or a great deal of experience.

For instance, as the years go by we hopefully learn perspective! Things never stand still. They go uphill and downhill. Triumph is followed by disaster, but fortunately, the opposite is true as well. As Rudyard Kipling said, in his poem "IF" —

> *If you can meet with Triumph and Disaster*
> *And treat those two impostors just the same;*
> *... Yours is the Earth and everything that's in it....*

Think about that. Triumph and disaster. Both of them are imposters. Neither one has the last word.

Previously, Paul had known triumph in his successful defense at the Council of Jerusalem, where the elders had decided he was indeed called by the Holy Spirit to take the good news of Jesus Christ to the Gentiles, and that they did not need to change ethnic backgrounds in order to become Christians.

But there had been disaster when Paul and his longtime companion, Barnabas, split up when they argued over the faithfulness of Mark, who had left an earlier missionary tour before it was completed. The great duo was in disarray, but that disaster led to triumph, as both men took the gospel to new places.

Triumph continued when Paul obeyed the message he received in a dream in which a man from Macedonia encouraged him to travel into Europe for the first time. The trip to Philippi resulted in the conversion of Lydia and the founding of at least two house churches.

The conversion of Lydia and her household was a great success! Then came a major church disaster. As is the pattern, we will see that it all turns out for the best. Paul continued to evangelize in Philippi. He and Silas were plagued by a slave woman who followed them, continually spouting prophetic gibberish, which her handlers interpreted for money. She was their big moneymaker.

As the woman followed Paul and Silas, she cried out on many occasions, "These men are slaves of the Most High God, who proclaim to you a way of salvation" (Acts 16:17). Most High God was the Gentile name for the God of the Hebrews. Evidently this began to annoy Paul after many repetitions, and when he was finally tired of being followed around, he turned and healed this woman of her demon.

This was not cause for celebration as far as her owners were concerned, because suddenly she stopped babbling and was worthless to them. Religion is one thing when it's good for business, but religion that destroys a person's cash flow is another thing entirely.

You can see the need for perspective, for climbing with the bear up the spiritual mountain to see what we can see. If we don't take time to get a good look around, to take a deep breath, to appreciate what God is doing in the larger picture, we will take each failure — and each success — far too seriously. After all, each success belongs to God. And each failure — are we all that important that we need to claim failure as ours, also? God's eventual victory is assured. Our part, like Paul's, is to stay in the game, to try, to attempt big things, knowing that God can do far more with our failures than we could with our successes.

Certainly, Paul at this point has run into a great brick wall — that place where Christianity meets economics, and where many Christians turn tail and run. The gospel has a cost, and it isn't just a case of going without chocolate once in a while. If we are truly to bring in God's kingdom, if we are going to live by the kingdom rules even when the world makes it impossible, we have to be prepared for the fact that we have to make hard economic choices if we are Christians.

Like asking the jeweler, when we're preparing to buy that engagement ring, if these are conflict diamonds we're buying, diamonds that are cheap because oppressors have cut off the hands and feet of those who have opposed them so they can run rampant with the diamond trade in their country. If Christians don't ask questions, diamond dealers will continue to buy precious stones without asking questions of their own!

A couple of years ago the National Council of Churches spearheaded a boycott of a major fast food chain in order to secure better wages for migrant workers who pick tomatoes. When Christians banded together to support the boycott, the workers ended up getting the raise they deserved.

We hear on occasions that major store chains are buying clothes from sweat shops. Christians have to challenge the buyers for these stores. And when celebrities put their names on clothing lines without checking the source of those clothes, we need to call them to account as well.

The world reacts fast when threatened by the economics of the kingdom. Because the slave's owner's profits were destroyed by the healing, they spread false rumors about Paul and Silas, which led to a brutal beating and arrest. Even though Paul and Silas were attacked, and had done nothing wrong, they were blamed for causing civil unrest and thrown in jail.

So what happened? How does God's Spirit work?

Instead of squelching the church movement, the missionaries' jail term led to the foundation of another house church! Paul and Silas were kept in the worst part of the jail. In the ancient world, jails were sometimes free enterprise affairs, where the jailer operated the facility for a profit. The jailer's own life would be forfeited, however, if the prisoners escaped.

While the jailer slept, a miraculous earthquake caused the shackles to fall off the prisoners and the doors to be left open. Waking up to find the convicts loose, the jailer began to despair, and rightly so. He assumed his prisoners had bolted and that he would be held responsible with his life for their escape. He prepared to kill himself. Paul and Silas assured him, however, that everyone was still inside the prison. What happened next was that the prisoners and jailer ceased to look at each other as population groups and started to see each other as people, and when that happens, church happens.

This is jailhouse rock with a vengeance. One earthquake, two prisoners, and a whole family of changed lives. And who knows where it ended, with the testimony of the saved jailer? There's no telling what this redeemed world can become once we all get into the act.

It's easy for people to label individuals as populations. It is easy to categorize a person as a store clerk, a librarian, a police officer, a bureaucrat at the unemployment office, an IRS agent, a prisoner, a jailer, or a homeless person. The key is to see each other face-to-face and know each other as people.

Authorities like the jailer can be outsiders just as much as the forsaken are. But those far off are now brought near (cf. Colossians 1:21-23). That's the deal God has made through the new covenant. Church is where you find it, at the riverside or in the jail, or in the neighborhood.

Were Paul and Silas fools for singing hymns in prison? Hardly. They might have been killed, and if they had, the Spirit would have used their martyrdom for the growth of the church. Certainly, that was the experience of the Anabaptists such as the Mennonites, who endured great persecution from both Protestants and Catholics. These Christians insisted on the separation of church and state. In an era where baptism meant entry into citizenship as well as membership in the church, they insisted that Christ's kingdom was more important than worldly kingdoms. These peaceable people refused to use violence (although for centuries other Christians spread false libels about them to that effect) and instead meekly endured horrific torture and executions for their faith.

The most famous example is that of Dirk Willems, who escaped from prison and ran across the ice to freedom. However, the man chasing him was heavier and fell through that ice and would have drowned had not Willems turned back to save him. This led to his recapture and his eventual death by fire at the stake. Willems has been held up by Christians as an example of the way that the love of Jesus trumps even concerns for our own safety. In the book of Revelation, John sees martyrs like Willems rejoicing in heaven, vindicated as part of the heavenly choir singing to God's glory, doing just fine, thank you very much.

That's the point of Easter, and the Easter season, when you come down to it. It's not simply a trick, a dog and pony show, an amazing act. Jesus is not raised from the dead to amaze us, but to transform us, to change the way we look at the world, and each other. The book of Acts follows the early church as people are changed, as racial barriers are knocked down, as the economic hierarchies are knocked sideways and forward and six ways from Tuesday.

In the book of Revelation, we read about the tree that is set in the middle of the New Jerusalem, and we are told that the leaves of the tree are for the healing of the nations. The book of Acts chronicles our forays among the nations. And you know, the story isn't over.

Let's cheat for a moment and sneak a peek at the end of the Acts of the Apostles. We follow Paul all the way to Rome, where under house arrest he continues the work of the gospel. We read: "He lived there two whole years at his own expense and welcomed all who came to him, proclaiming the kingdom of God and teaching about the Lord Jesus Christ with all boldness and without hindrance" (Acts 28:30-31).

And the story stops. We're on our way to a big trial in Rome, and we never do find out what happens. What kind of an ending is that? An arrest, danger and intrigue, a shipwreck, the arrival at Rome, Luke writes a real page turner, and suddenly the book of Acts stops. It doesn't end. It just stops.

There's a reason. The book of Acts is not about Peter or Apollos or Priscilla or Paul. It's about the gospel of Jesus Christ, and how it moves through the world. And that story isn't over. It's still unfolding. And we're a part.

The book of Acts is a book about us. We have a part to play, and every time we share the good news we're writing a new page. "Men of Galilee, why do you stand looking up toward heaven? This Jesus, who has been taken up from you into heaven, will come in the same way as you saw him go into heaven." Hey! Get to work!

Be healed. You are a citizen of heaven. You are allowed to sing. You can make noise. You can break down barriers. You can change the world. We can change the world.

And if you're feeling just a little bit cautious, a little bit scared, let me tell you something. Our next stop is Pentecost. The Spirit still lives among us. Easter season may be over on the church calendar, but it's never really over among believers. Once upon a time, the early Christians observed Easter Sunday every Sunday. It should be the same now.

The bear went over the mountain to see what he could see. It's worth it to climb with that bear and get a look around, to see what God has in store. We'll see the other side of that mountain all right — it's the mountain of the Lord and it's the kingdom of heaven we'll see, and the world that is so changed that at the name of Jesus every knee will bow. The Philippians learned that, because Paul not only wrote those words to them, he also lived those words, changing the lives of a rich woman like Lydia, a slave girl, and an outcast like the jailer. It didn't matter. Red and yellow, black and white, all are precious in God's sight. Jesus loves all of us little children of the world. Amen.

# Sermons On The First Readings

## For Sundays
## After Pentecost
## (First Third)

### *Wisdom's Delight*

### Stan Purdum

The Day Of Pentecost
Acts 2:1-21

# The Undoing Of Babel

Several years ago, my wife and I took a vacation where we drove to Mexico City in an old Volkswagen van. Neither of us speak Spanish, but along the primary route down and in Mexico City itself, we had no trouble communicating because many people there spoke English. After spending a few days in that city, we decided to make our exit from Mexico by driving up a highway along the west coast of the country. That route provided us many attractive views of the Pacific Ocean and, as we got farther north, the Gulf of California, the body of water between the Mexican mainland and the Baja peninsula.

As we got away from the more populated areas, we found fewer people who spoke English. We were carrying most of our food in the vehicle, so we didn't have to negotiate restaurants away from the main cities, and we were able to purchase gas for the van without much difficulty, because both we and the attendant knew what we were after. We had learned to understand the money exchange, and had memorized a few Spanish phrases that enabled us to ask where the bathrooms were, to say, "Thank you," and to convey that we didn't speak the language. We ambled along without too much problem.

Then one day, spotting a beautiful and mostly deserted beach, we decided to stop and swim. After we were there a few minutes, we noticed a man and a boy some distance out in the water, and they seemed to be trying to push a raft of some sort toward the beach. They appeared to be having some difficulty, so I waded out, grabbed hold of the raft, and helped them maneuver it to shore.

They were quite appreciative and the man began speaking rapidly in Spanish, pointing to the rocks placed on the raft. Adhering to the rocks were oyster-like shells, and as the man continued to speak, he pried open a shell and pulled out the material inside. I guessed that this was abalone, and the man handed the material to me, indicating with his hands that I should eat it, raw, something I wasn't accustomed to. At the same moment, my wife was saying to me in panic, "Don't let them give *me* one of those!"

But I gathered that this was their way of saying, "Thank you," and I didn't want to appear rude, so I ate it. Then the man launched into a new monologue, which, of course, we couldn't understand, but he was using his hand to point toward a hut not far way and was making motions that finally led me to believe he was inviting us to join his family for dinner.

I would have loved to accept the invitation and to have the experience that such a visit would bring, but because we couldn't communicate effectively, I felt the whole thing would be awkward and exhausting. So using my own hand motions, I indicated that we had to be moving on, and after a profuse exchange of "Gracias," we made our way back to the van and drove off.

It was an occasion where I wished for some sort of device such as the one that supposedly exists on the old *Star Trek* series — a little machine called the Universal Translator. In the series, it takes the language of any interplanetary species and converts it accurately so that the individuals involved can communicate freely. Of course, *Star Trek* is science fiction, and I have my doubts that such a device will ever be invented that will handle every language automatically and accurately. Communication is never a simple thing.[1]

But thinking about the difficulties of communicating across language barriers brings us to the stories from our two scripture readings for today.

Once upon a time, so the older story tells us, the whole world spoke the same language. The people had heard God's command to fill the earth and spread out over the land. Some, however, thought they knew better than God. They didn't want to scatter over the earth, so they built a city with a high tower, one designed to cause them to be praised as a great people, and to make them powerful enough to defy God's command.

What they were doing was an act of rebellion against God, so God came amongst them and confused their language so that they could no longer understand one another. Work on the city and tower became impossible, and in the end, the people scattered as God had wanted in the first place. The city and the unfinished tower came to be called Babel, which actually meant "gate of God," and was an early version of the name Babylon, but it sounded much like the Hebrew word *balal*, which means "confuse." Because of what happened at that place, the word Babel came to mean confusion. We could say that at Babel, the Lord made babblers out of the people by confusing their language.

That old story is a myth, probably told by ancient people to account for the existence of an unfinished tower somewhere or to explain why the people of the earth do not all speak the same language. But it is significant that the people imagined the world before Babel as one where everyone could understand one another. The way God meant the world to be from the beginning, so the thinking went, was that people could communicate clearly and without confusion.

When you think about it, that's not a far-fetched idea. Consider how much trouble we have in life because of communication difficulties — even between people who share a common language. How many marriages, for example, have problems because neither of the partners talk to each other about what's actually on their hearts, or when they do talk, one doesn't really listen to the other, or one lectures the other? Or even further, when both parties *are* trying to communicate and *are* working at paying attention, they still hear each other through the filters of emotion, weariness, momentary lapses, different understandings of the meaning of certain words, resentments, preconceived notions, defensiveness, self-centeredness, and so on.

But communication difficulties are not limited to marriage. Back when my wife was in college, she had to write a paper for a geography class. The professor handed out a sheet with the topic of the paper, but when you read it, you were left wondering what in the world he was talking about. My wife talked to a couple of her classmates, but they were as much in the dark as she was. She showed the sheet to me, and I was baffled as well. It happened that I knew the geography teacher at the local high school, so I suggested she talk to him about it. She did, and though that teacher wanted to be helpful, he wasn't sure what the professor was looking for, either.

Finally, my wife decided to simply answer the question as literally as possible, which resulted in a paper only a page and a half long. When she got to class, she discovered that most of her fellow students had papers ten to twelve pages long, so she was convinced that she had misunderstood the assignment, but having nothing else, she handed the paper in.

At the next class, the professor was angry that students had wasted his time with such "claptrap," as he described it. He said that only one student had done the assignment correctly, and he held up my wife's paper, with an *A* on it.

But the failure in that case was actually his. He had not communicated clearly, even though he was convinced that he had.

You no doubt have your own stories of miscommunications. Sometimes they are humorous, but often they are serious and result in damage to relationships, to partnerships, to friendships, and to other ways in which we humans try to connect with one another.

The other story from our scripture readings is the account of Pentecost, the celebration of the day when the Holy Spirit came upon the followers of Jesus. The major miracle of that day was one of communication. After the Holy Spirit fired up those followers of Jesus in the upper room in Jerusalem, they rushed out into the streets and began preaching. Because Pentecost was a major festival in the Jewish religion, the city was filled with pilgrims from every corner of the Roman Empire. The reading from Acts spells out the diversity of nationalities: "Parthians, Medes, Elamites, and residents of Mesopotamia, Judea and Cappadocia, Pontus and Asia, Phrygia and Pamphylia, Egypt and the parts of Libya belonging to Cyrene, and visitors from Rome, both Jews and proselytes, Cretans and Arabs...." These groups had no common language; each group spoke its own, but when the disciples of Jesus started preaching, all speaking Aramaic, everybody understood. The miracle was an undoing of Babel.

The story of Babel is often read on this Sunday of the year because it stands in contrast to the events of Pentecost. At Babel, the people started out with the ability to understand one another in a common language. They lost that ability and communication ceased. At Pentecost, people who did not speak the same language understood the gospel message clearly.

That reminds us that one goal of Christianity is to help us understand one another and to communicate without filters. But that is only part of the story. Jesus told us that we need to love our neighbor and our enemies. You see, it's possible to clearly understand someone but to disagree profoundly with them. I suspect that the Israelis and the Palestinians each have some pretty clear understanding of what the other side wants, but they do not agree that what the other side wants is valid. They have not yet communicated in the love that can set both sides free.

There is a sense that what Pentecost shows us is unrealistic. We can hardly envision a day when all communication barriers come down, and where there is no misunderstanding among humans. In fact, life as we experience it is more like the Babel story than the Pentecost account. Israelis vs. Palestinians, parents vs. children, husband vs. wife, employer vs. employee, student vs. teacher, "jocks" vs. "freaks," "preppies" vs. "Goths," and on and on. Even in the church, we find denominations that can't agree with one another and there are sometimes strong disagreements within single congregations.

But Pentecost is the event that started the church worldwide. Our beginning is marked by an event where factions were overcome and people of diverse backgrounds and languages not only understood one another, but were brought together with a common goal. Acts tells us that some 3,000 people became Christians that very day.

And so, though we have all too much experience with the inability to communicate clearly and with misunderstandings and disagreements, we also have the hope that Christianity holds out before us that the love of Christ within can break through those

233

separating barriers. I suspect that if there is one thing that will be different in eternity it will be that communication and agreement will be givens.

The fact is, however, that sometimes we see it happen even now. We could call it a foretaste of eternity, but it's also the reality that can occur when we give Christ full rein in our lives. Here's one example:

Writer, Anne Lamott, attends a Presbyterian church in northern California that has a racially mixed membership. In one of her columns, which I heard on an NPR broadcast,[2] she told about a man who began attending their church after he was diagnosed with AIDS, which he'd contracted from a male partner. The newcomer was white. Because of the AIDS, this man was weaker and more diminished each time he appeared in church. What's more, shortly after he started coming, his partner died of the disease. The man later said that Jesus slipped into the hole in his heart left by his partner's death.

In that church, there was a black woman in the choir who was very devout, but she was standoffish toward this afflicted newcomer. Raised in the South by fundamentalists, she had been taught that his way of life — that he himself therefore — was an abomination, and it was difficult for her to see him any other way. She was also a little afraid of contracting his disease. But he came to church almost every week for a year, and won just about everyone else over. Then, however, he missed a couple of weeks, and when he came back, he was emaciated and far gone.

On that Sunday, the first hymn was, "His Eye Is On The Sparrow," and when the congregation stood to sing, this man, rotting from AIDS, was unable to rise. He sat there holding the hymnal in his lap. After a moment, however, the black woman went to his side, bent down and lifted him up.

Hear the end of the story in Lamott's own words:

> She held him next to her, and he was draped over and against her like a child, and they sang. And ... the black woman and the man with AIDS, of whom she was so afraid, were trying to sing. But they both began to cry.

*Tears were pouring down their faces, and their noses were running like rivers; but as she held him up, she suddenly lay her face against his, put her black weeping face against his feverish white one, put her face right up against his and let all those spooky fluids mingle with hers.*

Lamott comments that she didn't know if what had happened was "an honest-to-God little miracle," but that it was "plenty of miracle" for her. But of course it *was* a miracle, the miracle of Pentecost, the undoing of Babel.

That kind of communication, you see, is a godly thing. It's no mere coincidence that the day the church was born, the day the Spirit filled Jesus' followers, was the day some people discovered they could communicate the love of God across previously uncrossable barriers. It was no accident that Pentecost undid Babel.

That's what the activity of the Spirit within us always empowers us to do. May we be open to let the Spirit work within us and God's love come through us.

---

1. My thanks to Carlos Wilton for this illustration, *The Immediate Word*, June 8, 2003.

2. I heard this broadcast sometime in the spring of 2003, but it comes from a column Anne Lamott wrote for *Salon Magazine*, January 6, 1997, called "Knocking on Heaven's Door." www.salon.com/jan97/lamott970106.html.

# Wisdom's Delight

I have a question for you, but let me tell you right up front that it is a trick question. The question is, "What did God create first?" If you are like most Bible readers, your mind will immediately jump to the first chapter of Genesis, and then it is a matter of trying to recall which part of the world God called into being first. In case you can't immediately bring that answer to mind, I'll tell you: It was the creation of light. Genesis says that in the beginning, "darkness covered the face of the deep." So as his first step in creating the world, God said, "Let there be light," and, the Bible says, light came into being.

But remember that I said I was asking a trick question, and so light is not the answer I am looking for. My question is a trick one because I did not ask which part of the *world* God created first, but what his *first creative act* was. The answer the Bible gives us to that question is found not Genesis 1 but in Proverbs 8. Actually, there may have been many creative acts before God made the world, but the first one the Bible records is God's creation of *Wisdom*. In Proverbs 8, Wisdom, speaking in the first person, says, "The Lord created me at the beginning of his work, the first of his acts of long ago."

Taken literally, that verse means that Wisdom was birthed prior to the creation of the world. What's more, in that same chapter, Wisdom, which really is an attribute of God, is personified as a woman. Bear in mind that Wisdom is not really a separate individual, but a characteristic of God on whom the biblical people put a female face to make it more understandable. We do the same kind of thing when we take a characteristic of our own and speak of it as though it were an entity outside of ourselves, such as, "My sense of fair play would not let me do thus and so" or "I had to keep my wits about me."

In any case, this personified-woman, Wisdom, says that while God was marking out the foundations of the earth, she was "beside him." In other words, Wisdom was God's companion in the process of creating the world.

In trying to impose some sense on that claim, we might be tempted to say that before God set out to create the world, he first created the understanding he would need to do the creating. That, however, sounds nonsensical. We are probably better to hear the claim of Proverbs 8 as a poetic way of saying that God imbued some measure of his divineness in the world he created.

In Old Testament Hebrew thought, there was a view that God had built the world and life itself to run best in certain logical ways. The idea was that if you could figure out what those ways were and then do your best to cooperate with them, your life would be happy and you would have well being. That understanding of life was called "wisdom," and as the word is used in the Old Testament, wisdom can be a skill, a body of knowledge, or, as in the case of Proverbs 8, an attribute of God.

Further, in those times, there were people who devoted their lives to discovering what God's wisdom consisted of. In fact, it became a career for some, so that moral guidance for Israel came not only from prophets and priests, but also from people known as "the wise." Some of these wise people were employed by kings to advise them on affairs of state and on personal matters as well. These wise men (and those who were officially among the wise in that patriarchal society were generally men, although some women were also known to be wise), issued their teachings in the form of sayings, fables, oracles, epics, riddles, poetry, and myths. Thus, eventually there was a whole body of written material called wisdom literature. In the Old Testament, Proverbs, along with Ecclesiastes, Job, and certain of the Psalms, are examples of this special category of writing. And unlike the historical or prophetic portions of the Old Testament, wisdom texts are intentionally instructive. Much of it has an outcome-oriented tone rather than devotional one, and it focuses on how one should act so as to make one's way successfully in the world while remaining righteous. Although not ostensibly religious in its outlook, the central theological claim of the wisdom writings is that "the fear of the Lord is the beginning of knowledge" (Proverbs 1:7).

In this section of Proverbs, Wisdom is in effect presenting her credentials. By portraying herself as the first of God's creations and of having been there with God at the birthing of the world, Wisdom is not claiming to be equal to God, but she is telling of her honored place next to God himself. Those credentials are important, for Wisdom wants her audience to heed her instructions, something they will only do if they are convinced that she is right. She wants them to listen, for she knows the value of her teaching. As she states it, "For whoever finds me finds life and obtains favor from the Lord."

All of that is well and good, but does it really have anything to say to us today? We may believe that God has so constructed life that it functions best in certain logical ways. And if that is indeed the case, then it certainly makes sense to try hard to cooperate with those laws of operation God has implanted in life, for we do want to be happy, healthy, and whole. But really, in this complex world, how do we know what all those principles are?

In my book, *Roll Around Heaven All Day*, I tell the story of my bicycle ride across America. On that ride, I met a young man in Kansas who was on a similar cross-nation trek by bicycle. His name was David, and he was in his early twenties. Since we were following the same route for a while, we spent five days riding together. Although the outward characteristics of our rides were similar, the inward meaning of the experience was significantly different for each of us. For me, the journey was basically an adventure and a way to scratch my life-long itch to see new places. For David, however, the journey was a pilgrimage. He had graduated from high school with no sense of what he wanted to do next. After working for three years at dead-end jobs, he decided he needed to do something to try to find himself, and so he settled on riding his bicycle across America. To help with his inner exploration, he had decided to try to read the holy books of the world's major religions. In fact, when I met him, he had a copy of a Hindu text with him and was working his way through it. I talked to him some about Christianity as we rode, and he listened respectfully, but without being persuaded. I've stayed in touch with David since then, and it doesn't sound as if he has kept up his reading of other religions, or has found the wisdom he seeks.

Perhaps most of us can identify with David, at least at some point in our lives. There may have been a time, especially in your youthful years, when you thought that at some point you'd have life figured out, that the answers to the deepest meaning of existence would be yours. And if you have sincerely embraced the way of Christ, you no doubt found that that commitment did settle *some* things, especially in the areas of morality, values, and eternal destiny. But if you are like many Christians, you'll also recognize that even following Jesus does not provide all the answers to life. As you get older, the remaining questions may not bother you as much, but they don't all get resolved either. What we call common sense and experience may fill part of the gap, but what the Old Testament calls wisdom remains an elusive quality.

Does that mean that the Old Testament's emphasis on wisdom is no help to us? No. We can read almost any portion of the book of Proverbs and find great pearls of down-to-earth advice about how to get along well in life. But there's more than that. In this section where Wisdom speaks of being beside God while he created the world, there is a statement that gives us another perspective. Here how it reads in the NRSV:

> *... when he marked out the foundations of the earth,*
> *then I was beside him, like a master worker;*
> *and I was daily his delight,*
> *rejoicing before him always,*
> *rejoicing in his inhabited world*
> *and delighting in the human race.*
> — Proverbs 8:29b-31

There is, however, one of those intriguing language puzzles in this statement. As it stands, Wisdom, being beside God "like a master worker" makes it sound like Wisdom helped with the creating process. And I understand that "master worker" is an acceptable translation of the original Hebrew. However, many Bible scholars think that the intent of the Hebrew word, which is admittedly difficult to translate, may instead be more like "little child."[1] The Revised English Bible follows that possibility when it renders this section this way:

*... when he made earth's foundations firm.*
*Then I was at his side each day,*
*his darling and delight,*
*playing in his presence continually,*
*playing over his whole world,*
*while my delight was in [hu]mankind.*

In both translations it is clear that Wisdom took great joy in the creation of human beings, but the second version enables us to see Wisdom as a child squealing with great delight as her parent, God, does marvelous things before her eyes, marvelous things like creating humankind. The child has great joy because of what her Father has made, and she finds human beings to be wonderful.

In that scenario, Wisdom is saying, "I remember as a child what great joy it was to watch my Father make you as he intended you to be." And the corollary to that is that God's Wisdom wants any who have strayed from the goodness in which God created us to come back and be Wisdom's delight again. Or, to say it another way, perhaps the greatest benefit of the pursuit of the meaning of life is not the answers we find, but the Creator we meet when we really search for wisdom.

To understand this more, it is helpful to look at Colossians 1:15-20, for in fact, the wisdom tradition continues there. James is the only whole book in the New Testament that fits that tradition, but there are a number of sections of other books that echo the wisdom teaching of the Old Testament, and these verses from Colossians are among them. In these verses, the Apostle Paul identifies *Jesus* as the "firstborn of all creation" and the one who "is before all things," which would seem on the surface to be a contradiction of Proverbs 8. But when we recall that Wisdom was simply a personification of a characteristic of God, then identifying Jesus as coming from God and participating in the creating of the world is a way of saying that the wisdom that dwells in God also dwells in Christ.

The writers of Proverbs did not have the benefit of knowing Jesus, as they lived centuries earlier, but from their point of view as expressed in Proverbs, they found it perfectly acceptable to urge people to seek wisdom rather than always urging them to seek God directly, for the reality is, seekers cannot go far toward wisdom without finding God.

In one of his books, E. Stanley Jones tells of New York City psychologist, Dr. Henry Link, who, because of his study of psychology, gave up Christianity as outmoded superstition. As he began treating patients, however, trying to help them untangle their snarled-up lives, he realized that he had to give them something outside of themselves to love. That made sense and was a wise decision, but to what should he direct them? As he pondered this problem, he eventually realized that the only permanent thing he could direct them to was God. And after realizing that, he soon found that he had talked himself back into being a Christian.[2]

This section from Proverbs tells us that God intended us from the beginning to be Wisdom's delight — God's delight, really. And by planting within us the urge to understand life, he also gave a path that leads us back to him.

To sum up, go ahead and look diligently for the meaning of life and for the principles that make life work best. But be aware that they are not ends in themselves, for the further you go in pursuit of them, the closer you are likely to come to God himself.

---

1.  See *The Interpreter's Bible*, Vol. 4, pp. 832-833.

2.  E. Stanley Jones, *Abundant Living* (New York: Abingdon Press, 1935).

# Choosing To Believe

Perhaps you recall recently when a burial box from the first century A.D. had come to light, on which was inscribed the words "James, son of Joseph, brother of Jesus." This revelation caused quite a stir in the world of Christian scholarship because, if authentic, it would be the oldest tangible link to the historical Jesus — evidence of his actual existence. While even many non-Christians agree that Jesus was a real person, no physical evidence from the first century has ever been conclusively tied with his life. So, when several experts in antiquities judged this box — or "ossuary" as it was called — to be authentic, it was big news.

But alas, now comes the news that it is not authentic. The latest investigations of the box declare that it may be a true burial box from the time of Jesus, but that the inscription was added much later. In other words, it is a forgery.

Now I don't know if that has had any effect on your faith, but I would guess that it has not. Most of us who follow Jesus do so because of an inner commitment, and we made that decision completely independent of any physical "proof." Thus the ossuary, if it had been authentic, would have been a nice confirmation of something that we already believe, but the debunking of the claim really doesn't make any difference in the solidity of our faith.

I raise the matter of this burial box because I want to talk about the foundations of belief, and the yes-it-is/no-it's-not story of the ossuary is a case in point.

Our text is from the Old Testament, but before going there, I want to point out something from a New Testament passage, Jesus'

243

parable of the rich man and Lazarus (Luke 16:19-31). As the story goes, there was a certain rich man who lived very well in a fine house and dined on sumptuous meals. Although his name does not appear in the Bible, he is sometimes called "Dives," which comes from the Latin word for "rich." Outside his gate was a desperately poor, sick man named Lazarus, covered with sores. He was so hungry that he wished he could have even the crumbs that fell from Dives' table. But Dives ignored Lazarus, and eventually the poor man died and was carried by angels to be with Abraham in paradise.

Not long afterward, Dives also died, but he went to Hades, the final destination of the unrighteous. There he was in misery. He called to Abraham to send Lazarus to him with a drop of water for his tongue, but it was not to be. Abraham responded kindly but plainly to Dives. During your life, Abraham told Dives, you had a life of plenty and Lazarus had nothing. But now things have reversed and following death, said Abraham, there is an uncrossable chasm separating them.

Dives then asked Abraham to at least let Lazarus go to Dives' five living brothers and warn them to behave more compassionately in their lives than Dives had in his. Abraham responded, "They have Moses and the prophets [that is, the scriptures]; they should listen to them." Dives replied, "But if someone goes to them from the dead, they will listen." In other words, if they get real, tangible proof, they will be convinced. But Abraham came back with, "If they do not listen to the scriptures, they won't be convinced by someone rising from the dead."

Abraham, you see, was exactly right. So-called proof can always be explained away if you want it to be. Consider this story from Lee Strobel, who at the time of this incident was an award-winning journalist with the *Chicago Tribune*. And he was also, quite plainly, an unbeliever. In fact, when it came to matters of faith, he identified himself as an atheist. In one of his books, he tells of the time when his newborn daughter was rushed into intensive care because of a mysterious illness that threatened her life. The doctors weren't certain what was going on, but it was clearly serious.

Strobel says that even though he was an atheist, he was so desperate that he prayed anyway, imploring God — if God existed — to heal his daughter. A short time later, his daughter, to everyone's surprise, did recover, completely. The doctors were left scratching their heads.

Did that convince Strobel that God was real? It did not. He thought, "What a coincidence! She must have had some bacteria or virus that spontaneously disappeared." He remained in his atheism.[1]

You see, you can always take any seemingly miraculous thing and debunk it if you are so inclined. You can explain it as an elaborate hoax, a coincidence, the ravings of a confused person, superstition, group hysteria, a lie, a hallucination, or something else. And there are also those spectacular failures among Christians that you can point to and say, "See, Christianity must not be real." Some time ago, a Catholic bishop in Arizona was arrested for a hit-and-run accident. Certain television evangelists have been exposed as money-grabbing frauds. Some pastors have abused children. The list goes on. We can always find reasons not to believe if we want to.

So Abraham is exactly right when he tells Dives that sending someone to his brothers from the dead would be ineffective and non-persuasive. They'd explain it away.

Which, of course, is what happened with lots of people when God *did* send someone to them from the death — Jesus himself. To this day, you can hear the speculations of people about what "really" happened on that first Easter, how Jesus' disciples were fooled or how his body was moved, or some other theory.

The same thing proved true of the account we read from the Old Testament of Elijah challenging the prophets of Baal. Those prophets begged their god to bring fire to their altar, but nothing happened, but when Elijah made a similar request to the Lord God about his altar, God's fire consumed not only the sacrifice, but also the altar, and even the water in the trench. Seeing *that*, the crowd of eyewitnesses was convinced. According to the Bible story, "They fell on their faces and said, 'The Lord indeed is God.'"

However, the person who had brought the prophets of Baal into the land was the king's wife, Jezebel, and she was not persuaded.

Apparently, she was not present to see the event, but she heard about it from her husband, who, as far as we can tell, did believe it, though it did not cause him to become a better man. When Jezebel learned what had happened, the only effect on her was to cause her to swear by the gods she did believe in to avenge herself on Elijah. And it's clear from the subsequent history of Israel in the Old Testament that the miracle on Mount Carmel had only a temporary effect in any case, for it didn't take long before the people were worshiping other gods again.

No, when it comes right down to it, accepting Christianity is a matter of *choosing to believe.* There's plenty of evidence to support belief in Christ and to justify taking the step of committing yourself to him, but if you wish, you can explain all of it some other way, or even simply refuse to consider it.

Do you remember the old Sunday school chorus, "I Have Decided To Follow Jesus"? It means exactly what it says: Following Jesus is a decision.

But here's the thing: For those who make the decision to follow Jesus, there is a different kind of certainty available. Jesus referred to it one time when he was challenged by some of his countrymen about where his teaching came from. He responded, "My teaching is not mine but his who sent me. Anyone who resolves to do the will of God will know whether the teaching is from God or whether I am speaking on my own" (John 7:16-17). In other words, it is only by embracing faith in God and by doing what you perceive as his will that you can gain a sense of the reality of Christ.

Saint Augustine put it this way, "Believe that you may understand...." That is not what we usually mean when we use the word "certainty," but it is what we call "conviction," which means that we are *convinced* on a deep, inner level.

Let me go back to Lee Strobel for a moment, the man who decided that his daughter's miraculous recovery was a coincidence. Much later, after his wife started attending church, Strobel investigated Christianity and eventually became a believer, but it wasn't any kind of so-called proof that changed him. He actually used his skills as an investigative reporter to look at the evidence for faith in Christ, and he says that that cleared away some of his objections.

But what happened after that was a pure choice. He says, "[I had] to overcome my pride ... to drive a stake through the egoism and arrogance that threatened to hold me back. [I had] to conquer the self-interest and self-adulation that were keeping my heart shut tight from God."[2]

In my own experience, I can tell you about two different times when I responded to the call of Christ, each time on a different level. One was when I was thirteen and attending a church youth rally where an invitation to follow Christ was given. I felt compelled to go forward and it resulted there in a gush of emotions and tears. Afterward, I felt new and changed. Later when I was in my late teens, and I had learned more, including many of the arguments against Christian faith, the emotional experience of my early teens was no longer sufficient. I remember things coming to a moment where I thought, "I have a choice. I can believe in God and Christ or not. What do I choose to believe?" Well, I chose to believe that God exists and that Jesus is the one I should follow. There was very little emotion involved in that decision. It took place simply in the arena of my mind. Confirmations that I made the right choice have come in several ways and at different times since, but none of it is what I can hand you in the sense of scientific proof.

It comes down to this: Do you want to know God personally and follow Christ? If so, there is plenty of evidence to support that decision. If you don't want that, then there are ways to deny the testimony of the evidence.

Among that evidence is the Bible itself. When Dives asked that Lazarus be sent from the death to warn his brother, Abraham said to Dives, "They have the scriptures; they should listen to them." In other words, "It's all there in black and white. They should take seriously what's there. But, if they aren't convinced by scripture then they aren't going to be convinced by a mind-blowing resurrection."

When you decide you want to know God and follow Jesus, there is that inner witness that Jesus talked about — do the will of God and then you will know whether or not the teaching is from God. Or we might say this in shorthand as "believe first and then you will be convinced." We might like it to be the other way around — "Convince me and then I will believe." In the end, though, it comes down to what we want and what we choose. If we choose to believe, our faith is not going to be strengthened by a burial box from the first century or shaken when it proves to be false.

Choose to believe in God and to follow Christ. The reward of belief is the fire and the peace of God's presence — and the inner conviction that you are on the right path.

---

1. Lee Strobel, *The Case for Faith* (Grand Rapids: Zondervan, 2000), p. 254.

2. *Ibid.*, pp. 255-256.

# The Kindness Of Strangers

In 1994, a 37-year-old man by the name of Mike McIntyre decided to confront his fears and the shaky path his life was taking. Living in San Francisco at the time, he left his job, his girlfriend, his apartment — all the trappings of his life, and decided to hitchhike across America, heading for Cape Fear, North Carolina, a location he selected for its name, which symbolized his fear of many things in life. He put a few things in a backpack, but to help him with this confrontation with his fears, he left behind the one thing most of us would not leave home without — money.

He decided he wanted to find some kindness in the soul of America, so he took with him absolutely no cash, no credit cards, no traveler's checks — no purchasing power of any kind. Instead, he decided, he would rely on the kindness of strangers. Even from them, he vowed, he would take no money, but would accept food, shelter, rides, and friendship. As he worked his way across the country, he found it was possible to do exactly that. He made the entire journey without money. He didn't eat as regularly as he would have if he were carrying cash, yet he received enough food to get by and was sheltered in people's homes along the way.

He stayed one night with an older woman who was caring for her brain-damaged granddaughter, yet she welcomed him, too. On another occasion, he found a sense of family on a South Dakota ranch. Elsewhere, he was taken in by a low-income couple that gave him a tent to take with him, even though it was one of their most valuable possessions.

Not everyone he met along the way was kind and generous, but most were. In fact, when he finally arrived in Cape Fear, he decided that the location was misnamed. In his book about the journey, appropriately titled *The Kindness of Strangers*, he writes, "The name is as misplaced as my own fears. I see now that I have always been afraid of the wrong things. My great shame is not my fear of death, but my fear of life."[1]

Consider now the experiences of another penniless traveler, Elijah, the prophet of God. His story is set against the backdrop of the reign of Ahab as king of the northern Hebrew kingdom, Israel. Ahab sat on the throne from 874 to 853, B.C. The chronicler who wrote 1 Kings says of Ahab that he "did evil in the sight of the Lord more than all who were before him" (1 Kings 16:30). Comments of that sort about Israel's kings were not so much judgments on a monarch's governing and political policies as on his religious leadership of the nation. It was a way of saying the king was an idolater, one who worshiped false gods. That was true about Ahab, but in his case, there was an added dimension. He took as his queen not a woman from his own people, but the daughter of the king of Sidon, a woman named Jezebel. When Jezebel came to Israel, she brought with her not only her own practice of worshiping the Canaanite deity, Baal, but also a whole entourage of professional priests of Baal. Ahab not only encouraged her, but went so far as to build a temple to Baal in Israel's capital city, Samaria (1 Kings 16:32).

When an extended drought settled in on Israel and the surrounding region, causing the crops to dry up and die, the historian was pretty sure whose fault it was. In fact, God's prophet Elijah presented himself to Ahab and told him in advance that the drought was coming, and that it was because of Ahab's sin. Indeed, the drought that came lasted over three years (1 Kings 18:1; Luke 4:25; James 5:17).

That was not to be the end of Elijah's work for God by any means, so through the long months of the drought, God made special arrangements for Elijah. First, God provisioned the prophet, causing ravens to deliver food to him by a small stream, from which Elijah drank. After that dried up, God instructed him to go to a widow in Zarephath, a town in Sidon, the land of the Phoenicians. That God sent Elijah among the Phoenicians rather than to a safe house in Israel is significant. For one thing, because Jezebel was the daughter of Sidon's king, for God to place Elijah there for safekeeping showed, if nothing else, that God has a sense of humor. It also implied, however, that Israel's God was superior to Jezebel's idols.

And that brings us to today's reading. When Elijah gets to Zarephath, he finds the widow to which God has directed him, but it is clear from the text that this woman had no idea that she was about to have a houseguest. It may have been God's plan for her to shelter and feed Elijah, but no one had informed *her*. Upon arrival, Elijah asks the woman for water, which she is willing enough to give him, but as soon as he adds a request for bread, she protests, saying that she has almost nothing, just a little meal and a little oil, which she had been planning to use for a final meal for her son and herself. Elijah instructs her to cook it up for him anyway, telling her that the provisions will not run out. She does as Elijah asks, and, as a straightforward reading of the story tells us, no matter how much meal and oil she uses from the container over the remaining time of the drought, miraculously, it never runs out.

When we take that story at face value, it seems to be a tale about the providence of God, who not only takes care of faithful Elijah, but also blesses anyone who helps the prophet. And, of course, that is *a* point of this story.

But let's go back a moment and look at what happened in this encounter on the purely human level. Here is a woman who is widowed; which was especially bad news in that society where women had little financial opportunity on their own. There is a drought over the whole region, so times are hard, and she has not only herself to feed, but a son as well, whom, we gather from the story, must be too young to be a contributor to the household income himself. So whatever she has on hand must be used wisely and carefully.

And now, a stranger — and a foreigner at that — shows up on her doorstep, asking for food. If you were in her sandals, would you start by telling him how much food you *actually* have, especially while you are still trying to decide whether the man at the door is an honest man down on his luck or a scoundrel with evil plans on his mind? Might you not say something like, "Well, I only have enough for a final meal for myself and my child"? Might you not, to protect your family, prevaricate just a little about the extent of what is in your pantry?

You see, whatever the truth about the amount of food she had on hand, the real miracle in this story is that, in the end, she is moved to open her home to this stranger in need. The Bible story makes the point that no matter how much flour and oil the woman used while she hosted Elijah, neither container emptied. Whether that was because God kept refilling them or because the woman actually had a few more resources than she at first admitted is beside the point. While the providence of God is one theme in this account, another theme is the hospitality of the woman.

Only the most senior among us today are old enough to remember the Great Depression, but that period would be something like the time of Elijah and this widow in ancient Israel. Several people I've talked to who lived through the Great Depression have told me of memories of their mother making a sandwich for a unemployed man who came to their door requesting help. More than one farmer in those days allowed men who were on the road or riding the rails in search of work to sleep in their barns. In hard times, especially, hospitality becomes one of the most valuable gifts that can be given.

Perhaps that is why in the New Testament, there are several references that commend hospitality as something appropriate for Christians to extend. Read, for example, Romans 12, where Paul instructed, "Contribute to the needs of the saints; extend hospitality to strangers" (Romans 12:13). The writer of Hebrews said, "Do not neglect to show hospitality to strangers, for by doing that some have entertained angels without knowing it" (Hebrews 13:2). In the book of Titus, where Paul is enumerating the qualities church bishops (spiritual leaders of the local congregations in those days) should have, he says, "For a bishop, as God's steward, must be blameless; he must not be arrogant or quick-tempered or addicted to wine or violent or greedy for gain; but he must be hospitable ..." (Titus 1:7-8). And in Luke, Jesus himself says, "But when you give a banquet, invite the poor, the crippled, the lame, and the blind. And you will be blessed, because they cannot repay you, for you will be repaid at the resurrection of the righteous" (Luke 14:13-14).

Note that God did not send Elijah to the home of some wealthy citizen of Sidon, someone who could really afford to take care of the prophet. That should come as a reminder to us that the call to be hospitable is not something that goes only to those in the higher income brackets. During Mike McIntyre's journey across America, most of the assistance he received came from people who were not especially well off. Some were not far from being penniless themselves.

Well, how, in this day of great risk from strangers, when there is no shortage of scam artists, sex offenders, and outright thieves on the street, do we Christians live out the biblical admonition to be hospitable? Very cautiously, it would seem. But then, hospitality doesn't always mean opening our guestroom to strangers. In fact, it's not that often that such opportunity or requests even come along today, although there are notable exceptions. On 9/11, after the planes were flown into the World Trade Center and the Pentagon, the United States closed its airspace. A number of planes had to be diverted elsewhere, and several landed in Newfoundland, where the local citizenry quickly organized to house and feed the passengers. Some passengers, especially the elderly and in at least one case, a pregnant woman, were taken into people's homes.[2]

That, of course, was an exceptional day, but occasions when kindness can be offered to a stranger do come along. And when they do, we will have to use our best judgment, guided by two biblical admonitions: One is Jesus' call to love our neighbor as ourselves and the other is his instruction to his disciples when he sent them out to spread the gospel — "See, I am sending you out like sheep into the midst of wolves; so be wise as serpents and innocent as doves" (Matthew 10:16).

Let me suggest four other ways the spirit of hospitality can and should express itself in the lives of Christians today.

First, we should be friends to our friends. That may sound odd, especially since hospitality often has to do with how we treat strangers, but consider how often in our busy lives we treat friends as strangers. Our lives are full of many activities, and when we are at home, we have got chores to catch up on and the television to fill any other moments. Friends are fine, but do we ever think, "Don't call too often, and don't lay your problems on me. I've got enough of my own"? Doesn't friendship mean at least that we are hospitable to one another? Doesn't friendship mean that the other person is important enough to that he or she is worth letting our chores wait and shutting off the television?

A second thing hospitality can mean today is that we accept that interruptions can be important parts of life. Sure, there are planned hospitality events, such as when we hold a dinner party or invite people over for an open house. In these cases, we intend to be in the role of host or hostess. But where hospitality really shines is when we practice it in moments when we weren't expecting to, when an Elijah of some kind suddenly shows up and interrupts our plans. (In terms of the widow who took Elijah in, we should notice that initially, she had no idea he was anything more than a hungry man with no money. It is not until days later, after her child dies and Elijah restores him to life, that she realizes that there is something special about him. At that point she says, "*Now* I know that you are a man of God" [1 Kings 17:24, italics added].)

Sara and Paul Fried operate a house of hospitality in Winona, Minnesota, a place that welcomes strangers every day. The Frieds, while acknowledging that there can occasionally be danger from a stranger, have found that more often, strangers can be teachers, friends, and maybe even Jesus Christ in disguise.

Sara Fried says that sometimes the first contact with a stranger comes as a phone call to their hospitality center, a call that is an interruption to their schedule or plans. But she says, "We've found in those interruptions ... beautiful examples of God."[3]

A third form hospitality can take today is providing a safe ground for people to talk freely. This is a recognition that in the critical matters of life, people do not always agree. Yet often, the best learning comes from listening to one another's viewpoints. Whether you are hosting people in your home, leading a small-group discussion at church, chairing a committee for the school, teaching a class, or anything similar, it is possible to conduct those

254

endeavors in a spirit of hospitality, where you serve as a kind of referee, allowing people to express their views even when you do not agree with them, so that growth and learning can take place in an environment where people feel comfortable and safe saying what they really believe.

And fourth, hospitality can be a way to bless someone. I found this out in a very direct way in my first church appointment. We had a youth choir in that church, and they were pretty good. So good, in fact, that my father's congregation invited us to bring our choir to their church to perform in a weekend of special services. Bring the kids, my mother said, and she would arrange for them to be housed with church members. Our youth were quite excited about this invitation, and they all planned to go. Then, a couple of days before we were to make the trip, our choir leader called me, upset. She had just learned that Althea, our best soprano, was not going to be allowed to go. Althea wanted to go, but her mother had said, "No." I agreed to talk to Althea's mom — Mrs. Smith — to see if she might reconsider.

I drove over to Althea's house, where Mrs. Smith welcomed me graciously. I told her the whole story of the invitation and the housing plans. Thinking that she might be worried about the chaperoning arrangements, I named the responsible adults who were going along. Mrs. Smith listened politely to all I had to say, but then said quietly, "You know, Althea is a *black* girl." And at once, it dawned on me what her concern was. We were a predominately white congregation. Mrs. Smith's family was one of only two black families on our membership roles, but they were so well integrated into our congregation that it never crossed my mind that race issues would be a concern when taking the kids elsewhere.

Mrs. Smith, however, knew what it was like to grow up black in a hostile environment. She herself had come from a community where racial prejudice was the norm and nasty expressions of it were common, and she didn't want to take a chance of her daughter being exposed to the same thing.

In the end, the matter was resolved well. I got Mrs. Smith's permission to investigate the housing arrangements with her concern in mind. I phoned my mother, who spoke with the family who would be housing some of the girls. The mother in that family then called Mrs. Smith, and told her that she'd love to have Althea as a houseguest, and Mrs. Smith allowed Althea to go. The weekend was a great success, and Althea came home telling her mother what a good time she had, including staying with the host family. Hospitality, you see, is a way of blessing someone.

There are certainly other ways hospitality can be practiced today as well, but in summary, it is important to recognize that the people of the Bible understood hospitality as a virtue. The early Christians thought so much of it that they *required* it of their leaders and urged all believers to practice it. In our day and age, it may not always be practiced in exactly the same ways, but hospitality is still an important way we put our Christian faith into practice.

---

1. Mike McIntyre, *The Kindness of Strangers: Penniless Across America* (New York: Berkley Publishing Group; Berkley trade paperback edition, 1996), pp. 245-246.

2. There are several accounts of the hospitality on that day. One is from Clare Ansberry, "Diverted on Sept. 11, Stranded Fliers Make Enduring Connections," *The Wall Street Journal*, November 7, 2001. An earlier report, titled "Delta Flight 15," apparently written by one of the passengers, circulated by email in October 2001.

3. Darrell Ehrlick, "Catholic volunteers find spiritual strength in strangers' messages," *The Winona Daily News*, August 1, 2004, www.winonadailynews.com/articles/2004/08/01/news/3strangers_01.txt.

# When Desire Goes Bad

Nathan, a boy I read about recently, is seven years old. His second grade teacher gave his class an assignment. They were to draw a picture and write an essay about what they would need to have a perfect life. Nathan drew a house and wrote beneath it, "My Home." Also, he drew himself and his dog. Next he drew a checkerboard with faces inside each square and wrote "My Friends" beside that. His essay was titled, "The Perfect Life for Me," and here's what it said:

> *A perfect life for me is the life that I'm in right now.*
> *Because I have a lot of friends and have a big family,*
> *too. I do not need a perfect life.*[1]

We might hope that young Nathan, who sounds wise beyond his years, will continue to be that content all his life, but if he is like most of us, he probably won't; the yearning for more than what we have at the moment is very common. And the affluence and advertising of our age encourages it.

Of course, wanting is a very necessary part of being human. It is a form of energy and motivation that drives invention, discovery, mastery, improvement, and accomplishment. The fruit of healthy desire is achievement and satisfaction.

But like any appetite, it needs to function with some restraint, because when it goes too far, when it becomes our *primary* motivation, it becomes destructive, both to us and to others. The Bible's

257

word for desire gone bad is "covetousness," and the fruit of covetousness is injury and discontent.

We encounter the word "covet" in the tenth commandment. The other nine commandments stake out the boundaries of the outer limits of decent conduct. Obviously, that few number of commandments can't address every specific behavior. So the final one, "You shall not covet," comes to us addressing this root motivation — desire — that drives so much of our action. Basically, it warns us about letting desire run rampant.

To covet is to desire something inordinately, *without due regard for the rights of others.* If I desire something you have to the point that I reach out and steal it, I am breaking not only the eighth commandment, about stealing, but also the tenth one, about coveting. In short, covetousness is *predatory* thinking. We could paraphrase this commandment as "You shall not harbor thoughts that can lead to breaking any of the aforementioned commandments."

This prohibition is different than the commandments against stealing, bearing false witness, murdering, or committing adultery, for those address specific behaviors that are to be avoided. The tenth commandment, on the other hand, begins with what is in our minds, where the sequence of feelings, thoughts, and scheming that leads to the breaking of the other commandments begins.

One of the most flagrant examples of covetousness in action is found in our scripture reading for today.

A man in Israel named Naboth had a vineyard next door to the palace of King Ahab. Ahab wanted the vineyard for a vegetable garden, and offered to buy it. But, because it was Naboth's ancestral inheritance, Naboth didn't want to sell. Ahab went home resentful and sullen, and sulked around the palace, too depressed even to eat. Finally, his wife, Jezebel, reminded him of the power he held as king, and in his name, she ordered trumped up charges brought against Naboth so that he was stoned to death. Once Naboth was dead, Ahab seized possession of Naboth's vineyard.

A more recent story of flagrant covetousness comes from the early 1990s. A Texas mom named Wanda Holloway tried to hire a hitman to kill a cheerleader and her mother. Her intention was that with the intended victims out of the way, Wanda's daughter would get the chance to become a cheerleader. Holloway plotted to have Verna Heath murdered by the hit man, hoping the death would upset Heath's daughter, Amber, so much that the girl wouldn't make the cheerleading team. That would improve Holloway's daughter's chances of making the squad. Both girls were thirteen at the time. Mrs. Holloway, who offered her diamond earrings and cash in this murder-for-hire plot, ended up sentenced to ten years in prison. Following the sentencing, Verna Heath, the intended victim, said, "I've always wanted to see Wanda Holloway show some remorse. I think her only regret is getting caught."[2]

Clearly, the tenth commandment prohibits that kind of predatory thinking. But the problem for us with reading either King Ahab's story or Wanda Holloway's is that most of us who are Christians don't connect with them. We may want more than what we have, but we don't want it at somebody else's expense. If we were in Ahab's sandals, and Naboth refused to sell us the vineyard, we'd simply shop elsewhere. And if our daughter faced tough competition to make the cheerleading squad, we'd try to help and encourage her. We wouldn't set out to ruin or kill the competing cheerleader or her mother. We figure there's plenty to go around, so we just want to be included in the bounty.

Where we do connect with covetousness is when we feel shortchanged. Do you envy someone else their good looks, or their good grades, or their good income, or their good fortune? Those feelings are quite normal and certainly not wrong, but they can make us miserable. What this commandment asks us to see is that honoring God and treating our neighbor right, has its root not in how we act, but in what we let our minds dwell upon. Proverbs puts it succinctly when it says, "For as [a person] thinketh in his heart, so is he" (Proverbs 23:7 KJV).

So this commandment warns us to examine that which we hunger after. Greed, envy, jealousy, and lust and similar ugly thoughts are the sources from which bad deeds spring. This commandment calls us to put our minds on better things.

Well, just exactly how do we do that? We may be able to control our actions, but how do we control our thoughts and feelings?

For one thing, we can replace them by providing good experiences that lead to better thoughts. For example, instead of resenting someone because they have more than we do, we can instead do something helpful for someone who has less. Or, instead of begrudging someone a promotion, we throw a congratulatory party for them. We do something the opposite of what the envy would lead you to do. Often, better thinking and feelings follow our actions.

For another thing, we can remember that life is more than arriving at goals. Life is what we do as we head toward our goals. Life itself, not acquisition, is the main event.

For a third thing, we can focus on the example of Jesus. Ask church youth today what WWJD means, and most can tell you. "What would Jesus do?" has become a standard by which many church kids trying to do the right thing have learned to measure themselves. And we can do the same. I may resent that I am feeling left out or shortchanged by something, but what would Jesus do in my situation? And then do it.

WWJD is not just a cautionary statement — it's not just a reminder against taking wrong action. Jesus offers us a life filled with discipleship joy. Instead of tying us to an ever-spiraling clamber up the world's ladder of "success," Jesus offers us purpose. Jesus offers us service. Jesus offers us God's pleasure. Jesus offers us God's peace. Jesus offers us redemption.

There's an old rabbinic teaching: "Who is wealthy? The one who is content with his life."[3] Young Nathan had it right. We don't need a perfect life. We need a contented one, one that is rich in generosity and acts of kindness, and is faithful to the example of Jesus.

---

1. Laura Schlessinger and Stewart Vogel, *The Ten Commandments* (New York: HarperCollins Publishers, Inc., 1999), pp. 297-298.

2. Terri Langford, *The Detroit News*, September 10, 1996.

3. Schlessinger, *op. cit.*, 307.

# As Seen From
# The Solitary Broom Tree

I'm not sure when the term "burn out" ceased being only a description of what happened to a campfire when you ran out of firewood to a term describing the experience of long-term exhaustion and diminished interest, usually coming immediately after an extended period of overwork, but the expression seems to fit that later situation, doesn't it? Exhaustion, deep weariness, all used up, nothing more to give, wiped out, burned out — call it what we will, its symptoms are all too familiar to many of us. A study back in 1993[1] showed that people who work in the care industries, such as nurses and social workers and others who have frequent intense or emotionally charged interactions with others are especially susceptible to burnout. But burnout can affect workers in any field.

Take prophets, for example. Since many prophets were commissioned with the idea that most of those to whom they prophesied were going to reject their message, burnout was practically part of the job description for being a prophet.

Ironically, burnout does not always come on the heels of failure or projects that do not produce. Sometimes it even appears to be brought on by success. A while back I read a biography of Leslie Weatherhead, a British clergyman who was quite well known in the mid-twentieth century, both for his hugely successful ministry and through the several books he wrote. The biography was written by someone in a position to know Reverend Weatherhead well, his son, Kingsley. Here's something the author said happened to his father during a time when things were going especially well:

*He was himself, I suppose, at 62, intellectually and spiritually at the height of his powers; if religious matters can be measured in words of the world, he was a success. Through huge congregations and through broadcast services which were relayed to all parts of the globe, his voice was reaching more people than ever before.*

The author went onto tell of the many who wrote to say how Reverend Weatherhead's preaching had helped them, and how well things were going at the church and at the accompanying mental-health clinic Weatherhead had established. But then the author added:

*For himself though, he increasingly felt that ... he had crossed a watershed ... He found that he wasn't much interested anymore in new proposals in the church; they didn't come to him as a welcome challenge, but as merely another item on a committee agenda ... His letters register ... his sense of the dullness of his days.*[2]

If we can understand how that can happen then we can understand what was going on with Elijah the prophet in our reading for today. He had just had a major success. In a confrontation with some 450 prophets of the god Baal and 400 prophets of the goddess Asherah, Elijah, alone representing Yahweh, proved that his God was the only one with power. You can read the details of that encounter in 1 Kings 18. But here in chapter 19, Elijah is anything but pumped up from his resounding triumph in the name of God. In fact, hearing that Israel's queen, Jezebel, is after him because he trumped her prophets, Elijah hightails it out of the area. Then, when he is safely away, all his energy leaves him, and he begins to feel sorry for himself. He has had it with being a prophet and he wants to resign his commission. He is burned out.

Now in saying that, we are not merely *guessing* at Elijah's state of mind. This is one case where the biblical author tells us what's up with the prophet using both metaphor and by quoting Elijah's own words. The metaphor is in the detail that Elijah, alone in the wilderness, "sat down under a solitary broom tree." That is a poetic way of conveying how Elijah felt — all alone like that single tree. Then Elijah's words let us look into his mood: "It is enough; now, O Lord, take away my life, for I am no better than my ancestors." What happens next, however, tells us that God is not about to let Elijah give up. The prophet goes to sleep, but God twice sends an angel to wake Elijah and give him food — nourishment for what is to come. God then directs Elijah to make a forced march to Mount Horeb, where instead of looking for a fresh vision or renewal, the prophet promptly takes refuge in a cave. That apparently was not what God had in mind, for God comes to Elijah in the cave and says, "What are you doing here, Elijah?"

The prophet's response is whiney and shows again how burned out he feels. "I have been very zealous for the Lord, the God of hosts; for the Israelites have forsaken your covenant, thrown down your altars, and killed your prophets with the sword. I alone am left, and they are seeking my life, to take it away." (Actually, that was quite an exaggeration. There were thousands in Israel who remained faithful to God, but when we are exhausted, we often fail to see the hopeful reality of a situation.)

God tells Elijah to go outside the cave and witness what God is about to show him, but Elijah won't go. So God sends first a great wind, and then an earthquake, and then fire, but none of these things cause Elijah to budge from his hidey-hole. Then, however, after all the pyrotechnics of nature are over, there is nothing but the "sound of sheer silence," and it is that which finally lures Elijah to move to the mouth of the cave. At that point, God again asks the weary prophet, "What are you doing here, Elijah?" Yet all the demonstrations of nature and all the enticements of God haven't brought Elijah out of his burnout, for he answers with the exact same lament as previously: "I have been very zealous for the Lord, the God of hosts; for the Israelites have forsaken your covenant, thrown down your altars, and killed your prophets with the sword. I alone am left, and they are seeking my life, to take it away."

This time, however, God gives Elijah more work to do: "Go, return on your way to the wilderness of Damascus...." When he gets there, he is to anoint new kings for Aram and Israel, as well as

263

begin schooling a new prophet who will eventually be Elijah's successor.

God doesn't end up being very sympathetic, does he? Here is poor Elijah, physically, mentally, emotionally, and spiritually exhausted from his work as God's prophet, with people out to kill him, and God won't even let him rest — won't even let him hunker down in this cave in peace. God calls out the forces of nature and then the voice of silence itself to get Elijah back on his feet. And when the weary prophet finally does stagger out of the cave, God adds new work to Elijah's to-do list!

But here's the real surprise: That is what works. God tells Elijah to get back to work, and Elijah does it. He goes on to again work successfully for God right up through his final hours on earth.

Well, what about you and me? We have lots to do, also, and some of us know what it's like to be overloaded and feel unable to cope any longer. There is today no shortage of advice available to tell us how to deal with burnout, or to prevent it in the first place. Here, for example, is a list of suggestions from the website of the Massachusetts Institute of Technology, MIT, given with some tongue-in-cheek counterstatements they call the "MIT View":

1. **Stop Denying.** Listen to the wisdom of your body. Begin to freely admit the stresses and pressures, which have manifested physically, mentally, or emotionally.
   - **MIT View:** Work until the physical pain forces you into unconsciousness.

2. **Avoid Isolation.** Don't do everything alone! Develop or renew intimacies with friends and loved ones. Closeness not only brings new insights, but also is anathema to agitation and depression.
   - **MIT View:** Shut your office door and lock it from the inside so no one will distract you. They're just trying to hurt your productivity.

3. **Change Your Circumstances.** If your job, your relationship, a situation, or a person is dragging you under, try to alter your circumstance, or if necessary, leave.
   - **MIT View:** If you feel something is dragging you down, suppress these thoughts. This is a weakness. Drink more coffee.

264

4. **Diminish Intensity In Your Life.** Pinpoint those areas or aspects that summon up the most concentrated intensity and work toward alleviating that pressure.
   - **MIT View:** Increase intensity. Maximum intensity = maximum productivity. If you find yourself relaxed with your mind wandering, you are probably having a detrimental effect on the recovery rate.
5. **Stop Overnurturing.** If you routinely take on other people's problems and responsibilities, learn to gracefully disengage. Try to get some nurturing for yourself.
   - **MIT View:** Always attempt to do everything. You *are* responsible for it all. Perhaps you haven't thoroughly read your job description.
6. **Learn To Say, "No."** You'll help diminish intensity by speaking up for yourself. This means refusing additional requests or demands on your time or emotions.
   - **MIT View:** Never say no to anything. It shows weakness, and lowers the research volume. Never put off until tomorrow what you can do at midnight.
7. **Begin To Back Off And Detach.** Learn to delegate, not only at work, but also at home and with friends. In this case, detachment means rescuing yourself for yourself.
   - **MIT View:** Delegating is a sign of weakness. If you want it done right, do it yourself (see #5).
8. **Reassess Your Values.** Try to sort out the meaningful values from the temporary and fleeting, the essential from the nonessential. You'll conserve energy and time, and begin to feel more centered.
   - **MIT View:** Stop thinking about your own problems. This is selfish. If your values change, we will make an announcement at the corporation meeting. Until then, if someone calls you and questions your priorities, tell them that you are unable to comment on this and give them the number for community and government relations. It will be taken care of.
9. **Learn To Pace Yourself.** Try to take life in moderation. You only have so much energy available. Ascertain what is wanted and needed in your life, then begin to balance work with love, pleasure, and relaxation.

- **MIT View:** A balanced life is a myth perpetuated by liberal arts schools. Don't be a fool: the only thing that matters is work and productivity.
10. **Take Care Of Your Body.** Don't skip meals, abuse yourself with rigid diets, disregard your need for sleep, or break the doctor appointments. Take care of yourself nutritionally.
    - **MIT View:** Your body serves your mind, your mind serves the Institute. Push the mind and the body will follow. Drink Mountain Dew.
11. **Diminish Worry And Anxiety.** Try to keep superstitious worrying to a minimum — it changes nothing. You'll have a better grip on your situation if you spend less time worrying and more time taking care of your real needs.
    - **MIT View:** If you're not worrying about work, you must not be very committed to it. We'll find someone who is.
12. **Keep Your Sense Of Humor.** Begin to bring job and happy moments into your life. Very few people suffer burnout when they're having fun.
    - **MIT View:** So, you think your work is funny? We'll discuss this with your director on Friday, at 7 p.m.![3]

Those suggestions and others like them probably would help if they were undertaken before burnout sets in, but when we have lost our zest for life, when we are truly wiped out, we seldom have the energy to take remedial actions. In the case of Elijah, God seems to know that. God never tries try to talk Elijah out of his depression and gloom. God does not argue with the prophet's ridiculous notion that he is the only one left that is faithful to God. Instead, God provides Elijah with the one thing that sometimes does help when we have lost our way, and that is a new purpose. By giving Elijah a new assignment, one that will affect the course of history, Elijah has a reason to go on, to take the focus off of his own woes and to starting looking out for others.

In the end, that may be the best thing that we learn from this biblical story — that when we feel all used up, then it is time to take the focus off of ourselves. Or as I once heard it worded, "When you dig another out of his troubles, you find a place to bury your own."

I've got a file full of examples of that, but here's one I heard about recently: During the recent presidential election, we learned a little about Elizabeth Edwards, the wife of the Democratic vice-presidential candidate, John Edwards. One of the things we heard was that the Edwardses had a lost their son, Wade. At sixteen years of age, this promising young man was killed in an auto accident when a freak wind blew his vehicle off the road. Frankly, there is nothing like the death of child to knock the stuffing out of a parent. But not long after her son's death, Mrs. Edwards quit her job as a bankruptcy lawyer and threw herself into creating a computer lab for underprivileged high school students. She set it up right across the street from the high school Wade had attended. She did it because she recalled that Wade had once gotten extra credit for writing a term paper on a computer, and it struck Mrs. Edwards that that was an unfair advantage over less fortunate kids who attended the same school.

The lab opened in 1996, funded by donations. For the first several months, it was staffed mainly by Mrs. Edwards and her husband, both of whom worked directly with the students. She continues to be involved there today.[4]

There are all sorts of reasons we can find ourselves feeling like Elijah did, depressed, alone, grieving, burned out, and feeling that there is nothing left for us to live for. That is life as seen from the solitary broom tree. But let us learn the lesson Elijah learned — that God calls us to serve, and that in serving, especially in God's name, we find meaning and purpose, and even the strength we need for whatever comes next.

---

1. By D. W. Cordes and N. J. Doherty.

2. A. Kingsley Weatherhead, *Leslie Weatherhead: A Personal Portrait* (Nashville: Abingdon, 1975), pp. 244-245.

3. "Burnout Prevention and Recovery," http://web.mit.edu/wchuang/www/humor/college/MIT-views.html.

4. Shailagh Murray, "Accomplishment, Grief Mix for Mrs. Edwards," *The Wall Street Journal*, July 7, 2004, A4.

# The Smell Of Bread

One of the most popular television shows ever was *M\*A\*S\*H*, which ran for eleven seasons, from 1972-1983. If you didn't see it when it was originally on network television, you've probably seen it in reruns on cable stations. The show was about life in a mobile Army surgical hospital during the Korean War, and the reoccurring characters included the surgeons. One of those surgeons, named Charles Emerson Winchester III, was a pompous, upper-class doctor from Boston who had been drafted into the medical corps. He felt that his fellow doctors were beneath him in breeding and sophistication, and he didn't hesitate to let them know that. Nonetheless, he did his job and in fact was an excellent surgeon.

Of course, being near the front lines, that medical unit saw a lot of people die, and in one episode, Charles began wondering what happens when someone passes away — what is on the other side of that dark barrier? To try to find out, Charles decided to question a dying soldier as he was slipping into eternity. Going to the dying man, Charles shouted, "What is happening to you? What do you see?"

The man replied, "I smell bread." And then he died.[1]

Theology has a way of showing up when we least expect it, doesn't it? With that simple, three-word response, the writers of that show affirmed for viewers something about the life to come that jibes with what little the scriptures tell us about the dying process. For many people, particularly those generations that would have grown up in the days before the Korean War and the ready availability of store-bought loaves, the aroma of freshly baked bread was a scent they associated with their homes. Many would have recalled coming home from school to find that their mothers had just baked some bread. They'd have dropped their books, taken a seat at the kitchen table, received a glass of milk and chunk of that soft, aromatic bread spread with butter, and been nourished. As children, few realized what a great experience that was, but the day would come, when far from home, the smell of freshly baked bread emanating from some bakery or somebody else's kitchen would trigger glad memories.

So if bread is the smell of home, then the writers of that *M\*A\*S\*H* episode were preaching some pretty good theology when they had the dying man say what he said, weren't they?

That, in essence, is the gist of my sermon today, and I haven't even talked about the text yet. But of course, that deserves attention as well.

The reading from 2 Kings 2 is the story of the prophet Elijah's last day on earth. The account begins with Elijah, with his disciple Elisha in tow, making a journey from Gilgal to Bethel to Jericho to the Jordan River. At each of the destinations, Elijah tries to leave Elisha behind, telling him to remain there because the Lord was telling Elijah to move on. But each time, Elisha refuses and sticks like glue to Elijah. Also, at each destination, bands of prophets (sort of the divinity students of that day) come to Elisha and tell him that the Lord will take Elijah from him that day. To each group, Elisha says that he knows all that, but will not let them say more. Finally, after Elijah miraculously parts the waters of the Jordan so that he and Elisha can cross, the pair reaches the other side. All at once, a chariot of fire and horses of fire appears between them, separating the two, and then a whirlwind comes and carries Elijah into heaven. Elisha, witnessing all of this, cries out "Father, father! The chariots of Israel and its horsemen!"

Now, this is a story with some peculiar elements. First, the journey from one place to another seems pointless. Elijah performs no ministry at any of those locations and even the order in which he visits them is roundabout and odd. Gilgal, where they start, is near the Jordan, where they end up. Bethel is a little distance off, but then they go to Jericho, which is back near Gilgal. The only point of this journey, if there is one, is that at each place, Elijah tries to leave Elisha behind, as if to say, "Where I am going you cannot come."

And then this business with chariot and whirlwind. Centuries of Bible readers have looked at this story and concluded that Elijah did not get to heaven by the route the rest of us do — by way of death — but rather that he was taken there directly without first dying. That's pretty strange.

Be those things as they may, however, in some respects, this story has parallels to the last hours of other people as they approach death. For one thing, there is the matter of Elijah trying to leave Elisha behind. I have seen people who had a terminal illness who for some time tried to stay upbeat and positive for the sake of their loved ones. I have also seen some of those folks come to a point where they can no longer carry the load of tending those who have gathered around them. Perhaps there is a point in the dying process where that kind of energy is gone, and the person seems to withdraw from the gathered family and friends, perhaps beginning the transition to the realm where the others cannot go. They come to a point where they leave others behind and begin to slip away alone. Like Elisha, those of us around them don't leave — won't leave, shouldn't leave — but the dying person has begun to sever the ties to those who remain behind. That may have been what was going on with Elijah on that journey.

The vision of chariot and horses parallels the experience of some as well, both dying and those who gather to be with them. Elisha's cry about seeing the chariots and horsemen of Israel — God's people — was an utterance of praise at the power and glory of God. He sees the glory of the God who is stronger than death — so much stronger that in this case, Elijah is taken up without even going through death. And sometimes, at the dying of a loved one, some of us sense the power and glory of God as well.

What's more, this story comes to us with the assurance that death is not the end; that God's power does indeed transcend the grave. It tells us that when our loved ones die, they pass into the hands of God who never lets them go.

271

There is no mention of bread in this story but there is the clear sense that whatever happens during the transfer of this righteous person to the heavenly kingdom is not a fearful thing.

Knowing that death awaits all of us someday, we might wish that we knew more about it. Doctors, of course, can tell us about the physical aspects of dying, and researchers like Elisabeth Kübler-Ross have helped us understand what happens to us emotionally as we near death, at least when we know it is coming soon, but what is the transfer to heaven like?

Some of the old Negro spirituals, such as "Deep River" and some of our hymns, such as "On Jordan's Stormy Banks I Stand" and "Shall We Gather At The River" portray dying as the process of crossing a river, with a better land on the other side, but we might wish that the Bible gave us more information about it.

Yet, what the Bible does give, at least about the death of those who serve the Lord, is good to hear. In the Old Testament, death is sometimes described as "going to one's ancestors" or "being gathered to one's people." (see, for example, Genesis 15:15 and 49:33) That's a comforting thought — going to be with relatives and friends who have gone before. And in the New Testament, death is often described simply as falling asleep. (see, for example, 1 Thessalonians 4:14-15)

There are also a few Bible verses we should hear on this subject. One is from the book of Revelation, where John of Patmos hears a voice from heaven that says, "Write this: Blessed are the dead who from now on die in the Lord" (Revelation 14:13). To die "in the Lord," whatever that may mean in terms of physical experience, means only good things in terms of the spiritual realm.

Another verse is from 2 Peter, where that apostle tells his readers, "... entry into the eternal kingdom of our Lord and Savior Jesus Christ will be richly provided for you" (2 Peter 1:11). That adjective "richly" means a lot, doesn't it?

Still, another does not address dying *per se*, but it clearly applies nonetheless. To the Romans, Paul wrote, "For I am convinced that neither death, nor life, nor angels, nor rulers, nor things present, nor things to come, nor powers, nor height, nor depth, nor anything else in all creation, will be able to separate us from the love

272

of God in Christ Jesus our Lord" (Romans 8:38-39). Well, if neither life nor death can separate us from the love of God in Christ, then it is not likely that the transition stage between the two can separate us from God's love, either.

As yet one more biblical testimony, hear Jesus' own words on the subject: "Do not let your hearts be troubled. Believe in God, believe also in me. In my Father's house there are many dwelling places. If it were not so, would I have told you that I go to prepare a place for you? And if I go and prepare a place for you, I will come again and will take you to myself, so that where I am, there you may be also" (John 14:2-3).

"In my Father's house there are many dwelling places." Well, what are the dwelling places in a house but the rooms? And one way to understand those words from Jesus is that this realm we call life is one room in our Heavenly Father's house, and the realm we call eternal life is another room in the same house. In one of his books, the late Peter Marshall tells of a home he knew of where a little boy was ill with a terminal disease. His parents had not told him he was going to die, but they were burdened with that knowledge. As time went along and the boy did not improve, he figured out for himself that death was coming. One evening, after his mother had read to him the story of King Arthur and how so many knights had died in battle, this boy asked his mother, "What is it like to die? Does it hurt?"

The mother had not been expecting that, and made an excuse to leave the room for a moment. When she was alone, she prayed for guidance and strength, and suddenly both were given to her. She returned to her son and said, "Do you remember how when you were younger and you played hard, that sometimes you got so tired you fell asleep wherever you were, with your clothes still on? Yet you always awoke the next morning in your own bed with your pajamas on. Do you know how you got there? Daddy carried you there and put you in your pajamas. Dying is like that. You just wake up in another room, carried there by a loving Father."

That answer seemed to satisfy the boy, for she noticed her son visibly relax.

But return to Jesus' words in John for a moment. I've taken a look at the Greek words that underlie these verses, especially at the word that's translated "prepare." That word is *hetoimazo*, and one of its meanings is "provide," which is related to word "provisions," which is another name for food.

So I think there is some justification for reading Jesus' words this way: "In my Father's house there are many dwelling places ... And if I go and bake bread for you, I will come again and will take you to myself, so that where I am, we can enjoy bread together."

---

1. Thanks to Elizabeth Achtemeier for connecting this illustration with 2 Kings 2, in her book, *Preaching and Reading the Old Testament Lessons With an Eye to the New, Cycle B* (Lima, Ohio: CSS Publishing Co., 2001), p. 79.

# Washing In Old Jordan

I know a man who has a severe back injury and lives with constant pain. He has seen the best doctors he can find. He has gone to a major medical center. He has taken thousands of dollars worth of treatments, but he has found no relief. He has also visited a chiropractor. He has tried acupuncture. The last I knew, he was planning to go to a faith healer.

I can't blame him. It must be awful to suffer constantly — and to have little hope of healing. There are millions like him, people who have an ailment or an agony or an anxiety and are unable to find a cure for it.

Naaman, whose story is told in our scripture reading, was one such person, inflicted with a dreadful disease that in his day was quite incurable.

He was a high-ranking officer in the army of Syria, a country that was one of Israel's enemies. He was an important man who had the ear of Syria's king — but he had leprosy.

Leprosy was a terrible disease of the skin. It gradually ate away skin, then bones and joints, often resulting in deformity or paralysis, and eventually death. (If you've seen the movie *Braveheart*, you may remember the father of Robert the Bruce, whose face was being eaten away by leprosy.)

Anyway, we can imagine that Naaman had already consulted the leading doctors of Syria. Because he was a friend of the king, it is likely that the king had even made his personal physicians available to Naaman, but it had done no good.

Now it happened that Naaman had a young Jewish slave girl in his home, and she told him about the Hebrew prophet, Elisha, and his power to heal. Naaman was so desperate that he was willing to try anything — even going to the land of his enemies to visit a prophet he didn't believe in. After all, what did he have to lose?

But when Naaman and his entourage arrived at Elisha's door, they were insulted to find that Elisha himself did not even bother to come out and greet them. Instead, the prophet sent a messenger out who told Naaman to go and dip seven times in the Jordan River to be healed.

That was hardly what Naaman expected to hear. His sense of propriety was offended. He was to dip in dirty old Jordan, a river in his enemy's land?! What an insult! Why there were at least two rivers in Syria that were cleaner than the Jordan, and they were on home ground at that. Why couldn't he wash in one of those?

Naaman turned his crew around and left in a huff. Fortunately, one of Naaman's servants was a little more level-headed and persuaded his master to try Elisha's prescription. Naaman did. He went and dipped seven times in Jordan, and emerged completely healed.

What interests me in Naaman's story today is his resistance to Elisha's instructions, for it is not unlike the resistance some of us may feel to some of the church's prescriptions for the healing of our souls.

We've all heard those time-worn prescriptions from the church:

- read your Bible
- pray every day
- attend worship every Sunday
- trust and obey
- do unto others
- take up your cross
- believe in Jesus
- and the like ...

We may well say to ourselves, "Why, I've heard those things ever since I was a child. They are okay, but my problems today are too big for such simplistic advice. I need some real help."

And even if we don't feel that way ourselves, we can certainly understand why a person might take such a position. After all, most of us have already discovered that a life of faith, even when supported by a regular devotional life and consistent church attendance, just does not solve all our problems.

In fact, there have been times for most of us when we have discovered help from sources outside of the church and religion.

For example, if we have been saddled with a personality quirk that interferes with our inner peace, we may have found more help for that particular problem from psychology than from religion.

Or if we have been anxious and overworked, we may have found more relaxation and refreshment from recreation, such as going boating or playing golf on a Sunday morning than by attending church.

The fact is, there are many sources of help for the specific difficulties that plague we mortals. Medical science, for example, has made tremendous contributions to quality of human existence, and quite frankly, it would be foolish to ignore medical help for our ailments and then expect God to miraculously heal us.

Or consider the development of human reasoning, the education of the mind. The cultivation of thinking and general learning is certainly done better by colleges and universities than by the church.

In fact, for almost every aspect of human life, we can name an institution, a science, a method, or a school of thought that has been created to respond to problems in those areas:

- if you are physically ill, you can turn to medicine;
- if you are mentally upset, you can turn to psychiatry;
- if you have trouble expressing your emotions, you can join a sensitivity group or an encounter group; and
- if you are in poverty, the government is probably a better source of long-term help than the church.

Many of the secular "rivers" of help are very fine; thank God we have them. And further, some of them even complement spiritual growth.

Nonetheless, despite all this help, life is more than just a healthy body, a sound mind, a strong will, stable emotions, and a comfortable personality. The fact is, a person can take their healthy body, sound mind, strong will, stable emotions, and comfortable personality and use those resources to plan a bank robbery, cheat their friends, or be unfaithful to their spouse.

One of the sad realities of life is that many otherwise sound and talented people suffer from a kind of spiritual leprosy. And when that is the case, medicine, psychiatry, education, and the like are not, by themselves, the source of healing.

What is needed for spiritual wholeness is for the various aspects of the human life — body, mind, conscience, emotions, reason, will, and so forth — to be organized around a human spirit that is committed to God. That spirit then becomes the "manager" of the other dimensions of life and helps to keep them in the proper perspective — focused toward God.

I know a woman who is a committed Christian. But despite her strong faith, she went through a period when she suffered some emotional distress. She decided to visit a professional counselor. She later told me that some of this counselor's advice and therapy was very helpful, but that a few of his suggestions encouraged attitudes that were so self-focused that they could be harmful to others, even to people she loved.

Fortunately, because her God-committed spirit was the managing center of her life, she was able to accept the advice that was helpful and to reject that which was obviously inconsistent with her Christian commitment.

In other words, her faith gave her a context in which to evaluate the other sources of help offered to her.

You see, what we are talking about is not whether the secular sources of help and inspiration — like Naaman's preferred rivers of Syria — are more appealing than the spiritual sources. The real question is, *what can cure us of our spiritual leprosy?*

And the answer to that question is already known to us: Go wash in the Jordan and you will be healed! Or, to put it into a more familiar phrase: "Believe on the Lord Jesus Christ and you will be saved!"

278

The problem is, most of us have heard that advice so often — many of us from childhood on — that it has a trite ring to it. But think with me for a moment about what following the way of Jesus really means.

For one thing, it means being a part of the believing community that we call the church.

- What other institution is there that sanctions the pursuit of holiness, compassion, the meaning of life as legitimate enterprises?
- What other alternative is there that so fully provides the resources for spiritual growth?
- What other place is there where children are nurtured in faith?
- What other place energizes the examination of societal issues not only in terms of what would be helpful but also in terms of what would be right?
- Where else are deaths mourned but mourned in the hope of eternal life?

Those of us for whom church attendance is a regular practice are doing a great thing for our lives. That's because week after week we have the opportunity to view our lives from a faith context, to reorient ourselves and to keep in perspective the other rivers of help. We here share our lives with fellow worshipers who struggle with issues of their own lives in light of faith. We learn again the power of praying for one another, of caring about one another. Even when a worship service, like the dirty old Jordan River in Naaman's story, is less appealing than some of the secular sources of help, it is still a place where spiritual wholeness was promoted.

Many of us, I think, stand with Naaman pondering strange instructions. Naaman's instruction was, "If you want to be cured of your leprosy, go wash in old Jordan." Ours may be, "Learn to pray." But at the root, we and Naaman are hearing forms of the same advice that the church has been giving for centuries: "Trust God and be made whole."

It may not be the sentence we were expecting, but it's the one we need to hear.

# The Sign Of God

Most of us have wrestled with questions like these at one time or another:

- What career should I pursue?
- Whom should I marry?
- Where should I attend college?
- What church should I attend?
- Should we have another child?
- Should I accept a job offer that moves my family far away from our hometown?
- What community responsibilities should I accept?
- And so on ...

You recognize, of course, that questions of this sort are much more significant than simple ones like, "Should I wear my green shirt or my gray one today?" What we decide about which shirt to wear, and other questions of that ilk, generally has no bearing at all on the direction of our life. But what we decide about jobs, marriage partners, and relocating often makes a considerable difference in how our lives go.

Some Christians maintain that for these bigger questions, these life questions, God wants us to make one particular choice or another, and that our job is to try to ascertain what his will for us is in the matter.

That God has a definite will in some things is clear from scripture. In Matthew 12, for example, Jesus is out teaching some crowds when someone tells him that his mother and brothers are at the edge of the crowd, wanting to speak to him. There is no indication that he refuses to see them, but first, he takes the opportunity to say something to the one who brought him the message. He points to the crowd and says, "Here are my mother and my brothers! For whoever does the will of my Father in heaven is my brother and sister and mother" (Matthew 12:49-50).

So Jesus plainly tells us that God has a will to which we should conform. But what is less clear is what that means. There is no question that God's will for all of us is that we should live righteously and love our neighbor. But beyond that, does God have a detailed plan for each of us that includes what sort of job we should take, whether we should marry, and if so, who should we marry and how many children we should have? That is less clear from the scripture, though many Christians believe it.

E. Stanley Jones, who for years was a Methodist missionary in India, tells about his early career decision. He had given his life to Christ at seventeen, and at 23, he was asked by a college president to teach at the college. The president said to him, "It is the will of the student body, the will of the townspeople, the will of the faculty, and we believe it is the will of God for you to teach in this college." But at the same time, he had a letter from a friend that said, "I believe it is the will of God for you to go into evangelistic work here in America." He also received a letter from the Methodist Board of Missions saying, "It is our will to send you to India." And at the same time, he had the notion that God's will for him was to go as a missionary to Africa. He describes this as a "traffic jam of wills." In the end, Jones prayed about all of these opportunities, asking God to make clear the Divine will, and eventually Jones became convinced that he should go to India, which he did.[1]

Our reading from Amos today also tells us something about the nature of God's will. The setting for the reading is from the eighth century before Christ, during the time when the Hebrew people were divided into two kingdoms. The southern kingdom, Judah, had its worship at Jerusalem. The northern kingdom, Israel, had its center at Bethel. Jerusalem had the temple, and there was a shrine dedicated to God at Bethel.

Unfortunately, there were some unholy things going on in Israel. The rich lent money to the poor, and when they could not pay even a small debt, the lenders sold the debtors into slavery. There were lavish buildings being built while the uncared for poor and sick sat at the gates begging. Dishonest merchants used fixed scales. Court decisions could be bought. Idolatry was widespread, but even those who avoided idol worship and prayed to God instead were sometimes guilty of observing only the outward forms of religion while failing to love their neighbor. They had convinced themselves that the injustice, dishonesty, perjury, fraud, and inhumanity did not matter as long as the pious customs were maintained. Worst of all, the prosperous considered their very prosperity as a sign of God's approval of how they were living. These people clearly were not doing the will of God.

At that point, God needed someone to point out their sins and call them to repentance. There were plenty of priests in Bethel, but they had become just as corrupt as the people around them.

In the southern kingdom, however, in the village of Tekoa, there was a herdsman named Amos. He was a devout man, but not trained in religion. Yet when he was called by God, Amos responded. At God's instruction, Amos traveled into the northern kingdom, to Bethel. When he got there, he began to preach in the streets. First, he mentioned the sins of some of Israel's neighboring nations, passing judgment on them. This likely pleased the crowds, but then Amos started talking about the sins of Israel herself. He warned that unless the people repented, they would suffer God's wrath just as their unholy neighbors would. He talked about holding a plumb line in the midst of Israel, and the people being far "out of plumb" spiritually.

Naturally, these words did not please his audience. As the crowd became angry, Amaziah, the chief priest of Bethel, stepped forward to confront Amos. Amaziah reminded Amos that he was a foreigner. If you want to prophesy, Amos, go home to Judah and tell them about their sins, but leave Israel alone, Amaziah said.

Amos responded by saying, "I am no prophet, nor a prophet's son; but I am a herdsman, and a dresser of sycamore trees, and the

Lord took me from following the flock, and the Lord said to me, 'Go, prophesy to my people Israel.' "

To put this in a contemporary setting, Amos was saying, "Look, I'm not preaching here because I've got a yen to be a minister. I'm a layperson, a farmer, but God has called me to speak to this situation, and I've got to obey him."

In effect, Amos was saying that his life had taken one of those unexpected turns. In his wildest dreams he never imagined that he would ever do anything other than herd sheep and tend sycamore trees. Yet here he was, preaching for God in another country. I suspect Amos would understand the banner I once saw in a church that was shaped like large footprint, across which were the words, "The sign of God is that we are led where we did not intend to go."

It struck me at the time that often when we end up doing something we didn't expect or prepare for, we may think it is a result of poor planning, but sometimes the unexpected changes of direction in our lives are evidence of the activity of God. Amos never planned to preach, but apparently he had the abilities and courage God needed to deliver the message.

Of course, not every impulse we feel to go in a direction not previously planned is a call of God's will, and we need to test those calls. Amos does not tell us how he determined that God was calling him. He only says, "God took me from following the flock, and ... said to me, 'Go prophesy....' " But here are some things Christians through the years have found helpful:

1. Do the obvious. Some principles Jesus made clear for us. For example, if one direction is obviously in line with the idea of loving our neighbor and another is not, then the one that shows love is the one most likely to be God's will.

2. Do what is clearly at hand. God may be calling you to work for him on the other side of the planet, but if the needs you keep seeing are the ones in your own community, those are ones to which God is most likely directing you. There is a story about Abraham Lincoln, before he became president, seeing a slave auctioned off. He was so disturbed by what he saw that he said, "If I ever get a chance

to hit that, I'm going to hit it with all I have." And of course, that opportunity came, clearly at hand, and Lincoln acted.

3. Consider your abilities and talents. Some things we can rule out because we are not capable of doing them. I, for example, have very little talent in art — so little that it seems unlikely God would call me into any kind of service where I'd need to do much with it.

4. Test your call by the Christian community. Among the silent-meeting Quakers, there is a practice called the "clearness committee." This is a group of five or six members whose sole function is to meet with a person who is trying to make a difficult decision and ask the person questions. They do not give advice, but ask the sort of penetrating questions that help the person discover for him or herself what the course of action ought to be. While we don't have such a formal structure, there is always wisdom in checking out a call with a few fellow Christians — asking them to listen objectively and probe your motivations.

5. Use your best God-given judgment and pray for clarity as you proceed. A man once said, "I prayed for advice but got no clear answer, so I just used my common sense." Of course, God can use common sense as a way to communicate with us. So ask yourself what seems most likely to be the direction you should go? One way to test that is to pray, "Lord, I think you want me to do thus and so. I am going to begin in that direction. If this is not what you want, please let me know in some way." Oswald Chambers, a devotional writer from an earlier era, wrote, "If we are saved and sanctified God guides us by our ordinary choices, and if we are going to choose what he does not want, he will check, and we must heed."[2]

6. Allow for the direct workings of God.

One such case is the story of Dr. Steven Kopits. Although of normal size himself, he became the one of the few surgeons in the world who specialize in medical care for people who are born dwarfs, or as they prefer to call themselves, little people. Although that term is also sometimes applied to midgets, there is a difference in the two. Midgets are simply small people, but their limbs and torso are proportional to their size. Aside from being small, they look normal. Dwarfs, on the other hand, suffer from a genetic condition that causes them to be born with severe deformities, including club feet, bowed legs, splayed hips, and limp spines. Their limbs and torsos are disproportionate. But the biggest problem of dwarfism is dysplasia, an abnormal alignment of bones and muscles that causes pain, crippling, functional disability, and even death if left untreated. As an orthopedic surgeon, Kopits works to correct these problems so that these little people have a chance to lead reasonably normal lives.

One thing that sets Dr. Kopits apart from some of his colleagues is how involved he gets with his patients. "I love them," Kopits admits. "The preached doctrine is that you cannot be a good physician if you get emotionally involved with your patients. My doctrine is that you cannot be a good physician unless you *do* get emotionally involved." He also reports that his major motivation for working with dwarfs is not because they are dwarfs *per se*, but because "they are a disabled population that was not being helped."

Kopits didn't set out to treat this population. He simply became an orthopedic surgeon because that field interested him. But after a patient with dwarfism came to him, and Kopits was able to help, others began to come as well.

Here's what I want you to hear: Kopits has helped many of these little people, but he refuses to take all the credit. He says, "Always I have felt that I was being taken by the hand. If you can say nothing else about me, you can say that I am a man who is doing exactly what he was meant to do."[3]

And so, it seems was Amos. And so can we. God's will doesn't normally come to us written on a cloud or spoken as an audible voice. But God's will can be ascertained nonetheless, in the opportunities that present themselves, in the talents he has given us, and in the inner nudges God gives us.

Our job is to listen, test, and intend to follow his direction.

1. E. Stanley Jones, *The Divine Yes* (New York: Abingdon Press, 1975), pp. 68-69.

2. *My Utmost for His Highest* (Westwood, New Jersey: Barbour and Company, n.d), p. 155.

3. Kopits' story from Brad Lemley, "Loving Healer of Little People," *Reader's Digest*, May 1985.

**Proper 11**
**Pentecost 9**
**Ordinary Time 16**
**Amos 8:1-12**

# When Nothing More
# Can Be Done

Colleen was a good woman with a bad heart. She had been a member of my last congregation for more than thirty years, ever since she'd married a man who'd grown up in our church. But for several years, she had been living with a weakened heart. It was just one of those things that afflict some people, and she'd been doctoring for it for some time. Initially, she'd kept working, but as she missed more and more days on the job because of the problems from her heart, it eventually became clear that she could not continue. By the time I arrived at that parish, Colleen, in her late fifties, was essentially homebound.

Because of the limits imposed by her health, she hadn't been able to come to church in more than two years. I'd visited her in her home a few times, and I also saw her at the hospital during several stays where she underwent various treatments and procedures. In fact, she'd been hospitalized for a few days right before the particular visit with her that I am about to narrate to you.

When I'd seen her in the hospital a couple of days earlier, she had not yet received the final report from the doctor, but she'd hoped that he'd have some new therapy or medicine to relieve her of her deepening weakness. So on the first day she was back home, I stopped by her house to find out what she'd learned.

I found her there alone. Her husband was out on an errand. After she invited me in, I asked what her doctor had said.

When she answered me, there was the sound of astonishment in her voice. What she said was, "He told me, 'Go home and prepare to die!' "

Frankly, I didn't know what to say. Certainly, nothing I'd learned in seminary or from my previous experience provided a clue about an appropriate response. Finally, I asked, "Is there nothing at all that can be done?"

"No," she said. "My overall health is too far gone. He said I probably won't live out the week."

It was a surreal moment. There we were, sitting in her sunlit, tidy little home surrounded by the glory of awakening nature in early spring. And there was Colleen, who, except perhaps for looking a little tired, appeared to be fine. And in that homey, friendly, bright environment, Colleen was calmly saying that she probably had less than a week to live. It was one of those times when the evidence all around you makes it difficult to accept what your ears are hearing. In fact, I asked her about the possibility of a transplant or seeing other specialists, but Colleen explained that all those things had been explored. There really was nothing more that could be done.

And, as it turned out, in less than a week, I was called to conduct Colleen's funeral.

Colleen came to my mind a few years later when I was watching the movie, *Titanic*. There is period right after the great ship has hit the iceberg where things still seem to be okay. The officers know that something has happened, but for the moment, the ship appears to be steaming on as usual. The passengers, after having been jarred a bit by the bump, have returned to their activities and things are carrying on as before. The ship's designer is on board, however, and he goes below to inspect the damage. He sees the water pouring in and makes some quick calculations. Then, in the movie, he meets with the captain and other officials. After explaining his calculations, he states his conclusion: within a few brief hours, the ship is going to go down. And there is nothing they can do to prevent that from happening.

Can you imagine what the men at that meeting were thinking at the moment? "He can't be right. The ship is still going along all right. There must be some repairs we can make. After all, this ship was built to be unsinkable." The evidence seen by their eyes was screaming against the information they were hearing, but as we know, that information was correct, and the ship went down that night, taking more than 1,500 people with it.

If you can put your mind into the startling effect of either of those there's-nothing-more-that-can-be-done incidents, then you are in a position to understand how the prophet Amos must have felt when he received the word from God that is recorded in today's reading. God's message must have come as a jolt to Amos. In the earlier part of the book, we see this prophet delivering the message he had received from God, and while it was filled with judgment against the people for their sins, there was at least still an element of hope in it: If the people will repent and turn from their sins, disaster could be averted.

The people have resisted Amos' call for repentance, however, and so now, in chapter 8, Amos hears a new word from God. In a vision, Amos sees a basket filled with summer fruit. God then explains to Amos the meaning of the vision, saying, "The end has come to my people Israel."

Actually, we'd have to be able to read this passage in the original Hebrew to make the connection. The Hebrew word for summer fruit is *qayits*, and the word for end is *qets*. The two words are not related in meaning, but they sound similar, and that is the basis for the association.[1] The message Amos hears is, "Israel's summer is almost over and the harvest of judgment has come." Essentially, God is telling Amos that the people have gone on too long in their sins and have passed a point of no return, and the nation will suffer an unwanted fate. And that is exactly what happened. Less than thirty years later, Israel fell to the Assyrians and many of the people were dispersed to other lands.

So Amos, too, hears the word that nothing more can be done.

There is a moment with a similar kind of impact in the New Testament, when Jesus prayed in the garden the night before his crucifixion. He prayed, "My Father, if it is possible, let this cup [meaning his arrest and crucifixion] pass from me" (Matthew 26:39), but what he evidently hears from his Father is that it is not possible, not if Jesus is going to be faithful to his Father's will. Nothing more could be done, and so Jesus adds, "Yet not what I want but what you want." At that moment, it might have still been possible for Jesus to get up and run for his life, but he chose to remain.

We, too, have faced awful circumstances where nothing more could be done. We've gotten that unwanted diagnosis. We've seen cherished relationships come abruptly to an end. We've seen great opportunities forever lost. We've seen irrevocable choices we've made end in horrendous consequences. We've heard the finality of the words, "It's too late." We've had to learn the meaning of the phrase, "It's terminal."

So what can we say to all of this darkness? We can say this, that great affirmation all Christians share: *In Christ, the end is not the end.* In Christ, what we call the end is the great beginning of eternity. That affirmation is true whether you are a Baptist, a Lutheran, a Catholic, a Methodist, or any of the denominations into which Christians divide themselves, for we hold in common that powerful reality that Jesus both taught in words and demonstrated with his resurrection: *The end is not the end.*

It is true that Christians share a belief in an end of *this* age, but we should note that such a doctrine is not really about ending. Rather it is about a new beginning, the beginning of God's kingdom fully come and the beginning of true life in its enduring form. Yes, we observe and remember the crucifixion of Christ, but our highest holy day is not Good Friday; it is Easter. Ultimately, while the whole Christian year, in one sense, marches us toward the cross, it does not leave us there. It pauses there, to be sure, but eventually it delivers us to Easter.

That sense of eternity sometimes comes out in the darkest moments of finality, the time when it is suddenly clear that nothing more can be done. On 9/11, Madeline Amy Sweeney, a 35-year-old mother of two small children, was one of the flight attendants on board American Flight 11, the plane that eventually was the first to be rammed into the World Trade Center. As the hijacking was under way, Sweeney, in the rear of the plane, managed to phone an American flight service manager in Boston. With remarkable calm, she told the manager what was happening, identifying the hijackers by their seat numbers. They included Mohammed Atta and four others. Sweeney reported that two flight attendants had been stabbed and that a business-class passenger had been killed by a hijacker who cut the man's throat. Moments before 8:46 a.m., she spoke of seeing water and buildings. And then, after a brief pause, when she apparently got some glimpse of what was about to happen, came her last transmission. She exclaimed, "O my God! O my God!"[2]

What was that? A cry of astonishment and terror certainly, but more, I think. In an instant when we suddenly comprehend that nothing more can be done, that things really are ending, from somewhere deep inside us sometimes comes the realization that the only refuge we have left is God himself. And there may only be time for the briefest of prayers: "O my God!"

When all else is gone, that is our only plea, our only prayer, our only affirmation of faith and our only claim on eternity. "O my God, receive me!" It was the prayer of Jesus on the cross — "Father into your hands I commend my spirit" (Luke 23:46) — and it is ours. Commending ourselves to God is what can be done — *the only thing that can be done* — when nothing more can be done.

Thank God!

1. Peter C. Craigie, *Twelve Prophets*, Vol. 1, The Daily Study Bible Series (Philadelphia: The Westminster Press, 1984), p. 181.

2. I gleaned Sweeney's story from several accounts of her actions on 9/11. One is a notice published in *The Boston Globe*, September 14, 2001, www.legacy.com/ LegacyTribute/Sept11.asp?Page=TributeStory&PersonId=91761.

# Sermons On The First Readings

## For Sundays
## After Pentecost
## (Middle Third)

### *The Hard Task*
### *Of Truth-telling*

## Lee Ann Dunlap

Proper 12
Pentecost 10
Ordinary Time 17
Hosea 1:2-10

# A "Somebody Done Somebody Wrong" Song

*Humpty Dumpty sat on a wall; Humpty Dumpty had a*
*great fall.*
*All the king's horses and all the king's men couldn't*
*put Humpty Dumpty together again.*

This is a nursery rhyme we learned as children, and somewhere along the line in history class we were taught that its composer, "Mother Goose," was, in fact, a political satirist. If we look between the lines of these playful rhymes we will find some kind of hidden message poking fun at royalty. (I guess you had to be there to get the joke.)

Whether Sir Dumpty was some courtier destroyed by political intrigue or a giant egg as once depicted in a children's book only historians can say for sure. But, political or not, there is a truth to be told by his story: Some things and some relationships are just so fragile that all can be lost in one wrong move. Knock over Grandma's antique hurricane lamp and it is junk, no matter how much glue or scotch tape you use to put the pieces back in place; and don't tell me you haven't tried that approach. Broadcast a story alleging a politician's misconduct in office and a career can be destroyed even if libel is proven. To quote the Berenstain Bears (from *The Berenstain Bears and the Truth* by Stan and Jan Berenstain), "Trust is something you cannot put back together once it is broken."

Take marriage, for instance. Two people can carefully create a world together, can share their lives and their bodies with one another, can make babies, and build a business; and all of it will crumble by the weight of a lie.

"I, John, take you, Mary, to be my wife," so the vows go, "for richer, for poorer, in sickness and in health, 'til death us do part." According to the National Center for Health Statistics, more than eight people per every thousand made that promise in 2001; and four people in every thousand broke it through divorce.

The reasons for these disastrous statistics are as complicated as the relationships themselves; but most certainly a major factor is broken trust. We lie to ourselves and our spouses about lots of things — like addictions to alcohol or drugs, or the money we spent and where we spent it, or in more recent times the amount of time spent on the internet. And there is the all-time favorite topic of country music and soap operas — the cheating heart. Most marriages are lost by a combination of these factors. Once the lies are revealed, the wounds are nearly impossible to heal completely even if the marriage survives. Like Grandma's shattered lamp — the cracks are always there.

That is why the story of Hosea, son of Beeri, seems so personal even these centuries later. It is a parable lived out in real life not only by the prophet but by nearly four out of every thousand people in our neighborhood. Such betrayal may even be in your story as well. But more than all that, Hosea claims, it is *God's* story.

In the beginning, the prophet, presumably a young man, is ordered by God to "take for yourself a wife of whoredom and have children of whoredom." (That's the RSV translation.) Whether this female is a common street prostitute or part of a pagan fertility cult is debated by scholars even yet. In a matter of six verses the command is accomplished; Hosea marries Gomer and three children are born and given names of prophetic significance: Jezreel ("cast away"), Lo-ruhamah ("not pitied"), and Lo-ammi ("not my people").

Why anyone would deliberately marry an unfaithful partner could jump-start a lot of speculation on our part. Bringing children into such a union would not be considered wise family planning, to say the least. One might suspect the prophet discerned God's handiwork in these events *after the fact*. That God would orchestrate such a fiasco is difficult to accept. That Hosea would oblige should raise an eyebrow, as well. Still, we must admit that, in our own day, marriages are consummated and children "begat" for reasons that are equally questionable. Some have contemplated this story from the perspective of Gomer or her progeny in an effort to make sense of it. Such speculation can provide useful insights into our modern domestic relations but it misses the point of the book altogether. Ultimately the message is not about Hosea and Gomer and their struggles of the heart — it is about God and the covenant people. God makes the reason clear even if not logical. "The land commits great whoredom by forsaking the Lord."

Hosea used his family struggles as a way to speak to his people about their own idolatry. In the tragic last days of the northern kingdom, Israel's throne saw six kings in 25 years. With the impending threat of Assyrian expansion into the territory, political maneuvering and diplomatic gamesmanship became a way of life. First came one treaty and then another, tribute after tribute, taxation upon taxation, courting one military alliance after another in the name of domestic tranquility. These were turbulent times and the nation's political, economic, and religious leaders were caught up in the currents, living as though God were not God and as if the covenant made at Sinai had no claim on their actions.

Hosea is not the only biblical writer to use the marital relationship as a metaphor for God's relationship with Israel, but he certainly pursues that image with maximum emotional intensity. Stories of the deities of many of Israel's neighbors also ascribed to their gods' personal characteristics like jealousy or anger or fury in the face of betrayal, but no other nation's gods relate so directly with human beings or are so concerned about their ethical behavior. No other god fights so passionately for the human community nor expects such fidelity from it, and none expresses such heartache when things go awry. Not that we would think of a Hank Williams' song as divine lyrics, but "Your Cheatin' Heart" could well be the title of God's lament over Israel.

No soap opera or romance novel could write the drama better. But more surprising and intriguing than the human infidelity related by this story is the divine response: the promise of reunion and reconciliation. "In the place where it was said to them, 'you are not my people,' it shall be said to them, 'Children of the living God' " (v. 10). Beyond the heartache and lament is an undying commitment "to love, honor, and cherish" even when that love is scorned and abused. Where does one summon such forgiveness, such stubborn commitment to love? Only from the heart of God.

The cheating heart story is far too familiar to the human drama, whether it is Gomer, or Israel, or the bride of Christ. To invest one's heart in another is incredibly risky; and to betray that trust is to bring disaster upon oneself. That anyone would take such a risk is a testimony to love's hope and strength. That the Creator of the universe would do so for the sake of humanity is nearly incomprehensible. That this God would continue to pursue and woo us despite our faithlessness is almost beyond belief. Those who insist "you can't put Humpty Dumpty together again" don't know God's power or Christ's mercy.

Still, the task of such reconciliation is not easy. Ask anyone impacted by an extramarital affair. Before love can be restored, there is a lot of "hell to pay" — a lot of screaming and a lot of silence to be endured; a lot of confession to be made and tears to be shed; a lot of hard work before trust can be re-established. Israel paid a heavy price for its flirtation with pagan idols and betrayal of God's compassion. About 721 B.C.E., Samaria was crushed by the Assyrian army and its people exiled. The northern kingdom came to an end.

A hard lesson learned by a people long ago, yet we flirt with similar disaster when we forsake Christ to pursue selfish ambitions. In our efforts to secure material possessions, financial stability, social esteem, or institutional survival, we give obeisance to false idols and devote our energies to powers and principalities that promise the best deal or the easiest shortcut. We wheel and deal as if Christ is not Lord and as if loving God and neighbor is not his prime directive. We have abandoned our prayer life, tossed our Bibles onto a shelf, and neglected worship. We have ignored the membership promises we made to the church to give God our time, talents, and treasure. Such betrayal ultimately leads to judgment. Keep it up, and Sir Dumpty's "great fall" will not be long in coming.

Some of us, individual Christians or communities, may already have learned such truth the hard way, and our lives may even now be splattered at the foot of the wall. Amidst the heartache of broken lives, depleted bodies, and fractured relationships we find ourselves empty and hopeless. Considering the mess we've made, we wonder if redemption is even possible.

Thank God for Christ's mercy and God's stubborn love toward us. The God who raised Jesus from the dead can indeed restore our fractured lives and make us new. The wounded can be made whole, the sin can be forgiven, the relationship restored, and trust mended. Our cheating hearts can be made pure once more. All this is possible, not through our own efforts but by the love of Christ and the renewing power of the Holy Spirit. All that is required is that we turn in repentance. Call to God and you will once again receive pity. Cry out and you will again be called, "My child."

Proper 13
Pentecost 11
Ordinary Time 18
Hosea 11:1-11

# A Father's Heart Cry

Steven and LaDonna had been married nearly ten years before they were finally able to conceive a much-desired child. To their surprise and concern, little James arrived prematurely, weighing a scant four pounds. He required several weeks in the hospital's incubator and lots of prayers before he could finally go home.

In the years since then, Steven has often shared how his firstborn, and only child, changed his life forever. Having that little life depend on him made him a better man and better husband. And beyond that, he confesses, becoming a parent changed his relationship with God. He has committed himself to being a top-notch father and James is an adoring and adorable son. Through that effort he has emerged as a spiritual leader, not only for his child but in his church and community.

Theirs is a happy story, one that needs to be told, because, as we know, not all parents' stories turn out so well. Being a parent can be great, of course. Those homemade Mother's Day cards, or presents wrapped by little fingers are more precious than the finest jewels. A hug and a kiss or an "I love you, Daddy" can bring satisfaction beyond measure.

But not every parent gets to celebrate. In the same church that Steve and LaDonna attend is another set of parents who have been called numerous times in the middle of the night to go the emergency room when their son has attempted suicide. At other times, the calls have been from the police. They have loved their son no less than their other children, and no less than other parents love their children. They have tried their best to follow the experts' recommendations, but the cycle of mental illness, depression, and alcohol abuse continues to challenge their best intentions, and the possibility of their son's self-destruction looms constantly overhead.

What if you have a child in whom it is difficult to take pride or delight? I'm not talking about the baseball through the picture window or the raging hormones and insane arguments of the "terrible teen" years, when boundaries get challenged and nerves get tested. What happens when a child's action brings true shame?

Take, for example, the parents who courageously turned their own son into authorities after they realized he was a sniper who had been terrorizing their city for several months. Or, consider the plight of "good parents" whose children end up in prison or even on death row because of drugs, mental illness, or other circumstances beyond parental control. These days, nearly all parents live in fear of their child being a victim of school violence, but what if *your* child is the anxious, unhappy, bullied adolescent who does the shooting? What do you do when *your son* is convicted as a sexual predator? These are a parent's worst nightmares.

Sometimes, despite the best efforts of dedicated, diligent, and loving parents, the child just turns out terribly warped. So what is a parent to do with a *true* problem child? That is the dilemma that rips at the heart of God in today's passage from the prophet Hosea.

Earlier in the book of Hosea, the prophet used the example of marital infidelity to reveal a fundamental breach in the nation's corrupted relationship with God — Israel is condemned as a cheating spouse. A marriage gone bad is one kind of heartache, but a rebellious child is another matter altogether. You can't divorce your children regardless of how much you might want to sometimes. The parent-child relationship holds a different kind of passion — and, when things go awry, a different kind of grief.

"When Israel was a child, I loved him," God pronounces, "and out of Egypt I called my son. The more I called them, the more they went from me." Nearly every parent can relate, one would think. "Stay in the driveway," we call to the four-year-old on a tricycle, and he immediately makes a beeline for the street. "You shall worship no God but me," declares the Lord as the first commandment, yet "they kept sacrificing to the Baals, and offering incense to idols." Hosea's portrait of God as Father is not new to the biblical tradition, but it would seem to be unique amongst world religions. No other deity relates to human beings in quite the same manner or with quite the same passion, with the same loyalty or the same jealousy. Threaten a child and you will arouse a parent's strongest fighting instinct. Betray their love and you unleash their greatest heartache. God's passion is no less intense, Hosea reveals.

The prophet Hosea most likely wrote during the reign of King Hoshea. As the nation of Assyria struggled to gain control of an already unstable region, smaller nations were caught amidst powerplays for security and control. Treaties were made and conveniently broken with those military forces making the best promises or the worst threats. The king's latest bargain at the time of the prophet happened to be with Egypt, and it was a costly one at that. To accept protection from a foreign nation meant paying tribute — extracted from the ranks of the poor and the weak. Such tribute robbed the nation of its gross national product disrupting the national economy; and, as always, those on the brink of survival suffered the most.

Dependence on these foreign armies also meant accepting their culture and giving obeisance to their gods. Given Israel's history, this was an ironic return to the nation that had once enslaved them. Hosea rightly saw such dependence as a rejection of what God had done in the Exodus. Israel was living by pagan standards and not God's family values. In today's terms we might say that because the nation did not trust God's protection, Homeland Security became more important than "liberty and justice for all."

The nation had abandoned the covenant and rebelled against God, and Hosea knew this meant disaster. Given his own marital and family dysfunction, he likely knew a parent's grief firsthand. Earlier chapters tell of his courtship and marriage to an unfaithful wife and the impact of children born into the affair. "Jezreel," "Loruhamah," and "Lo-ammi" bore the impact of the infidelity — much like "not-pitied" children of broken homes bear the emotional scars today, emotionally disowned as "not my people." And, like many of today's youngsters they acted out their anguish in rebellion. Those of you with less-than-perfect children might, perhaps, have an inkling. But a few of you, who have perhaps personally parented persons who are hell-bent on self-destruction, are better positioned to grasp the heartache of God amidst Israel's spiral toward disaster. While the airwaves are loaded with "cheatin' heart" songs, we hear very few broken-hearted parent songs, quite likely because such anguish most often runs too deep for lyrics.

"My people are bent on turning away from me," God says. As we examine our own world we could well ask, "Are we any different?" Our own nation, like Israel, was called into existence by God, or so we say. Although not the military underdog that Israel was in Hosea's time, we are still trying to pursue our own course toward domestic tranquility without heed of covenant loyalty. In our pursuit of individuality and self-reliance are we not equally guilty of believing we can fix our own problems (or even the world's), without God? Our military, political, or economic solutions may differ in content but our "keep religion out of politics" attitude reveals the same fundamental breach with the heart of the Creator.

It's not just the nation who has strayed. As the church, we are a people called out of bondage by the blood of Christ. Yet we worship at our convenience — if at all. God is great and all that, but an hour on Sunday is enough, isn't it? And why should I miss a good ball game or my quiet time with the Sunday paper for that, either?

We practice our ethical teachings — until they become uncomfortable. "Love honor and cherish" sounds good in the wedding vows, but something (or someone) better is bound to come along, and don't we owe it to ourselves to be happy?

We receive God's blessings but skimp on our charity toward others. A tenth? Are you *kidding* me?

We ask for God's mercy and protection, but rarely share our testimony with unbelievers. We don't want to offend, after all.

Such behaviors pave a path toward self-destruction and this grieves the heart of God, just as parents' hearts are rent when a son or daughter's rebellion hurls them toward broken relationships, economic ruin, or even a prison cell. "The more I call, the more they went from me." What is a loving God to do?

As we said earlier, Hosea is not the only one in the Bible to speak of God as a loving Father. Perhaps it was Hosea that Jesus had in mind when he told his followers the story of another father in another place. This father also watched in pain as his younger son left home intent on making his own way in the world — a way that did not include his father's family values, but did include the son's share of the family wealth. Jesus told the story in dramatic fashion as this son squanders the resources of his inheritance in an ever-descending spiral that many parents today know all too well. Perhaps it was Jesus' own knowledge of his Heavenly Father's compassion which led him to reveal how this father would respond. This father watched, and he waited in hope for the moment when his prodigal son would appear on the horizon. And when his broken and humiliated child did return, this father ran to greet him with open, loving arms and tears of joy.

Jesus knew the love of the Father as well as his anguish, just like Hosea had known it. "How can I give you up, Ephraim? How can I hand you over, Israel?" the prophet asks. "My heart recoils within me; my compassion grows warm and tender." "I will not execute my fierce anger; I will not again destroy Ephraim; for I am God and no mortal, the holy one in your midst, and I will not come in wrath."

The good news is that in the end God's love always outweighs God's punishment. That was the experience of the Jews who wrote the Hebrew Scriptures, and that is the experience the church proclaims. As much as God fumes over our idolatry, hypocrisy, and self-centered ways, and much as God aches over our self-destructive addictions and community-dividing behaviors, God will not abandon us and God will not reject us when we plead for mercy.

In the end, God's heart cry is a love song for us. God calls to us like God called to Israel. It is a song of reconciliation sung by Jesus of Nazareth on the hill of Calvary and it is echoed by the Spirit in our own hearts and lives. It is a song that will flow out of us when we stand willing to watch and to wait in patience and to receive and forgive others despite our own anguished hearts. This is God's promise: The heartache will end, but the love will not, because, in the end, this is a love song that promises to resonate through all eternity.

Proper 14
Pentecost 12
Ordinary Time 19
Isaiah 1:1, 10-20

# Star-spangled Justice

In just a few more weeks we will be winding down the official summer season. The children start back to school and we all have one final summer fling during the Labor Day holiday weekend. Patriotic holidays like Flag Day, Independence Day, and Labor Day are best celebrated in the hot summer sun or watching "the rocket's red glare" under the stars.

Summer holidays have a tradition all their own: hot dogs and charcoal-grilled burgers, potato salad, baseball games, and fireworks. These times are fun for everybody — well, most everybody. If you happen to work in the emergency room or the recreational industry — a state park or a marina — holiday memories might include drunken boaters, burn injuries, or four-wheeler accident victims.

Things like parades and speeches and flying the flag are traditions, which perhaps get a bit closer to the spirit of the season — the more solemn side of the occasion. In much of the country national holy days like Labor Day and the Fourth of July have come back in vogue in recent years — a stirring of our patriotic spirit. Such celebrations have long been recognized as essential to good citizenship. By singling out particular moments in history like the signing of the Declaration of Independence, or celebrating the establishment of labor unions and collective bargaining, our culture expresses the values upheld by the collective community, and we reflect on the struggle of those who have sacrificed to establish and uphold those community values. In doing so, we hope to shape the attitudes and values of future citizens.

In the United States, the common patriotic values we hope to pass along are focused upon freedom, both political (as with Flag Day and July Fourth) and economic (Labor Day). "Liberty and justice for all" is the theme that binds together the various people and ideologies into a common national myth expressing the best of what we hope to be as a nation. During our national holidays we remember and reflect upon the stories of those before us who have struggled to achieve our national ideals: the Minutemen of Lexington and Concord, the Continental soldiers of Valley Forge, the bloody battles fought to free slaves and maintain unity of the states, as well as those who have marched in picket lines and protest movements to gain fair wages and safe working conditions.

And more than merely remembering, we seek to honor those who still struggle and sacrifice to ensure liberty and justice for all even today — by speaking for it in the public arena on behalf of those who have still been denied, and by fighting for it against those who would yet deny it to others. It is the American way, or at least it is the hope to which we strive.

But before it was ever the American way, it was biblical mandate. Those in our nation who would speak of liberty and justice while seeking to remove God from the public forum had best remember our history and the biblical foundations upon which it was laid.

While we need to be honest in telling our national story and to confess the harm we have often done in the name of God and country (that is another sermon entirely!), we must also give fair recognition to the good and noble things America has inherited from the faith traditions of our founding ancestors. The Liberty Bell in Philadelphia's Independence Hall bears the inscription: "To Proclaim Liberty Throughout the Land," but many civil libertarians who would separate church from state forget those words are straight from the Hebrew Scriptures. Before Congress ever passed a Labor Act or Thomas Jefferson ever penned the Bill of Rights, there was the prophet Isaiah. "Cease to do evil, learn to do good; seek justice, rescue the oppressed, defend the orphan, plead for the widow."

Isaiah knew the intricacies of politics. He knew monarchies first hand: Uzziah, Jotham, Ahaz, and Hezekiah — he knew them all. He paid close attention as they struggled as a pawn amidst the larger military campaigns of their powerful neighbors. First it was Egypt and Assyria who wooed and courted and then threatened and coerced; later Babylon and Persia would join the fray. He watched as these kings depleted their national economy in order to pay tribute to these superpowers that promised military security, a security purchased on the backs of the poor. In the political maneuvering and gamesmanship, Israel's statesmen had forgotten their own national history — and Yahweh's place in it. "Leave religion to the festivals and the high places," was the politically correct policy. Honor Baal, and Ashterah, and any other idol that promises success and fertility. Appease potential allies and their gods at any cost. "Religion and politics don't mix" we hear them cry in our own language. "Do what works for you."

But Isaiah did remember God, and he spoke out. Religious talk without the walk is useless, he insisted. Worse than useless, it is an abomination and an insult to God, who forged this people out of the suffering of slavery and delivered them from bondage to the very nation they were seeking to court as their protector. This God had created them from nothingness just as God had created the sun and the stars, the earth and the sea. To court this God with offerings while flirting with Baal and others for a better deal amounts to adultery. To offer sacrifices in God's temple and then ignore the demands of the covenant is hypocrisy, and an insult that will prove disastrous, Isaiah declared.

National security depends on national righteousness and not our military spending or diplomatic maneuvering. National righteousness means being who we say we are, practicing what we say we value, and putting our national budgets where our mottos are.

Our national anthem extols "the land of the free and the home of the brave"; yet our initial public response to the terrorist attacks of September 11 has been to curtail personal liberty and due process of law in the interest of safety. Such a response is practical, but hardly brave. We have paid for added security in our public places by diminishing our spending on public welfare. We condemn other nations' arsenals of weapons of mass destruction while

311

investing in our own: a practical national policy perhaps, but hardly a brave or honest one.

In New York harbor, the Statue of Liberty stands as an icon of what America aspires to be. Inscribed in her foundation are words by Emma Lazarus that stir our patriotic spirits:

> *Give me your tired, your poor,*
> *Your huddled masses yearning to breathe free,*
> *The wretched refuse of your teeming shore.*
> *Send these, the homeless, temptest-tost to me;*
> *I lift my lamp beside the golden door.*

But our immigration laws bespeak quite another message: "Only the employed and educated from certain regions of the globe that are favorable to our way of life need apply." Practical national security perhaps, but not too brave.

Anyone listening to Isaiah's words to *his* nation can't help but hear a message to *ours*: National security depends upon national righteousness. The best defense against those who would destroy our freedom or prosperity is to live out our democratic ideals without abandon and to practice generosity without fear of want. Or, in Isaiah's words, "Seek justice, rescue the oppressed."

What we also need to hear from Isaiah is that this call to national righteousness is not one option to be considered amongst several others, any more than Yahweh was just one god to be worshiped along with Baal or Ashterah, or the deities of Egypt or Babylon. This is not a matter of "whatever works for you." In the end, righteousness is the only viable option, just as God is the only living God.

Isaiah knew, just as we know, that to abandon this truth in favor of what is convenient, or comfortable, or politically correct is to invite judgment and even destruction. National hypocrisy, like personal hypocrisy, is an abomination. We must be who we say we are, practice what we say we value, and put our money where our mottos are, or we will cease to be. "If you refuse and rebel, you shall be devoured by the sword," God said to Judah and says to us.

Fancy worship that dazzles and entertains won't cut it. Neither will strict dispassionate adherence to doctrine and regulations. Worship without service is as useless as service without worship. What is required is radical trust in God's faithfulness (Love God) that finds its way into radical obedience to God's command, "Love your neighbor."

"Come now, let's reason together," says the Lord. ("Let's argue it out" is the NRSV translation.) "If you are willing and obedient, you shall eat the good of the land." God desires to bless us, just as God desired to bless Isaiah and his people, and, through us all, to bless the world. But, before that can happen, we must bless God. We must bless God through our words and prayers and hymns of praise; and we must bless God in the words we speak to one another, and in the deeds of justice and peace that we perform in God's world.

**Proper 15**
**Pentecost 13**
**Ordinary Time 20**
**Isaiah 5:1-7**

# Song Of The Vineyard

Some of the best prophetic voices of any culture are its troubadours. Historically, the term refers to traveling musicians who once strolled the streets and pubs of medieval Europe singing love songs in exchange for food and lodging. Today they travel by jet or private coach filling auditoriums with screaming fans and recording "greatest hits" albums. Regardless of the time or language, music has an almost supernatural power to affect the human soul and even change the course of the human community. It lifts our spirits, bolsters our courage, and points out injustice. A single melody can change our minds and hearts; or at least it has that potential.

It seems there's not a lot of social justice music on the airwaves these days, not like the songs that penetrated the souls of those growing up in the '60s and '70s. Most of the socially significant music has to be squeezed in around the more popular stuff that sells CDs. Some of you may remember the first time you heard "Blowin' In The Wind" by Peter, Paul, and Mary. They put in an occasional appearance on public television, but haven't made most radio playlists in years. These days, Elvis Presley can still be heard singing, "You Ain't Nothing But A Hound Dog"; but his version of the Mac Davis song, "In the Ghetto," gets precious little airtime. Judgment seldom sells well in our marketplace.

One of the more intriguing social critics in the country music realm is making a posthumous comeback. During the heyday of his career, Johnny Cash — "the Man in Black" — became a voice for the downtrodden and ignored. Although nearly forgotten himself in Nashville, Cash hit the charts one last time only months

315

before his death with a music video on MTV of all places, inspiring a new generation of fans while confronting the darker side of life and death.

Regardless of the culture or the language, music has the power to touch both mind and heart, literally at a different level. Studies indicate that music stimulates a different part of the brain than the written or spoken word alone. That's why songs like "We Shall Overcome" have such power even today. It is also why church folk have such strong sentiments about our worship music — contemporary, traditional, chants and praise choruses, and everything in between. And, we are not the first. It is no coincidence that the most frequently quoted scripture within the Bible is Psalms, the hymnbook of ancient Israel.

Some of the best prophetic voices of any culture are its troubadours; so it should be no big surprise that Isaiah, one of the Bible's best known prophets, begins his long and effective career with "let me sing a song." Scholars doubt that the words were ever put to music, but this "Song Of The Vineyard" functions more like an introduction to a weightier message. It is likely the parable was preached early in Isaiah's ministry, and is possibly connected to the harvest festival.

It's not hard to imagine. Like any festival, the crowd is in a good mood — maybe even a bit intoxicated. After all, it is the grape harvest and what better way to celebrate? It could be that the band had already sung a few of the crowd favorites about good times and good wine.

Then Isaiah gets the microphone and changes the tune.

The crowd wants to hear "God Bless Judah" songs but Isaiah sings them a "somebody done somebody wrong" song — a tale of "my beloved (friend) and his vineyard." We can imagine the shock as the party turns silent and sullen.

"I will break down the (protective) wall, and the nation shall be trampled," promises the Lord.

We can imagine how such a message might be received in one of our own national celebrations. Imagine a gathering on the White House lawn for Memorial Day. The invited music star suddenly changes the program from "Proud To Be An American" to "One

Tin Soldier." For those too young to remember — that is another of those social justice tunes from the '70s. The chorus urged us to hate our neighbors and cheat our friends in heaven's name because, in the end, we could justify our actions. Look up the lyrics on ScoutSongs.com to get the whole story — but trust me — it made sense back then.

This would be quite a different message — quite a different effect.

So what was Isaiah's point?

When Isaiah compares God's people to a vineyard, he presents their spiritual dilemma in terms to which the crowd could relate — especially a crowd of farmers and vinekeepers. All the proper agricultural techniques were applied: the right area, sunshine, and fertile soil protected from the chaos of the environment by a sturdy wall. The right resources were provided in proper quantity and cultivation done with due care. This was no experiment — it was a long-term investment in hard work.

By all calculations, the grapes should have been exquisite. Instead, the project was a disaster — literally "stinking grapes." It's kind of like harvesting skunk cabbage instead of coleslaw after a season in the garden. These "stinkers" are described in detail in the verses that follow: hoarding, drunkenness, and pleasure-mongering, all-the-while ignoring the truths of God.

The prophet is quick to name the core sin — contempt toward creation and ingratitude toward the Creator. Not only did Judah not measure up to her promised potential, but the nation had putrefied the very blessings lavished upon them. In the relationship between Yahweh and the covenant people, this was infidelity of the highest order.

I asked for justice, God declares (*mispat* in the Hebrew), and instead got bloodshed (*mispah*). I planted righteousness (*sedaqah*) and instead got a cry (*seaqah*). This harvest was a failure. "What more can be done?" the vinedresser asks the feasting audience.

Nothing. That is the commonsense answer. There is little one can do with rotten crops except toss them on the compost heap in hopes they will fertilize a new and better harvest. And, there is little a faithful God can do with a corrupt and rebellious people except use their coming disaster as a lesson for future generations. This was indeed a hard lesson to learn — a lesson taught with sorrow and tears — tears of the prophet as well as the people.

It is a lesson to which our own nation must pay attention. We are a people planted in rich soil drawing nutrients from the faith and courage of our ancestors. We are blessed with abundant resources, enriched by a wealth of cultures. We have thrived in freedoms that most of the world has never known and we are protected by military capabilities unmatched anywhere on the globe. God has blessed America and yet we are systematically ejecting God out of our public life. The Ten Commandments can no longer be viewed in our courts, biblical religion is no longer accepted in our schools, and religious symbols are not welcome as part of our public holiday celebrations. Like those ancient Hebrews, we are in danger of forgetting our covenant past and polluting our divinely bestowed blessings.

This is a lesson to which the church must give heed. Most of us sit comfortably in our padded pews. We are surrounded by beauty and ample material possessions. We worship in freedom and (with few exceptions) safety. We are not persecuted or harassed for our beliefs. By all calculations, we should expect to grow and thrive, to produce spiritual fruit of spectacular quality; but not many do. Christ commands us to invite others in but instead we chase them out. Rather than the sweet wine of communion and grace, we offer the putrid vinegar of criticism, hurtful words, and indifferent attitudes.

Isaiah does not condemn his own people for their failure to measure up so much as for the corrupting of their God-given goodness. In far too many congregations across too many denominations, the sweet vines of grace planted by the "great gardener," have yielded "stinking grapes" — the product of our ingratitude and contempt of God's love. Material blessings inspire greed instead of generosity. Political power produces moral bullying rather than justice for the outcast, and pluralism yields an "anything goes" attitude (so long as it's not offensive to someone).

What is God to do with such produce? The commonsense answer is, "Pitch it!"

Here is the amazing part: God doesn't. God doesn't discard us even though we try to discard one another. God refuses to burn the field and start anew, at least not yet. The protective wall still stands, and we are protected from our enemies and the world's raging chaos that threatens to undo us.

We have to ask, "Why not?" But Easter people know the answer: It is *Jesus.*

Jesus wrote for us a new covenant, sealed in his life's blood. He has taken the "stinking grapes" of our sin and "trampled out the vintage" of forgiveness and new life. "This is my blood, shed for you and for many for the forgiveness of sins. And as often as you drink it — remember me."

What kind of song is best sung to a cheating lover? Many a wounded heart might respond with the title made famous by Travis Tritt, "Here's A Quarter, Call Someone Who Cares." But through Jesus, God has taken away our "beatin' and cheatin'" lyrics and has sung to us instead a most amazing love song.

Regardless of the time or language, music has an almost supernatural power to affect the human soul and even change the course of the human community. Of all the songs ever composed and all the singers who ever sang, none can compare with Christ. His divine love song was sung from the cross of Calvary and resounds in the triumph of the empty tomb. The melody still rings on the lips of those whose lives he has restored and it promises hope for our human destiny.

*There's within my heart a melody Jesus whispers sweet
and low:
Fear not, I am with thee, peace, be still, in all of life's
ebb and flow.
Jesus, Jesus, Jesus, sweetest name I know,
Fills my every longing, keeps me singing as I go.*
— "There's Within My Heart A Melody,"
words and music by Luther B. Bridgers, 1910

319

**Proper 16**
**Pentecost 14**
**Ordinary Time 21**
**Jeremiah 1:4-10**

# The Hard Task Of Truth-telling

Carrie's[1] high school guidance counselor noticed she had been acting out a bit in school recently. She had appeared depressed and had been having some authority issues over rules and such. The guidance counselor set Carrie up with a local pastor who had been volunteering a few hours each Friday after a teen suicide a few months before. Most of the other students who came to see the pastor just needed someone to listen to their usual teen issues and heartaches. But, shortly into their time together, Carrie began to open up about some real grown-up problems. In due course she revealed that she was, for the most part, raising herself as well as a younger sibling — preparing meals (when food could be found), doing laundry, and getting them both up and dressed for school each day. Her mom and live-in boyfriend were usually high, drunk, or both.

The pastor knew the authorities needed to be notified, but Carrie was terrified of just what would become of her and her family. By law, the neglect had to be reported, but the pastor was hesitant to force the aftermath of this notification upon the teen without her consent. For the next ninety minutes the two wrestled with just what to do next.

This woman-child was also wrestling with her faith in a God she'd only heard about but never known. She was not convinced this God even existed, let alone loved her. In the end she chose to trust the pastor and the school staff who sought to help. She found the courage to tell the truth. Child welfare was notified and the intervention was begun. Some of her fears materialized and she

321

did, in fact, experience some repercussions. There was no storybook ending; but with the help from friends she didn't know she had she found within herself a strength she never knew existed. It wasn't "happily-ever-after" but she did live through it, and was eventually able to laugh again.

Carrie's story is all too familiar, unfortunately. Even in her small rural school her experience is not unique. Other children, even younger than she, in any number of other places, are daily forced into these kinds of hard decisions — finding the courage to seek out help and to speak the truth about alcohol and drug use, sexual exploitation, and domestic violence in their homes and families.

Youth, like adults, quite often don't know what they are able to do until the moment comes when their "metal" is tested. Most are terrified by uncertainty and a sense of inadequacy to live into what must be done or to speak what must be told. But when they step up to the task, they gain strength that can last a lifetime.

Jeremiah was one such youngster. We don't know exactly how young. The Hebrew word can mean any age from infant to teen. Little else is known for sure beyond a few brief verses beginning the book that bears his name. He came from Anathoth, we are told — the village to which David's friend and priest, Abiathar, was banished by King Solomon. We can only speculate how, or if, such history played a factor in Jeremiah's own tension with royal authority in his adult years.

Just where he was when called into service we are not told. We know only that God initiated the encounter. "The word of the Lord came to me," he would later relate. This was no mystic teen at a youth retreat on a quest for divine truth. Like Abraham, Moses, and Gideon before him, it was God who issued the draft notice by name.

It was not a commission Jeremiah would have chosen for himself. His family lineage may well have prepared him to be a priest perhaps, to offer sacrifices in the Jerusalem temple and pronounce God's blessing upon those who still came to worship. He could have made a decent living in the quiet safety of the temple institution. But to proclaim God's word of judgment — to announce the doom and destruction of that temple, of the world as he knew it — this was a task most adults would not desire. For a youngster like Jeremiah such a message must have seemed downright terrifying, especially when the orders were coming directly from the Almighty. Like Moses and Gideon before him, and countless others who would be called thereafter, Jeremiah recognized immediately that God's plan needed some adjustments — like, "Hey! umm, you got the *wrong person* to carry this off. I haven't even started speech class, yet!" In the presence of such a holy and awesome God, and given the cosmic nature of the message, which of us would *not* claim to be vocally impaired, if not totally tongue-tied?

Notice how unimpressed God seems to be with Jeremiah's logical objections. No lightning bolts or angry thunder are emitted from heaven, no "how dare you defy me!" No divine anger, but not much sympathy, either. Only the assurance of God's providence is given. "I will put the words into your mouth." It would be easier, perhaps, if God would promise success rather than just presence. Something like, "Don't worry, they'll love you. It'll be great," would bolster so much more willingness on the part of Jeremiah, or any one of us. Instead he gets, "I will be with you to deliver you." To some folks' way of thinking, that implies hazardous duty rather than a good time had by all.

Few rational people, young or old, are eager to engage in the hard and thankless job of truth-telling — particularly if pronouncing the truth brings pain to those we love. Condemning the sins of our enemies or nameless strangers can bring satisfaction to some, but announcing doom to a nation or a community to which we ourselves belong — that is tough duty. The spiritually wise have learned that, usually, the harder it is to speak words of judgment — the more ache that pronouncement brings to our hearts — the more likely it is that the message is of godly origin instead of human vindictiveness. The harder it is for a prophet to speak the message, the more it is likely that the prophet speaks the truth.

To speak the truth even when it breaks our hearts — such a divine calling prompts few volunteers. Yet, day after day, countless numbers are called to just such service:

- children like Carrie who find the courage to report domestic abuse and neglect;
- the battered wife who confides in her pastor;
- the corporate manager who risks his livelihood to blow the whistle on professional misconduct;
- the athlete who tells the truth about steroid abuse amongst his closest teammates; and
- the factory worker who risks destruction of the town's economy by reporting an environmental or safety hazard.

From time to time God calls nearly all of us to the hard task of truth-telling, even when it means alienating those we love. Most of us recognize our own inadequacy to such a task and offer our own form of protest. Not everyone answers the summons. Jeremiah did. Some might wonder why.

It was God's promise to be present that turned the tide from Jeremiah's fear and self-doubt to empowered obedience. "I will be with you. I will put the words in your mouth." God had more confidence in Jeremiah than Jeremiah had in himself. The one who made Jeremiah knew better than any just what Jeremiah was made of, and that was all that was necessary. Jeremiah came to understand it wasn't about his own abilities or even his flaws.

It wasn't about Jeremiah at all — it was about God. It always is. It is about God's passion for righteousness and God's unwillingness to let Judah (or any of us) continue to live a lie, because living the lie will ultimately bring its own destruction.

It is no different today. Regardless of the denominational affiliation or theological perspective, the church, is called, as Jeremiah was called, to the thankless and often painful duty of truth-telling. Unfortunately, in far too many of our churches what is passed off as prophecy is hardly more than badgering those who believe or behave differently with threats of divine retribution. We engage in far too much condemnation and far too little enlightenment. Real prophecy, the truly courageous truth-telling inspired by God, consists of denouncing the lies our own people most desperately want to believe, in casting a vision few are able to see, and in illuminating a path hardly anyone wants to follow.

Where does that path invite us to go? What is the hard task to which the church is uniquely called today?

In this world of armed conflict, we are called to live "pro-peace" instead of "anti-war," to practice what we believe to be right rather than merely condemn those we think are wrong. We are called to model "the more excellent way" of mercy and compassion.

In a world where "money is power," we are called to advocate for the poor and disabled, whose concerns and needs are usually the first to get erased from our public budgets and consciousness. In a world of "better living through science" the church is required to point to realities beyond that which can be seen or measured.

In a society fragmented by issues like abortion, capital punishment, and "right-to-die," we are called to proclaim a message that is both "pro-life" and "pro-choice" by inspiring and empowering others to "choose life."

The church is called to expose all these false idols by pointing to the one, true God. Not only must we refuse to give homage to whatever would claim our ultimate loyalty, but we must strive to live in loyalty to the Christ who ultimately claims us.

Who of us is eager to assume such a task? Who of us is adequate to speak such invisible truths? Like Jeremiah and his fellow prophets before us, we plead our own incompetence and beg to be discharged from such service.

But God is not so willing to excuse us from duty, because God is unwilling to let the word go unspoken or the truth go unproclaimed. God is no more willing to let us perish in our lies than God was willing to let Jeremiah's audience abide in theirs.

Each of us, at some point in our life, is called upon to do "tough stuff" — to make hard decisions, to proclaim painful truths, to expose convenient lies, and to live by unpopular standards. In those moments we receive from God no assurances of success or rewards for endurance. All we are promised is God's sustaining presence. Amidst our protests of fear and self-doubt all we get is the knowledge that the God who made us knows what we are made of, and believes in us even more than we believe in ourselves. We find the courage to speak the word, which comes from beyond us because we, too, discover that in the end it is not about us — it is about God.

And that alone is enough.

---

1. Carrie is a fictional name.

Proper 17
Pentecost 15
Ordinary Time 22
Jeremiah 2:4-13

# Have We Been "Slicked"?

In many small towns across America the annual Volunteer Fireman's Fair is the social event of the year, or at least it used to be. In days gone by, a typical carnival might have the usual carousel or Ferris Wheel, sometimes pony rides, and always there were the games of chance. (Today we might frown upon these as "gambling" — but back then it was just small-town fun for a good cause.) Bingo was usually preferred by the adults; but the youngsters had other ideas. For a boy named David in Freeport, Ohio, the hands-down favorite was the nickel toss.

At the time, the county was a world leader in pottery production and the firemen would purchase boxes of "seconds" (dishes and cups with slight imperfections) and extras from the factory in Scio and lay them out on a flat board. The object was to toss a nickel into a bowl or plate or cup or saucer and thus win the dish. One could make an evening of this game and take home a set of dishes to boot. Young David, and others like him, could easily spend $5 worth of nickels for $1 worth of mismatched dishes. Not really a good deal, his siblings tried to convince him, but he kept at it year after year, proudly bringing his treasures home for Mom — cups and saucers, meat plates and soup bowls, dinner plates and salad bowls.

Today, this mismatched pottery sits amongst the most prized pieces in his mother's cupboard — to be treasured more than the finest china. But at the time the family had a different attitude.

"You got 'slicked,' " they would say. "Snookered" is the expression used by others. The phrase was a local one derived from

327

one of those town characters found in nearly every community. People called this particular gentleman "Slick" or "Slicky," because he'd developed a reputation as a wheeler-dealer who nearly always got the better end of the bargain he offered. He just had a way of talking people into things. You kind of figured that folks would know better after a while, but they just kept dealing. Fall for the smooth talk once and people might have sympathy, but after that the local folks would just shake their heads and say, "You got slicked!"

We all get "slicked" from time to time. It happens when we give up something valuable in exchange for what is cheap, like tossing away $1 worth of nickels to get a ten-cent coffee cup. Most of us get cheated from time to time regardless of how carefully we live; but sometimes we plunge right into a bad decision based on half-truths and flowery promises we want to believe.

How often in our own lives have we given up what is truly valuable for the cheap stuff — like routinely giving up time with our children for that time-and-a half overtime pay, or trading fidelity in marriage for a temporary fleeting passion? As one preacher remarked, "I've never heard anyone at the end of their life say 'I wish I'd worked more hours' or 'I wish I hadn't wasted so much time playing with my kids.' " How often have we ourselves exchanged the glory of a sunset for a recliner and the evening news?

Then come matters of the spirit. How easily and readily we exchange an encounter with the Almighty for a sit-com and commercials, or a morning of Sunday worship for an extra hour of sleep. Too many folks have listened to the smooth talk and empty promises in the world around us, and too many of us have invested our lives in that which is useless and fleeting. At day's end, we feel empty and cheated, never daring to admit we've been "slicked."

When the prophet Jeremiah looked around in his own place and time, he recognized that his own people were getting "slicked." Concerned with self-preservation, they were investing their life's energy in the acquisition of material possessions while starving their widows and orphans. In their quest for "homeland security" they were seeking to bolster the military budget but ignoring the sick and the elderly. Kings and courtiers were cutting political deals for profit and safety and then conveniently forgetting their promises when the winds shifted.

The issues were not just secular or political. No such thing as separation of church and state existed in ancient Judah. Cutting a deal for protection with Babylon included honoring their deities in addition to financial tribute to their king. Pledging loyalty to Egypt meant offering obeisance to their gods as well. To those nations who worshiped many gods it was no big deal — the cost of doing business. But for Judah — the nation that on Mount Sinai had pledged to serve no God but Yahweh — such a betrayal amounted to adultery.

Jeremiah spelled out God's grief and anger over the nation's conniving ways. The corruption pervades all levels of the social realm:

> *The priests don't seek God, the courts don't know God's law, the leaders defy God's rules and even the prophets speak for other gods.*
> *... they went after worthlessness and became worthless.*
> *... they have forsaken me, the fountain of living waters, and hewn out cisterns for themselves, broken cisterns that can hold no water.* — Jeremiah 2:8, 5, 13

Rural folk who have lived in a dry country such as Palestine get the picture. A functional cistern holds water for a time, just to get you by during a dry spell. It will do for bathing and watering crops and livestock, but its contents are stale and even brackish — certainly not preferable to fresh well water. Abandoning an artesian spring for even a good cistern is definitely a bad choice — but exchanging it for a cracked cistern? That idea just doesn't hold water — *literally!* That is a bargain that can cost you your life. It's bad enough to trade our treasures for the cheap stuff — even worse to exchange it for toxic waste.

"If you are unwilling to serve the Lord, choose this day whom you *will* serve," Joshua had challenged the covenant people when they settled the promised land. "Far be it from us that we should forsake the Lord to serve other gods," the people had sworn (Joshua 24:15).

"Sweet talk" we call it today: Promises made in the passion of the moment only to be forgotten when commitments become inconvenient or unprofitable.

Do we behave any differently?

In our war against terrorism we are trading personal liberty for a promise of safety, the living water of our nation's history for the cracked cistern of national security. "You made my heritage an abomination."

We wave the flag with public ceremony and sing "God Bless America" but remove the Ten Commandments from the public courthouse. "Those who handle the law did not know me."

We have traded biblical truth for political correctness. "The prophets went after things that do not profit."

Precious nickels for cheap pottery. Let's face it: We've been "slicked."

Atheism (literally "no god"), is no more viable an option for our nation's survival than polytheism ("many gods") was for Judah. Both options leave us dry and dusty as a leaky cistern amidst the summer drought. Only God's living water can sustain. Only God's power can protect. Only God's righteousness can withstand the assault of the enemy. Anything or anyone else brings certain destruction.

So where can we go to find the good stuff — the fresh sparkling water that gives life?

"Ho, everyone who thirsts, come to the waters," our Lord invites us (Isaiah 55:1).

Centuries after Jeremiah's time another "young and fearless prophet" would again come to God's people offering the "good stuff." "If you knew who it was [that you are dealing with]," he invited a Samaritan woman at Jacob's well, "... you would have asked, and he would have given you living water."

The invitation is for us as well, and the living water is nothing less than the Spirit of Christ himself. "Whoever believes in me will never be thirsty" (John 6:35). He redeems our broken lives, our fractured integrity, and our empty promises and offers us joy and peace and truth. The bitter waters of despair are made sweet by hope and the toxic waste of anger and resentment is replaced by forgiveness and love. Cheap pottery becomes priceless treasure as he trades our useless attitudes and behaviors for what is precious and enduring. "Invest in me, and you'll never get 'slicked'; trust in me and you'll never lose out."

# God's Eminent Domain

What would you do if you opened your mailbox one day to find a letter from the city or county announcing that you have to move? That land your grandparents worked so hard to till, or for which you struggled so long to purchase is deemed the best land available for a new shopping mall. The appraisers will soon be checking out your home to determine its fair market value and you are expected to vacate.

For a group of homeowners in New London, Connecticut, this nightmare became reality when the city attempted to force them to sell their property to make way for a hotel and other private facilities. In June of 2005, the U.S. Supreme Court ruled 5-to-4 that their local government (and yours) has the power to confiscate private property, not only for public projects like roads and parks, but also in the name of economic development. A lot of folks disagree.

This authority, known as "eminent domain" is not new. Included in our Constitution's Fifth Amendment on private property is a "takings clause" which permits such confiscation for the purpose of roads, bridges, and public infrastructure like utility easements. What makes this decision different is that now governments are permitted to claim property for the benefit of private enterprise rather than public use alone. Opponents fear that the private property of poor and middle-class communities has been further jeopardized.

Most of us are not strangers to the impact of eminent domain. In the 1930s many farmers in Ohio's Muskingum River Watershed were forced to sell their homesteads for the cause of flood control. Whole towns were demolished as dams were constructed. Later, the Interstate Highway System would claim even more homes and farms, all in the name of progress. In 1960, the movie, *Wild River*, starred Montgomery Clift and Lee Remick. It depicted the plight of similar folks in the Tennessee River Valley. The tension focused on a sensitive and compassionate TVA agent (played by Clift), called in to remove an elderly matriarch who stubbornly refused to leave her ancestral home in the flood plain. Here were the graves of her husband and children and the home she had known all her days. Here it was that she intended to die. The movie called into question many assumptions and values of a changing country, and probed the tension between personal rights and public progress. As with most real-life stories about these events, the ending was bittersweet.

We, the people, determined long ago that roads, public recreation, electric power, and public utilities are all good things that come with a human price. Now shopping centers fit into this category as well.

Regardless of how we feel about eminent domain, it is here to stay, but in today's scripture lesson, the prophet Jeremiah reminds his nation about a greater and higher eminent dominion that must be recognized, even by the Supreme Court. To quote the psalmist, "The earth is the Lord's and the fullness thereof."

To assert God's claim to eminent domain Jeremiah uses a story from his own everyday experience, a kind of living parable. Perhaps we can walk with him a while as he journeys to the potter's workshop. Take a moment to look around to see the various bowls and pitchers in various stages of the process — some dried and awaiting the fire, perhaps a few finished pieces on display, and maybe even some that are cast aside as cracked or broken. At the center of it all is the potter himself, his attention fixed on the wheel and its clay. Watch with Jeremiah as the potter spins this lump, as it rises and takes its shape through the slight movements of the potter's fingers. A flick of the wrist, a slight movement in the fingers, and the clay becomes a bowl, maybe then a pitcher or vase. Another shift of the hands and it all collapses on itself and is again just a lump of clay with entirely new possibilities — all of it at the imaginative whim of the craftsman.

Here amidst the daily labor of an ordinary potter, Jeremiah discerns the wisdom of his nation's extraordinary God. "You are like clay in the crafter's hand," God says. It was precious clay — called into existence from the barren womb of Sarah and Abraham through a simple promise spoken by God. It was imported clay — scraped together by God's own mighty hand from the weak and helpless tribe of slaves, baptized in the waters of the Jordan, purified by a daily struggle for survival in their desert wanderings, and shaped by judges, prophets, and kings under God's watchful eye and attentive hand.

But this vessel proved to be less than intended. Marred by religious idolatry and political corruption its shape was contorted and now useless for its original purpose — to offer praise to God, and justice and hope to humanity. It was time to redesign. "Am I not free to do with this vessel as I choose?" God asks.

God's claim of eminent domain runs contrary to our twenty-first-century-American convictions. As others have pointed out, the Frank Sinatra classic "I Did It My Way" is popular sentiment in our culture, albeit poor theology. "It's my life" (or body), we say, "and I can do as I choose." Drugs and alcohol, sexual promiscuity, gluttony — "Don't tell me what to do. My destiny is in my own hands." Such sentiments are perhaps a comfortable security blanket, but they are no more realistic than, "It's my property and I can do what I please with it." It all sounds good until you test it out in court.

The people of Jeremiah's Judah snuggled protectively in the notion that they controlled their own destiny. When it came to politics, their leaders bargained with pharaohs and kings for the best deal they could get; and then changed sides when it suited their homeland security needs. Political wheels were greased with the sweat and blood of the poor and the powerless. Their covenant to worship Yahweh alone was watered down for the sake of the practical, the efficient, and the politically correct.

They paid a heavy price: Jerusalem sacked, the temple destroyed, their leaders deported. At the hands of their enemies the religious and governmental institutions that defined their world were demolished. Families were uprooted and sent into exile. They discovered the hard way just how fragile their dominion really was.

It is a lesson not lost on us today: like when our medical tests confirm our worst fears, or when our spouse suddenly walks out on the marriage. It is a lesson we learn when our child ends up in prison, or worse yet, the morgue. It is a rude awakening when the hurricane or earthquake or flood claims our earthly possessions, our community, even our lives. Our destiny is *not* within our grasp — and we *hate* that!

Neither is our destiny at the peril of merciless forces or cruel fate or even the Supreme Court. Amidst the agony of their exile, Judah found hope within Jeremiah's words. The same potter who destroys the vessel with a flick of the wrist has the power to rebuild and reshape the demolished lump of clay into a new work of art. Amidst the grief and confusion of life's chaos, they were taunted and tempted to believe that God is either powerless or cold-hearted. Ultimately, they chose another path. They chose to affirm, in the words of the children's prayer, "God is great *and* God is good."

Like it or not, in the end, true eminent domain is God's alone. When we acknowledge this fact, we are freed from our futile strivings for self-domination and from the anxiety such strivings produce. We cannot determine our own destiny; we can only receive it from the hand of God. When we relinquish all illusions of self-determination, we are freed to hear the good news: God is working on our behalf to give to us what we can never achieve on our own terms. Jesus gave his life to reveal God's love, God's goodness — and Easter revealed God's power. When called to obedience, even unto death, Jesus did not resist; and his affirmation of God's eminent domain changed the course of human history. And, just as miraculously, he has changed us!

Whether or not our culture chooses to acknowledge it, God is Lord of all creation and ultimately our human destiny is in God's hands alone. It's a good thing. Left to our own schemes we know the mess we can make. We can either deny this reality or we can yield to the Potter's hand. We can continue our futile efforts at self-domination, which can only end in brokenness and ruin, or we can work within God's eminent domain and experience the joy and peace of being who God envisioned us to be.

"Am I not free to do with you as I choose?" God asks each of us today.

Absolutely.

In the words of the hymn,

> *Have thine own way, Lord! Have thine own way!*
> *Hold o'er my being absolute sway.*
> *Fill with thy Spirit, till all shall see*
> *Christ only, always, living in me.*
>
> — "Have Thine Own Way, Lord,"
> words by Adelaide Pollard, 1902

# Tales Of The Spiritually Stupid

"Stupid is as stupid does." So says the now-famous quote from the movie, *Forrest Gump*. Nowadays, it would seem stupidity is an epidemic. Just type the words "stupid people dot com" into your internet search engine and you can find loads of websites where people share their tales, like the man who wrote: "My ex-wife once called me at a bar and asked, 'Where are you?' "

Another favorite story is told about a high school teacher who assigned her class a paper on World War Two. On the date it was due, one boy came in empty handed. "I went to every library I could find, but I found NOTHING on World War Two. I found a lot of books on World War 11, though."

Makes you wonder.

Most laughable are stories of the criminally dumb. Nearly any law officer could write a book on these. The following one came through the grapevine from a patrolman in Ohio in the aftermath of Hurricane Katrina. He was assigned to security detail at a New Orleans Wal-Mart that had been looted. Several days after the flooding ceased, a man brought a plasma television back to the store's customer service department. He'd "picked it up a few days earlier" (those were his words). But when he took it home and plugged it in the television didn't work, so he was bringing it back for replacement. It was obvious to all that the television had been stolen. The officer had a tough time keeping a straight face as the store rep explained that this problem was to be expected since that part of the city still had no electricity.

An Ann Arbor newspaper crime column reported that a man walked into a Burger King in Ypsilanti, Michigan, at 5 a.m., flashed a gun, and demanded cash. The clerk turned him down because he said he couldn't open the cash register without a food order. When the man ordered onion rings, the clerk said they weren't available for breakfast. The man became so frustrated he walked away.

Dumber still is the guy who walked into a Louisiana Circle-K, put a $20 bill on the counter, and asked for change. When the clerk opened the cash drawer, the man pulled a gun and asked for all the cash in the register, which the clerk promptly provided. The man took the cash from the clerk and fled, leaving the $20 bill on the counter. The total amount he got from the drawer? — $15.

Stupid behavior even has its own competition these days. In recent years, the Annual Darwin Awards have honored "the least evolved among us." Sometimes the competition is deadly — as in the 2005 winner. "When his 38-caliber revolver failed to fire at his intended victim during a hold-up in Long Beach, California, a would-be robber did something that can only inspire wonder. He peered down the barrel and tried the trigger again. This time it worked."

You have to laugh; but it makes you want to cry. These are somebody's children here.

Criminally stupid is one thing, but the spiritually foolish are another matter entirely, and with equally devastating consequences. Just ask the prophet Jeremiah. Year after year, he watched and warned his nation about the consequences of idolatry and religious corruption, of economic injustice and ecological abuse. His pleas fell on deaf ears.

In an earlier time, when Assyria had assailed Jerusalem, the walls had held, the supplies lasted, and the political winds had shifted before full power could be brought to bear. When the enemy departed many rejoiced that Yahweh had come to the rescue the chosen people, sparing the throne of David. Yet even as they gloried in God's power, they neglected God's covenant and its moral demands. The people continued their pagan worship ceremonies, and their leaders continued their flirtatious courtship with neighboring nations. Kings pledged their allegiance and a hefty tribute to whoever could offer the best protection; citizens offered their sacrifices to whichever god they deemed most expedient to meet their needs. Pagan worship thrived while the widows and orphans wasted away for lack of public compassion. Many fell into a false sense of security, believing that because God had spared Jerusalem and its people in the past, the city and its citizens remained inviolate forever. Not funny at all — but extremely foolish.

God declares, "For my people are foolish, they do not know me; they are stupid children, they have no understanding. They are skilled in doing evil, but do not know how to do good" (Jeremiah 4:22).

Such foolishness can only lead to tragedy and suffering. As Jeremiah looked toward his nation's future, he saw only death and destruction: the earth "waste and void," the heavens "had no light," the foundations of the earth shaken to the core. The fruitful land lay deserted and the cities were in ruin. From the depths of his soul, Jeremiah knew these desolations were not the victory of deities superior to Yahweh — a sign of God's weakness in protecting the nation — as some would later claim. This devastation was, instead, the ordained fate of the spiritually stupid. And Jeremiah wept, even as God wept. "Stupid children" they may have been, yet still they belonged to God.

Sadly enough, such foolishness is with us yet. Only a generation ago, Jeremiah's graphic images of quaking mountains and hills moving to and fro became a literal reality as men split the atom and its power was released in a mushroom cloud in America's southwest desert. Not long afterward, Hiroshima and Nagasaki became "cities laid in ruins." Images of the planet plunged into darkness with no light from the heavens have shifted from poetic language to an all-too-real possibility in our own world.

In the days since then, humans have not only split the atom but we have spliced the genetic code and trod on other divine mysteries, as well. Designer babies may soon be an option for those who can pay. Gene-specific germ warfare (killer viruses which can target a specific ethnic or racial group) may well be added to future war arsenals. Jet travel in the modern age means a deadly virus can be passed around the globe in a matter of hours.

"Miracles" have become human terrain while God is increasingly pushed from the public arena. While much good has been accomplished by the human pursuit of knowledge and control, we have also placed our own survival in jeopardy. Global warming, ozone depletion, worldwide pandemics are very real consequences of spiritual foolishness. We have usurped God's authority while failing to attain God's wisdom and in so doing invited judgment upon ourselves.

Yet spiritual foolishness need not be as large-scale as all that. Examples are evident in our own churchyard. Spiritual stupidity, like any other kind, happens when we don't stop to think about the long-term consequences of our actions, or when we refuse to listen to the warnings of others when the truth is right in front us. And believe this: We can be as obstinate and dense in our church relationships as any Darwin Award champion. Call it a "failure to evolve."

Pause for a moment to consider what we might call "stupid church behaviors" and most of us could fill a page or even two. To give a few examples:

- Those acrimonious theological arguments at ecclesiastical conferences when some people *quote* the Bible without having actually *read* it.
- Those "hissy-fits" made in the pew regarding noisy children or stains on the carpet of the youth room by people who then ask the pastor why the church has so few children. Duh!
- Church members who oppose making their building accessible to persons with handicapping conditions because, "We don't have anybody like that who comes here." Of course not — they can't get in the building!

When one church council adopted a goal to increase participation by children and youth, the pastor suggested the congregation start an after-school program. "Many of these kids get off the bus in our parking lot," the pastor observed. "Some of them stick around and play at our basketball hoop."

"But those kids don't belong to our church," came one member's objection.

Okay — that was sort of the point!

Then there's the pastor in Illinois who, like many others, scheduled her mornings in the office and afternoons doing hospital calls and home visitation. At her annual evaluation, part of the congregation complained they could never reach her because she was always out and about while others said she spent too much time stuck in the office.

RIGHT!

Makes you wonder.

If you want to talk about a "failure to evolve" consider the story of one church member who, while visiting friends, had been invited to attend a thriving United Methodist church in Los Angeles. She returned to Ohio rather indignant because the church was packed on their arrival and they were seated in the very back while the local street people, prostitutes, and addicts were given room in the front. Some of "those people" even participated in the service. She handed her pastor a newspaper article on the congregation and its pastor, inquiring whether this church received any of her church's apportionment dollars. If so, she was solidly against paying such mission askings. She did not want *her* dollars going to support such a thing.

Hello! Wonder where this church got such a notion? Could it be from someone who ate with tax-collectors and healed lepers with his touch?

Tales of the spiritually stupid: We've all heard them, even witnessed them. Rest assured these stories are not fiction. We have experienced such things in our own congregation. Could be we've been the source of a few "stupid church behaviors" ourselves — like when we invest our life's time and energy in the things of earth rather than the people of God, or when we care more about the church building than the ministry that happens there, or when we stop focusing on our relationship with Jesus only to be sidetracked by our doubts or fears or personal agendas.

"My people are foolish," we could well hear God say about us today. "They have no understanding." How sad it is — the pain and the heartache caused by our own stubborn pride and wayward actions. Makes you wonder how the church has survived all these years. Yet, miraculously we are here.

Stupid children we might be, but we belong to God. Suffer the consequences of our foolishness we shall, but God has a plan to save us, and all creation as well. And God does not relent either in judgment or in salvation. "I have not relented, nor will I turn back" (Jeremiah 4:28). In this, we have hope.

In later years, after terrors foreseen by Jeremiah had come to pass, a devastated people looked back through pain and sorrow. It was Jeremiah who helped them make sense of it all and it was his words, which inspired hope in Yahweh's redemptive power.

This we profess above all else: Redemption is God's specialty. "For God so loved the world, he gave his only Son," the Bible says. When all the hatred and fear and corruption in the human arsenal had been inflicted upon the Son of God in a place called Calvary, he bore it upon himself and took it to the grave. Scripture tells us the mountains quaked and the heavens grew dim, and the community of disciples sank into despair, much like the experience of Jeremiah. Then God raised Jesus from the dead, and all that hatred and corruption came to nothing. As the Apostle Paul would later write, "God's foolishness is greater than human wisdom." In this we have confidence.

When times are at their worst, when all we see in our church or community or in the mirror brings us to the brink of despair, we do not lose hope because God did not lose hope for the world. Because Christ does not give up on us in our foolishness, neither shall we give up on ourselves or others. Releasing our folly and clinging to Jesus we find forgiveness and hope for new life, not for ourselves alone but for the entire world. In this we have joy.

# Listening For The "Ching-ching"

When television producer, Dick Wolf, introduced a new "cop show" in the early 1990s, he could hardly have predicted it would lead to one of the biggest television sensations of its time. In the fifteen years or so since its first episode, the familiar "ching-ching" sound and opening credits of *Law And Order* have become cultural icons equivalent to Archie Bunker's *All In The Family* living room or the scrambling medical staff of *M\*A\*S\*H*. Since the original *Law And Order* debut *Special Victims Unit*, *Criminal Intent*, *Trial By Jury*, and *Conviction* have been added to the lineup with others on the storyboard. Predictably, each series has its own website where fans can log-in for the latest script details and chat about their favorite detectives and lawyers. No doubt we will one day see these characters in the Smithsonian Museum.

Part of the appeal of this series is undoubtedly the fact that these "dedicated police officers and district attorneys" always find the culprit and almost always are successful in putting the "bad guy" (or girl) behind bars. Even when they can't prove their case, the criminal usually gets a serious "comeuppance" by show's end. Viewers get a vicarious satisfaction in seeing justice executed and order restored — at least until next week.

For the most part, we take great satisfaction in seeing others pay for their sins, criminal and otherwise, particularly if we have been a victim. Reality-based court shows like *Traffic Court* and people like Judge Judy have been with us for decades — although not nearly as popular as the fiction. Seeing justice, even the make-believe kind, carried out before our eyes, helps our world to feel more stable, particularly amongst the chaos of our modern times.

Revenge can be sweet, even if it isn't so dramatic. Lots of you may remember uttering the so-called Parents' Prayer: "May you grow up and have children who are just like you." So many times this blessing (or curse) comes true and grandparents just smile knowingly when their children relay the misadventures of their own offspring. "Now I know why you did thus-and-such," the elders are told in a kind of prayer of confession. Rather than offering absolution, these elders often reply with an unsympathetic, "I told you so!"

Sometimes we would rather not see it happen, though, especially when the dire warnings involve our children or other loved ones. Reading about a tough sentence for a DUI or child abuse can bring satisfaction to a victim of these crimes, but for the family of the perpetrator, the pain is tremendous — even when they are a willing party in the prosecution's case.

What courage and conviction it takes for a spouse to report domestic abuse or a parent to have one's own child arrested for substance abuse. Dr. Phil occasionally does "intervention episodes" which focus on getting family members to confront addicts or offenders, forcing folks into action with the hope of empowering healing. The results (and the ratings) are great if the offenders acquiesce, but the pain is excruciating if they don't.

Perhaps some of you have been caught in that nightmare — loving someone who, for whatever reason, is hell-bent on self-destruction and taking others along for the ride. Whether it's a marriage, a friendship, or an employment situation, the most sensible solution is to get out — especially if you or others are in harm's way. How do we cope and what do we do when the "prophecy" comes to pass and the person gets their wish? Sometimes "told you so" is too sad to say — even if it is warranted.

In biblical tradition, Jeremiah is known as "the weeping prophet." More than any of the others, he expressed the heartache, the tragedy, the sorrow of being right in his truth-telling. For years, he warned his people about the consequences of worshiping false idols and abusing the poor and the helpless. For years, he had ranted and raved to kings about placing their trust in political gamesmanship rather than the God of the covenant. For years, he had condemned the religious institution and its leaders for receiving the people's sin offerings without condemning sin or teaching righteousness. Sometimes, it is as devastating to be proven right as to be wrong in our warnings.

> For the hurt of my people, I am hurt; I mourn, and dismay has taken hold of me.
> Oh, that my head were a spring of water and my eyes a fountain of tears; so that I might weep day and night for the slain of my poor people!
> — Jeremiah 8:21; 9:1

In this particular text from Jeremiah, it is hard to know whose words they actually are — the prophet's or God's. As long or loud as the judgment had been proclaimed, neither Jeremiah nor God has satisfaction when the judgment came to pass and the Assyrian Army began its siege. Later, the city and its temple would be razed and the leaders executed or deported. While escape would have been the most sensible course of action, Jeremiah remained with his people and suffered with them through the whole catastrophe. And, while God had every right to nullify the covenant promise in response to the people's blatant rebellion and religious apostasy, God chose to suffer with them amidst the exile.

This kind of lament in the scriptures serves as an affirmation of faith about who God is. In other non-biblical religions the supreme deity is impersonal and dispassionate — beyond the suffering of this physical existence. In many of these other religious traditions, the path to salvation lays in denying or escaping such passion and pain; and ultimately to escape the human existence altogether. Even among some who profess a biblical faith this is still an "end-goal." In some people's understanding, God is all about a kind of dispassionate policing of human behaviors, catching the "offenders" and ensuring they are brought to cosmic justice. Others experience a more personal, but vindictive, God who is "out to get me." This divine prosecution is sometimes for real guilt in our moral failures like marital infidelity and such; or, sometimes, to give meaning to various misfortunes unconnected with our human behavior, like natural disasters which destroy our communities and take innocent lives.

Even those of us who have committed ourselves to faithful living by God's commands may wonder at times if such faith makes any difference. We pray for years for the soul of a friend or loved one; we implore God to defend us amidst "office politics"; we tithe faithfully but still struggle to find a job that can pay the bills and provide for the family. We live the wholesome lifestyle prescribed by the scriptures but still experience chronic pain or sickness. We do our best to "trust and obey" but still we sometimes wonder if God even knows or cares.

But clearly the scriptures, both Hebrew and Christian, reflect a God whose heart aches for the abuser as well as the victims; for the lawbreakers as well as the enforcers. That is a place where few of us are willing to go emotionally unless forced there by circumstances in our own lives and families. When the accused is someone we love, even when they are guilty as charged, we weep a fountain of tears. And, even when our fountains run dry and all our compassion is spent, God continues to care.

Amidst the grief, the confusion, the chaos, and the uncertainty, Jeremiah points the way to God's own heart. This is a God who continues to care even for those of us "hell-bent on self-destruction." This is a God who refuses to give up even on us, and who continues to work redemption's plan.

"Is there no balm in Gilead?" the lamenter asks. "Why then has the health of my poor people not been restored?" The region famous for its healing medicine could not produce that which was necessary to heal the wounds of sin and despair. Centuries later an African-American spiritual would answer the prophet's plea:

*There is a balm in Gilead to make the wounded whole;*
*There is a balm in Gilead to heal the sin-sick soul.*

That balm, we profess, is none other than Jesus the Christ, the Great Physician. His was a ministry of touching the untouchable, embracing the social outcast, healing the bent-over, and forgiving the unforgivable. His was a death of suffering for the cause of the kingdom so that the unredeemable might find redemption. And, his was a resurrection which proved God's own commitment to the salvation of humanity.

In Jesus we encounter a God who has not abandoned us even in our sin, but rather has become invested in restoring what has been broken. Our God stands not only for "Law and Order" but for mercy and compassion. Because of that, we find the strength to look beyond our fountain of tears and live for the day when joy shall be restored. Rather than the "ching-ching" of *Law And Order* we await the sound of the trumpet announcing the day when "he will wipe every tear from [our] eyes," when "death will be no more; mourning and crying and pain will be no more, for the first things [will] have passed away" (Revelation 21:4).

# What A Deal: Investing In Hope

What is the most ludicrous business deal you ever got into (or *out of*) just in time?

In the tiny town of Flushing, Ohio, amidst the coalfields of Belmont County, stands a brick building which used to house the Citizens' National Bank. Like a lot of community financial institutions of its day, this bank specialized in small loans made to local farmers, sheepherders, and working-class folks in the nearby area and harbored the hard-earned dollars of their working-class neighbors. Their capital was fortified with investments of some local coal tycoons and a congressman from the area; and for nearly two generations, it served the community well until it was swallowed up by a much larger financial institution from a much larger city. Instead of the local farmers and businessmen who originally constituted the board of directors, financiers who have likely never set foot in the town, and probably couldn't even find it on the map, now operate the bank.

The story of this little bank is not much different from a lot of community banks in lots of small towns across the country that have similarly been bought by larger financial corporations. But what is most noticeable about this bank was its founding date — smack in the middle of the Great Depression!

One has to ask — who would invest money in a financial institution at a time when banks were going belly up and in a place where cash money was so scarce? Yet, that is precisely what this group of farmers, shepherds, and small-business operators did. And, for nearly two generations they succeeded in providing the capital that built homes, purchased equipment, expanded businesses, and paid college tuition for folks in that tiny town. But you have to wonder — in 1931 was it optimism or insanity that inspired the investors?

That kind of investment at that time in history was risky enough, but could anything be more ridiculous than buying property in a war zone? Yet that was precisely the deal offered to the prophet Jeremiah that we read about in this particular text.

The scene is nearly preposterous: the unbeatable army of Babylon surrounds Jerusalem. Jeremiah had been relentlessly foretelling the destruction of Judah. While other so-called prophets had sought to bolster fragile morale by assuring the populace that Yahweh would once again act to spare the Holy City, Jeremiah had stubbornly announced just the opposite message. During a temporary reprieve in the siege he had attempted to leave the city and encouraged others to do so, and consequently he was imprisoned for treason. Some even wanted him dead.

So there he was, under armed guard in the court of King Zedekiah, confined, and helpless — watching his people die of starvation and disease even as they clung to false patriotic hopes. Certainly, he was in no position to be planning his investment portfolio.

Yet, even then and there, Jeremiah discerned that God was still at work. Amidst all that destruction, came a ridiculous real estate proposal. Cousin Hanamel wanted to sell out, and most likely *get* out before all was lost. According to the very covenant tradition that Judah had been so flagrantly ignoring, when a kinsman fell on hard times and was forced to sell his family property, the responsibility fell on the nearest relative to purchase the property and thus keep it in the family. Jeremiah got first option to invest in property that was quite possibly already under foreign domination.

What a deal! Kind of like trying to sell oceanfront property just *before* the hurricane hits. Good strategy if only you can find somebody foolish enough to buy it.

Somehow, Jeremiah sees more than meets the eye. Like those farmers and shopkeepers who pooled their assets to start a bank amidst the Great Depression, Jeremiah could see beyond his present circumstances. Amidst that dark hour, just months before total disaster and the collapse of society as he knew it, Jeremiah changed his tune — from "doom and destruction" to "hope and restoration." This was no speculative business venture or a gamble to make money on Jeremiah's part. This rite of redemption of property had direct spiritual ties to the promise God had once made with Abraham and Isaac and Jacob, and later with Moses and Joshua. Underlying this Jewish redemption tradition was an understanding that the land is not property of any individual, but rather "the earth is the Lord's" given as a heritage to the covenant people.

Under God's orders, Jeremiah invested in the future, and he did so publicly. Even as Judah's social, economic, and legal system crumbled around him, the prophet took extreme care to follow procedure. He weighed out the money (a generous price considering the market) and secured the proper deeds. Then he arranged to preserve the documents, "in order that they may last for a long time." All of this was a public demonstration of confidence — not in the economy, nor in the government, but in the power and compassion of Almighty God. "For thus says the Lord of Hosts, the God of Israel: Houses and fields and vineyards will again be bought in this land." And Jeremiah backed up that confidence with his own savings account (32:14-15).

"Desperate measures for desperate times" we might be inclined to say. What have Jeremiah's words and actions to do with us? Our future is hardly in the same jeopardy. We have no enemy armies assaulting our perimeters, threatening to pillage our treasures, or carry us into captivity. Or do we?

Check out the national dialogue about church-state relations in our country and you'll find a lot of folks sounding the alarm. The present furor in the classroom and courtroom over "Intelligent Design" is a case-in-point. Judeo-Christian values that were once the cornerstone of our society are being challenged in our court system and assaulted in the popular media. Prayer in public schools is nearly a thing of the past (except for exam time!), and the pressure is on to blot out the very mention of God on our coinage, in our pledge to the flag, or at our public gatherings and sporting events. Books, movies, television shows, and public art espouse

353

values and behaviors in direct conflict with biblical commandments, and those who protest such moral corruption are labeled as radicals and told to "lighten up" or "get with the times." When Cecil B. DeMille directed *The Ten Commandments*, his work was received with much more appreciation by his peers than say, Mel Gibson's, *The Passion Of The Christ*, a few decades later — definitely a change in the cultural environment. "Organized Religion" is demonized in contemporary, secular thought much like it was during the Soviet communist revolution a century ago.

At present, mainline churches appear to be the biggest casualties of this modern assault. Traditional liturgies, worship styles, and ecclesiastical structures no longer communicate with the same meaning and power as previous generations. Theological controversies and social issues have fragmented many mainline denominations and sapped their spiritual energy and commitment to mission. Many members, and even clergy, are bailing out — either to other nontraditional fellowships or out of the church altogether. "Mainline Protestantism is dying!" some experts insist.

Most certainly, this challenge is not to be compared with other places on the globe where carrying a Bible or sharing the gospel is considered a capital offense and worship services are disrupted by deadly violence. Compared to that kind of hostility, American Christians are still living on easy street. But, even though the assault is more subdued and ideological, it is nevertheless a growing battle for survival.

Even amongst Christians in healthy congregations, daily living can feel like a siege against our faith. Illnesses like cancer or Alzheimer's disease assail the body; the death of a child cripples the spirit; a layoff from the factory tears at a community's social fabric. Marital infidelity shakes our faith in people. Natural disasters like hurricanes and floods leave us fearful and questioning God's trustworthiness. Like Jeremiah, we often watch helplessly as those around us are destroyed by allegiance to false idols and commitment to faulty values. At such times, investing more of ourselves in a struggling faith life seems about as absurd as Jeremiah buying into the future of Judah (literally) amidst the fiery arrows of the enemy.

What does it take to stand on such faith, to live with such assurance, to hope amidst such despair? Where can we find the confidence to continue to invest ourselves in hope when evidence of impending doom lies all around?

Like Jeremiah, we also stand on a promise: a covenant made by God and sealed in the blood of Christ. Despite the "fightings without and fears within" we have Christ's assurance of forgiveness and the Holy Spirit's presence.

The enemy will continue to besiege in some form or another. At times, such forces may breach the walls of our best defenses and possibly leave us crushed and wounded. The consequences of unfaithful living will have to be dealt with and our lives made accountable to God. These truths are inevitable, but they need not be fatal. Even if (or when) our worst fears about the future materialize, God's promise will not fail. God will continue to abide with us beyond all of it. Our bodies will grow old and die, but our lives are held in Christ. Our sinful actions will continue to create barriers in our human relationships, but Christ will never cease to offer forgiveness. Our social institutions will crumble and fail, but God's providence will continue. Political movements and military strength will rise and fall, but God is still the Master of history. The sun, moon, and stars will eventually implode into nothingness, the experts tell us; but we profess faith in God who is the Lord of creation.

For the founders of that little bank in that little town, investing their hard-earned cash money in the future of their community proved to be a good deal despite the economic climate of the Great Depression. But God offers us so much more. In Christ, we are given the strength to stand on hope when others are bailing out. In faith, we sign the deed to our lives over to him in full view of a skeptical public just as Jeremiah did so long ago. In confidence, we lay his claim on us out for all to see, even as he takes us unto himself to preserve us safe and secure for all eternity.

# Song Sung Blue

Some records are made to be broken — like Olympic speed skating; Cal Ripkin, Jr.'s, most consecutive baseball game appearances; and North Dakota's longest cow chip toss. Other records we'd prefer to let stand — the world's deadliest disaster, or the most active hurricane season, for instance. Years 2004 and 2005 will probably make the books as among the most dramatic in weather history. Hurricanes pounded the southern coast of the USA. Floods and blizzards battered the midwest. Earthquakes devastated parts of central Asia. And one of the deadliest of disasters — the tsunami — decimated whole villages in southeast Asia. Global relief agencies, both governmental and private, were stretched to the breaking point. Some experts are saying even these records might not stand for long.

In late summer of 2005, the wind and water of Hurricane Katrina cut a path of destruction stretching over ninety miles of the Gulf coast. Only a few weeks afterward, Hurricane Rita pounded Texas. Even yet, as the city of New Orleans, Louisiana, continues to mop up and rebuild, images of stranded homeowners atop their houses and frustrated evacuees pleading for help outside the Super Dome continue to linger in the national consciousness. Most of the nation remained glued to their television screens moment by moment as the disaster unfolded. The chaos amongst emergency service providers, the fear, the anger, and the dead bodies shoved aside, the starvation, the disease, the looting, and the violence — all played out live as the world watched on FOX and CNN and the evening news.

357

Although most folks would never recognize it as such, what played out on the airwaves and news commentaries in the ensuing months was what biblical writers knew as lamentation. The term "lamentation" is a written form musicians might call a dirge, such as would be used, or sung at a funeral. The book of the Bible we know as "Lamentations" was just such a dirge, adapted to fit the public forum. Scholars tell us it was originally written to corporately grieve the fall of Jerusalem after eighteen years of siege warfare. The city had been surrounded by Babylonian enemies and its inhabitants left to starve or die of pestilence or violence.

Imagine that, if you can — a city, say New Orleans — cut off from help and public aid — not for a few days or even a week — but for a year and a half. Imagine the condition of the Super Dome after eighteen months of the leaky roof, clogged toilets, and scarce supplies. Well, let's not — the thought is too traumatic to even conceive!

But the similarities are striking: Jerusalem and New Orleans, Judea and Mississippi or Alabama. Cities and people divided by time and geography, yet united by their experience of suffering and destruction — destruction not only of lives and property but the loss of public trust and cultural institutions. The shock, the despair, the blaming, and the search for a reason — whether in ancient Hebrew or American English (or Cajun) — the sentiment is much the same.

Yet, in some ways, the differences are equally striking — at least in the content of the laments. For days and even months after the hurricanes, the television news seemed to lay its lamentation at the feet of the government in general and at the feet of President Bush in particular. Not that earlier failure or oversight or indifference on the part of civic officials were not contributing factors to the overall disaster, but listening to some newscasters one would have thought the president himself had conjured the storm for political gain.

Subsequent investigation revealed there was enough guilt to go around, but assigning blame to the mayor or the governor or even the president just didn't get at the real issue for many. Just why did this happen? Meteorologists explained the science of a hurricane and the Army engineers explained the physics of water pressure on dirt levees. City planners and social analysts could pronounce theories about why so many folks could not or did not get transported to safety. But these answers just were not enough to satisfy the big question: Why did it happen *to us*?

A few religious extremists claimed that the city was experiencing God's wrath in response to convocation of homosexuals the city had welcomed. Others pointed out that a number of church assemblies were scheduled to convene there as well. At least these views, right or wrong, included God. Atheists had to look elsewhere.

How does a secular society, which separates religion from science, answer such a question? In recent years we have gone to battle over the constitutional validity of "one nation under God" in our Pledge of Allegiance and "In God We Trust" upon our currency. But that creates another dilemma: When God is removed from the public picture, who is left to hear the lament? The president may rightfully admit blame for an ill-prepared Federal Emergency Management Agency, but despite what some may want to think, even he cannot control wind and wave and the currents of the jet stream. Who, then, is accountable? Who is there to respond to the wounded and grieving soul when one's whole world has been washed away by a tidal wave, flattened by a tornado, or even devastated by a divorce or an inoperable tumor?

In the face of such calamity, we need to cry, we need to moan, we need to ask why. But who is there to hear when God has been eliminated from the equation?

That is precisely where the Bible departs from the secular worldview. When their world collapsed — when the temple was razed and Jerusalem lay in ruin, the Jewish believers took their grief and anguish directly into God's very presence. Their government could not help — it was literally held captive. Their priests were of no use — the temple and its altar of sacrifice were gone. Only God's Word remained. Only God's promise could sustain.

It took the destruction of Jerusalem and Judea, but the people did return to Yahweh. So far as we know, they did not address their lament to Baal, whom they had once worshiped in the shrines. They cried out to God as they had done in Egypt and Sinai and on Mount

359

Carmel. To their credit, the survivors of the Exile (on the whole) learned from their calamity. They acknowledged their sin and idolatry and asked for forgiveness.

It was this shift in attitude ("repentance" is the biblical term) that made all the difference in the world. They opted to cling to God rather than deny his power or his love. This faith decision not only changed the course of their history but also preserved them as a people and a culture. Their religious reflection on this experience inspired them to write or revise much of the Hebrew Scripture we read today. The faith and hope they found amidst the calamity became the bedrock upon which they built their subsequent faith story.

In the aftermath of personal and communal disaster, our human tendency is to blame everyone else. And it is the tendency of everyone else to blame the victim. Neither approach can diminish the pain — it is real and it is important, but it is also essential that in the face of any calamity we address that pain, that we learn from it, and that we grow through it. Only then can we draw power from it.

Only a few months after the New Orleans tragedy, a small town in West Virginia faced a calamity of its own — a tragedy on a smaller scale but equally devastating. Twelve of its citizens — fathers, sons, brothers, and friends — were trapped in the darkest reaches of the earth after an explosion in the local coalmine. While rescuers worked frantically to save them, an army of government experts and media reporters besieged the community to watch and wait. There in the public forum, in full view of the cameras, was the tiny little community church where the families waited — and prayed — and worshiped! They did not scream at the president, nor bemoan the economic realities, which sent these miners into such an inherently dangerous workplace. They revealed their inner strength and professed their faith in God even when word came that eleven had not survived.

The investigation into the cause of that explosion continues, at the time of this writing, and no doubt some very real human failures will prove to be factors. But, as much as much as we'd like to put human beings in charge of the universe, we are forced to acknowledge there are even yet forces out there that are simply beyond our control — like it or not. We do, however, have a choice in our response to such realities.

Radio commentator, Paul Harvey, closed his post-Katrina commentary with a story about a visit he had once made into the devastated area of Louisiana. He described how once upon a time, hundreds of years earlier, other winds and waves had toppled the magnificent trees of the bayou, leaving them underwater for centuries. Then he described how these fallen trees had been transformed into timber of such strength and beauty that modern loggers would brave the perils of the swamp to mine this underwater treasure. He reflected with awe and a touch of sadness upon the magnificent beauty of the swamp he had visited and how those very trees had tumbled into the depths of the bayou.

Then he finished with this profound observation: "And then the wind blows — and the present is decimated — and the future is renewed."

The Bible records how God once decimated Jerusalem, and how God used that experience to restore the future God had promised. Even now, as we face the calamities, which assail us all from time to time, the question remains: When the winds blow and our present is demolished, can we trust God to do the same for us?

# Sermons On The First Readings

## For Sundays
## After Pentecost
## (Last Third)

### *Profiting From*
### *The Prophets*

## John Wayne Clarke

# Foreword

The sermons contained in this book, with the exception of Deuteronomy, come from the message of the prophets, specifically: Jeremiah, Joel, Habakkuk, Haggai, Isaiah, Daniel, and Deuteronomy.

The prophets saw things to which other people were blind. But, this was not because of some poetic insight, or because of sharp intellect. They were not magicians, nor did they participate in cultic practices. The message they communicated resulted entirely from God's gracious gift to them. What the prophet saw was revealed to him by God. The prophet was not, however, some passive receptacle used by God. The prophet was called upon to be an active player in the unfolding history of God's people.

While they were inseparably linked to the past, they were very much aware of the present. Their writings reflect the "then and there" of their world. They were living in a world that was filled with political, economic, social, moral, and religious contradictions, and they were called upon by God to tell the truth about those contradictions, whatever they may have been.

The prophets stand in a long succession of witnesses that began with Abram. They were indebted to those who came before them in history, especially to the teaching of Moses, on whose foundation they all continued to build. To quote Malachi, "Remember the teaching of my servant Moses, the statutes and ordinances that I commanded him at Horeb for all Israel" (Malachi 4:4).

The sermons that follow attempt to throw light on the historical as well as practical aspects of the message of these giants of biblical history. Those who came before us profited from these prophets, and by the grace of God, we will also.

John Wayne Clarke

# Letters From A Loving Prophet

Jeremiah was the last of the great prophets to minister to the Hebrew people during the days of their political independence. His book is the longest prophetic book in the Hebrew Scripture. Because of the incredibly profound concepts which it contains, and because of the great spiritual advances which Jeremiah charted, he has been called by some the "greatest figure between Moses and Jesus."

In chapter 29, the prophet is writing to the exiles in Babylon. It is a message of hope, a message that contains within it something that had almost been forgotten, that is a message of having a future.

This section of Jeremiah is quite literally a letter of instruction. It is outlining for the captives in Babylon how to move ahead with their lives. The prophet here reminds the people that life cannot come to a halt during troubled times. They are to face the cold, hard fact that they are a people in exile. They are going to be where they are for a long time. They should, therefore, settle down, engage themselves in everyday normal activities that lead to some sense of normalcy. In this chapter, the prophet sheds much light upon his concept of God and religion. It also shows that he is now an impressive and influential person among his people. It is a letter that reveals an amount of raw courage that flies in the face of those who hold the people in bondage. Jeremiah dares to challenge and shatter any illusions and false hopes the exiles may have been told.

These verses, and the ones that follow, disclose that Jeremiah was a man of indomitable faith. He was honest enough to tell the people the cold, hard facts. He was openly pessimistic about the immediate future, but he was optimistic about the longer span of time. He was sure that God had plans for the people and that God would carry those plans to fulfillment.

This chapter also reveals that Jeremiah was a man of penetrating insight. He communicated a truth that the Apostle Paul and, later, New Testament leaders tried so hard to get across and that is that true faith is not dependent upon geographical locality. A person of faith can know God anywhere. That means in captivity in Babylon or in prison in Rome.

This important message also gives us a glimpse of the importance prayer held to the prophet. Jeremiah encourages prayer for the enemy. "... pray to the Lord on its behalf, for in its welfare you will find your welfare" (29:7b). This is the only place in the Hebrew Scripture where this is done. In a very real way, Jeremiah both personalized and universalized the religion of his people.

It is a message that is just as important in our own time as it was in the year in which it was written. All of us face unpleasant situations in life. All of us come to points of distress in our lives, and at times, feel as if there is no good reason to continue. It is hard, at such times, to remember that we were created to be partners with God and that God will not leave us alone. In fact, when we are held within the grip of trouble, it is then, more than any other time, that we are to rely on God in all areas of our lives. We are to pray diligently and move ahead, doing whatever we can to live life, rather than giving up because of fear and uncertainty.

We know we are to rely on God's Word to us for instruction. Jeremiah knew that he had a job to do in communicating to God's children that they would have a life, which was worth living regardless of current circumstances. One of the most important factors in surviving and even thriving while living in captivity was the ability to rely on and respect God.

In our world today, we still live in captivity. Don't get me wrong, we live in the greatest country on earth. But, we also live in a country where we are surrounded on all sides with contrasting ways to live life. Freedom always has a cost attached to it. We are inundated with values that run contrary to God's Word. We, like the

Hebrew people of Jeremiah's time, are faced with an uncertain future. We live in a world where security is no longer assured. Changing times and changing ways of looking at the value of life have caused a rift even between Christian communities. In all conditions of life, it is our wisdom and it is our duty to not throw away the things that have been the anchors of our lives. Jeremiah is telling the Hebrew people to seek the good of the country where they are being held captive. He wants them to know that if they live peacefully, the King of Babylon will protect them. They must, however, demonstrate lives that reflect in goodness and honesty; being patient in allowing God to deliver them in due time.

It is a request and a message that we need to hear today! We too, must live a life of faith, a life that faces the world in which we live with courage and dignity. We, like the people held in captivity, need to see past whatever circumstances seem to be holding us captive.

In many ways, this part of Jeremiah's message reminds me of the prayer that is so much a part of many people's lives that are in turmoil. You have heard this prayer, or you may live with it each day:

> *God grant me the serenity*
> *To accept the things I cannot change,*
> *Courage to change the things I can,*
> *And wisdom to know the difference.*

In some ways, it seems that Jeremiah's message embraces much of what is called the "Serenity Prayer." It is hard for us to accept the things that we cannot change. It was hard for the Hebrew people to whom Jeremiah was writing and it is just as hard for all of us. When we look at our world there are always things that we wish we could change. There are things that we know run counter to our Christian way of life and we would like to be able to do more to change those things whatever they may be.

One of the main themes of Jeremiah is that of individualism. Jeremiah kept himself apart from society, and even refrained from getting married, in order that he might serve God more fully. And, although he kept himself isolated to a certain degree, he engaged the world in telling them what was wrong with the way people and nations were living. He preached that the individual was directly responsible to her or his God. Other prophets had always emphasized the strength of the tribe and that they would be judged by God on their collective witness. They were told over and over that evil or good would come according to the present or past works of the nation as a whole. Jeremiah substituted individual responsibility, holding each person accountable for her or his actions.

The question presents itself, "What can I do, individually, to help myself while helping others in my own journey of faith?" Our lesson tells the people to do the things that all people do regardless of the fact that they are being held against their wishes. Get married, start a family, and be productive and responsible members of society. We are to learn that a majority opinion is not necessarily God's will. Rather, it is God's will that even in captivity we should prosper so that our family and our name will continue to live even after we are gone. There is, within this reading and this historical situation, the question of when God's people should rebel and not get along with their captives. At least, in the context of Jeremiah's letter, the answer is that, in this case, resistance is not the will of God.

Once again, individual choice and how that choice affects the larger group comes into play. Here, the people must act responsibly as individuals, so that they are not punished collectively. God will come when God will come. That is the difficult message for the Hebrew people in Babylon, but it should always be remembered that the people of the northern kingdom, those taken captive by the Assyrians in 722 B.C. did not, for the most part, survive their captivity because of their resistance. Jeremiah instructs the people to wait upon the Lord.

Although Jeremiah is often called the prophet of individualism, that title should not be mistaken for any sense of a loss of community. He was simply voicing a reality that needed to be understood by those in captivity. He reached deep within himself to find the strength and wisdom he needed to continue to be God's prophet. And it was in this same spirit that he tried to communicate the importance of the individual person learning to rely on God, especially when all around, the world seemed to be in ruins. But he never advocated individualism detached from the traditions of the people who were separated from the larger community. Jeremiah knew, as should we all, that we are strongest when we are within a community of the faithful. It is within that family that we individually and collectively find our ability to face the world and know that we are not alone.

How often within our own community of faith do we hear people say that they do not really need church? They run out that worn out idea that they commune best with God in private while walking in the woods, or on the golf course. The only thing that is even slightly accurate about that statement is the fact that people do tend to talk to Jesus more on the golf course than they do in church! But, when we face problems in our lives, both individually, and as a community of faith, we should be reminded of Jeremiah and his message. Like most prophets, he was not universally listened to or agreed with, but that did not change his message. Nor should it change the message of salvation as found in our Savior Jesus Christ. Jesus' life and ministry are a perfect example of individual and communal responsibility. He lived his life in a way for all to see how one should conduct the living of life while sharing that life at the same time.

Getting back to the question of what you or I can do to help yourself and others who find themselves in the middle of life, good or bad, Jeremiah tells us:

- the majority opinion is not necessarily God's will;
- although punishment for sin is severe, there is hope in God's mercy;
- God will not accept empty or insincere worship; and
- serving God does not guarantee earthly security.

My sisters and brothers in Christ, God comes to us in the midst of living. Jeremiah's call by God teaches how intimately God knows us. We know from both the Hebrew and New Testament Scriptures

371

that each of us has been valued by God before anyone else knew we would even exist. God cared for us while we were in our mother's womb. A God that would love us that much, even unto death, is never going to let us go, not ever!

Friends, "Build houses and live in them; plant gardens and eat what they produce. Take wives and have sons and daughters; take wives for your son, and give your daughters in marriage, that they may bear sons and daughters; multiply there, and do not decrease. But seek the welfare of the city where I have sent you into exile, and pray to the Lord on its behalf, for in its welfare you will find your welfare."

Amen.

**Proper 24**
**Pentecost 22**
**Ordinary Time 29**
**Jeremiah 31:27-34**

# New Covenant — New Testament

Our reading today from the prophet Jeremiah is one in which the Hebrew people, not knowing what else to do in terms of addressing their predicament, decide to blame it all on God. They believed their problems to be the result of their sins and the sins of their fathers. Of course, one person's sin does indeed affect other people, but all people are still held personally accountable for the sin in their own lives (Deuteronomy 24:16; Ezekiel 18:2).

This theme would later be taken up in the New Testament as the writers of the gospels brought forth a new idea that a person's sin, whatever that sin may have been, could and would be forgiven in and through Jesus Christ, who became the ultimate expression of a new covenant for us all.

The Hebrew people found themselves, once again, in an untenable situation. They cannot see how their negative situation can be turned into a positive one. The realization, however, hits them, as it does us all, that at some point, we are no longer able to fix the things we have broken. At some point, our frail nature as mere Homo sapiens, mere human beings stares at us from our mirror. What can we do? How can we ever rectify the things that we have done and make them right? No person, then or now, goes through all of life without knowing that they need intervention in some part of their life. Sometimes that has to be thrust upon us, and at other times we realize that we need to do something before we self-destruct and destroy those we love along with ourselves.

It is in the midst of this situation that we are shown a new vision of the ultimate restoration of the nation Israel. This section

373

of Jeremiah has been labeled by many as the most important part of the entire book of Jeremiah. It is easy to understand why, when one reads and reflects on the words from our reading today. These words are no mere expression of the reclaiming of some lost people and land. It is, rather, a new covenant between God and the people. It was, and is, so dramatic an idea that later writers would use it to name what has come to be called the New Testament, or New Covenant, in the Christian canon.

Jeremiah 31 anticipates the time when God will write the law on the hearts of the people, and reminds readers that at the core of the law is the covenant relation God establishes. The God who initiates this covenant is a God who comes to the people with a personal covenant, unlike any before.

Like most prophets, Jeremiah had to depend on God's love as he developed endurance. It was a lonely life being a prophet. Every time you opened your mouth, you were very likely going to say something that no one wanted to hear! At best, the audience would be apathetic, or at worst, antagonistic to what he had to say. Prophets were ignored; their lives often threatened. Jeremiah saw in his lifetime both the excitement of a spiritual awakening for the Hebrew people and the sorrow of their national return to sin. With the exception of the good King Josiah, Jeremiah watched king after king ignore his warnings and lead the people away from God. He saw his fellow prophets murdered. He himself was severely persecuted.

It is into this difficult setting that Jeremiah had listened and watched the people turn against God. Then, like now, people will do most anything to discover how they can live the good life (good=sinful) and still be on God's side. It is almost a daily dance throughout the world today, as well as in the time of Jeremiah, for God's people to step around the reality of sin. It is worse when we know that we are sinning. How can we deprive people of the basic necessities of life so we can have more stuff and still be God's people? Of course, we cannot live in sin and still be in covenant with God, because God is without sin. How dare we be so arrogant as to assume that we are somehow on an equal sphere with God, that we can simply do what we want when we want. How gracious of God to see our weakness and absolute inability to fix our world.

The greatest prophecy in Jeremiah is the new covenant passage that we read a few moments ago. And to build on the good news of this new covenant is the fact that this covenant will not be like the Mosaic covenant. History has a way of repeating itself and the people had not done a great job of keeping the Mosaic covenant. Therefore, a new one is given here. The collapse of the old covenant that resulted in the destruction of the nation, created a very important question. "How can a holy God maintain a relationship with a sinful people?" The answer is in this new covenant.

The new covenant involves both continuity and discontinuity. There will be continuity. Like the old, the new covenant will be rooted in, and rest upon, the divine initiative. In other words, God will act in sovereign grace. Also, it will have as its intent the full realization of a dynamic relationship between God and humankind.

For us as New Testament people, it is easy to forget how important a dynamic relationship with God is. This is a sign that God is not going to stay up on the mountain. God is not going to be a distant, scary, menacing, thunder-clapping God, in the fog and mist of the early morning. No, God is going to mix it up with us. We who are on this side of the New Testament might ask what all the fuss is. Jesus has come to us and lives with us and walks with us. But, we must put all of that into proper perspective when looking at today's text. For one thing, the new covenant is incorporated in the promise. Earlier, covenants were made, not promised. The taking up of the covenant into the promise marks the end of the history of God's previous dealings with God's people and a new history will begin.

In point of fact, the new covenant that is promised in these historic verses is only new in the sense that it will fulfill the original intention of the Sinai covenant. Maybe the best way to understand the difference between the Sinai Covenant and this new covenant as described in Jeremiah is to say that words must be lived, not only spoken. In the book of Exodus we hear "I am the Lord your God." It is the opening line of the preamble. This covenant was original with God. God initiated it. It was not a joint "arrangement" between Israel and the Lord, as between equals in a marriage. God is God and God's sovereignty was the ground and source of this covenant.

The command stresses the positive aspect of worship, insisting that Israel worship the Lord God and not any other. This made Judaism a distinctive monotheistic religion. It can be argued that the greatest contribution of the Jews to history and civilization was its ethical monotheism.

The Ten Commandments that make up this new covenant put God at the top of the mountain. This is a God that will give the laws that the Hebrew people will live by. These laws will be written in stone. The people are to stand away at a distance from God. Moses, as mediator, drew near to the thick cloud where God was, but not the people. God gave Moses the laws of the Sinai Code. Moses then delivered them to the people. The mood and impression of this revelation and experience is one of awe and mystery and the holy. God's transcendence and utter "otherness" is dominant. This God is separate and holy, and must be worshiped and respected as such.

But changes are coming as evidenced in our reading when we hear that the new covenant, "... will not be like the covenant that I made with their ancestors when I took them by the hand to bring them out of the land of Egypt — a covenant that they broke, though I was their husband says the Lord" (31:32). You see, do you not, that the people broke the covenant, not God? And one of the main reasons the covenant was constantly broken was because the covenant was not personal, it was quite literally written in stone. It was the cold, hard facts. Those of you who remember the television series, *Dragnet*, will remember that Sergeant Friday always prefaced his remarks by asking for "just the facts, ma'am, just the facts." He was always stone-faced, cold, and professional. Just so with the laws on stone. They were accurate and true, but they were not a part of the lives of those who heard them. They were laws to be obeyed, but not laws that the people had lived with.

In our reading we hear, "But this is the covenant I will make with the house of Israel after those days, says the Lord: I will put

376

my law within them, and I will write it on their hearts; and I will be their God, and they shall be my people" (31:33).

What a dramatic and powerful difference. The covenant will be inside the people. They will know this covenant because it will be a part of their daily life. You see the covenant involves the creation of new people through the action of a divine deed. God will put God's will straight into the heart of humankind so that the necessity of communication through external methods will be circumvented. This is Jeremiah's way of speaking of what we would call the work of the Holy Spirit in the making of a new person, who will light up God's Word by living a life that honors that Word.

It is the picture of a new creation. New women and new men forgiven and in fellowship with God in a new community, with the ability to discern and do God's will, is a new thing in the Hebrew Scripture.

But, it is not a new thing for those of us who name ourselves as Christians. Jeremiah lived and spoke in a time far removed from our Lord Jesus Christ, but the message remains much the same. Our salvation is personal, it is heartfelt, and has come to us in the carpenter from Nazareth.

The foundation of this new covenant for the Christian community is Christ (Hebrews 8:6). It is revolutionary, involving not only Israel and Judah, but even the Gentiles. It offers a unique, personal relationship with God, with God's Laws written on individual's hearts instead of stone. Jeremiah looked forward to the day of the fulfillment of his prophecy, the day of the Messiah. We who call ourselves Christian, already live within that fulfillment. The covenant is here in Jesus Christ. We have the wonderful opportunity to make a fresh start and establish a permanent, personal relationship with God. Praise be to God! Are you a part of the covenant? If not — why not?

Amen.

# Calamity And Hope

The little book of Joel has a big part to play in the overall story of the Hebrew Scripture. Its purpose is to warn of God's impending judgment against the people of Judah because of their sins, and to urge them to turn back to God. The book is written by Joel, the son of Pethuel, and it is directed toward the southern kingdom, and God's people everywhere.

The book itself is one of the literary gems of the Hebrew Scriptures. It is written and built up with care and dramatic effect. There are surely other prophets who write with greater passion and greater power; but there is hardly a writer in the Hebrew Scripture who shows proof of such careful and detailed and exquisite pains to give his work literary polish as does Joel.

We know very little about Joel. We know, as mentioned, that he was a prophet and the son of Pethuel. He may have lived in Jerusalem because his audience was Judah, in the southern kingdom. Whoever he was, Joel speaks forthrightly and forcefully in this short and powerful book. His message is one of foreboding and warning, but it is also filled with a sense of what might be, a real sense of hope. Joel states that our Creator, the omnipotent judge, is also merciful, and wants to bless all those who put their trust in God.

Joel begins this book by describing a terrible plague of locusts that covers the land and devours the crops. He warns that what the locusts will do is nothing compared to what will happen before the coming judgment of God, or as Joel puts it "before the great and terrible day of the Lord comes." The prophet, therefore, urges the people to turn from their sin and return to a place that is proper in God's presence. Implicit within this message of judgment and the need of the people to repent is an affirmation of God's kindness and the blessings God promises for all who follow. In fact, "Then everyone who calls on the name of the Lord shall be saved" (2:32).

The people of Judah had become prosperous and complacent. They were taking God for granted, they had turned to self-centeredness, idolatry, and sin. Joel warned them that this kind of lifestyle would inevitably bring down God's judgment. Of course, they, like us, fail to adhere to the warnings that tell us that we should slow down and take the time to reconnect with God. We are in so much of a hurry in our day-to-day living that we not only take God for granted, we fall into the mistaken notion that we are gods in and of ourselves. We can get along just fine without God, we don't need the bother of wondering what God would have us do, and we will do what we want!

Prior to the verses in today's reading, the people have been called to repent and return to God. Superficial emotionalism will not suffice as a way of getting God's forgiveness. God is seeking those who truly understand what is wrong and who are willing to sacrifice a part of their lives in order to find forgiveness and fulfillment in their lives. God will restore their harvests, making it possible for them to bring a proper offering when it is called for.

In verse 15, a new call goes out for a fast and solemn assembly. Old and young are called to gather together. These earlier verses are needed if we are to truly get the scope of what is happening. Repentance brings its promised reward. God rehearses those blessings with which God will empower the returning people.

It is useful to look again at our opening verses as a way of recognizing the importance of being called to gather as God's people. When we get together we will be happy because, "he has poured down for you abundant rain, the early and the later rain, as before" (2:23). Remember, in a land not blessed with large bodies of water; the promised rain is truly a gift from above, but it is more than that. It is the promise of life itself. We cannot live without water, we cannot live without God. The following verse (24) tells of the consequences of that rain, full vats of food.

Once we are filled with the goodness that only God can provide to us we will have no excuse for not being the people God has called us to be. Imagine in our twenty-first-century world, with all of the enormous benefits we enjoy, how much easier it is for us to ignore these verses and relegate them to the storehouse of history. It is so easy to forget who and "whose" we are. We live in a time when the world is smaller than it has ever been. News comes to us spontaneously, there is no delay. We have at our fingertips the most cutting edge technological advances ever conceived.

A bomb explodes in Iraq; a terrorist takes hostages in the middle of a major city; rockets take off from countries from around the world. Space exploration is commonplace in our time.

Power, strength, and might, and we stand in awe at the natural and man-made display, but these forces cannot touch the power of the one who created the creation. Volcanoes, earthquakes, and tidal waves unleash uncontrollable and unstoppable force. Every day we are reminded of the power of nature. But these forces, as powerful as they are, cannot touch the power of the omnipotent God. Creator of galaxies, atoms, and natural laws, the sovereign Lord rules all there is and ever will be. How foolish of us to live without God; how foolish of us to think we can run and hide from God like we could from our human parents. How utterly ridiculous to disobey God — but we do. Like the people of Joel's time, we have sought independence from God, as if, through our own methods, we can do what God can do. It is in the midst of all of this rebellion on our part that God still gives us an opening.

You see, it is about this day of reckoning that Joel is writing. It is the theme of this timeless little book. There will come a time when God will look us over. There will come a time when God will decide if we have measured up. It is so easy to think only of the immediate time in which we live. Joel is reminding the Hebrew people that God will take notice of what is going on. It is through Joel, to us in our own time, that this same message comes. A day will come for us, for all of us, when God will judge all unrighteousness and disobedience, all accounts will be settled and the crooked made straight.

It is so hard for us in our world to conceive of a God with whom we will one day have to reckon. It is God with whom we must settle accounts; not with nature, not with the economy, and not with a terrorist. We cannot ignore God forever. We must listen and pay attention to what God says through people like the prophet Joel, or we will face the kind of calamity that is outlined for the people to whom Joel was historically writing.

Within the Christian community, it is very important that we make the connection between these verses in Joel, and the New Testament message as it comes to us in the book of the Acts of the Apostles. Contained in verses 28 and 29 we have this message, "Then afterward I will pour out my spirit on all flesh; your sons and your daughters shall prophesy, your old men shall dream dreams, and your young men shall see visions. Even on the male and female slaves, in those days, I will pour out my spirit." The promise made in Joel comes to new life in Acts chapter 2 beginning in verse 14 when Peter brings to fulfillment the promise of Joel.

This is no small thing. The early church ran the risk of forgetting who it was and what it was to do. With Jesus no longer there to guide and instruct, the people, much like their ancestors before them, needed to know that they were not going to be left defenseless as they began to put together what we now know as the church. Peter connects the older tradition with the newer one. Peter, like Joel before him, understands the warning signs of history. He knows that the people need reassurance, need direction. Joel's prophecy reaches across time and Peter becomes for Joel a voice of one crying out from history that God will not leave the people alone.

In the final analysis, Joel presents us with a vision of the blessings that we can expect as God's children. We have a promise of immediate relief from trouble. God loves us and will not leave us to our own devices. God will not allow us to be forever afflicted with doubt and uncertainty. God will intervene as happened on the day of Pentecost. Joel had no way of knowing that his prophecy would be linked to a fisherman by the name of Peter, but God did. Joel takes up his stand as if some of his prediction had already taken place. Only a confident person can do such a thing.

We are to find that same confidence in Joel's message and, of course, in the life, ministry, death, and resurrection of our Lord Jesus Christ. When Peter stands in the book of Acts and speaks about Joel's prophecy, Peter becomes an eternal link in our personal relationship with Jesus.

It is so hard sometimes for us to grasp the incredible importance of a timeless message like this one from Joel. Indeed, in closing let us be reminded that we, that is the church, are related in a very real way with Joel and his contemporaries. They, like John the Baptist, were a voice crying out in the wilderness. In this case, that voice traveled through times of extreme oppression and extreme joy. Joel predicts the time when God will pour out God's Holy Spirit on all people. It will be the beginning of a new and fresh worship of God by those who believe in God, but also the beginning of judgment on all who reject him.

We are reminded once and for all that God is in control. Justice and restoration are in God's hands. The Holy Spirit present in Peter's life and message confirms God's love for us just as it did for the people of Joel's time.

My sisters and brothers in Christ, we must be faithful to God and do as Joel and Peter did before us and place our lives under the guidance and power of the Holy Spirit.

Amen.

Proper 26
Pentecost 24
Ordinary Time 31
Habakkuk 1:1-4; 2:1-4

# Living The Vision

In most congregational settings, the name Habakkuk does not bring people to their feet. He is not considered famous biblically speaking, like the more recognized names of Isaiah, Jeremiah, and others. In point of fact, most people do not know who Habakkuk is or what he did.

Habakkuk was a prophet who undertook to sustain the faith of the nation through one of the most hopeless periods of Hebrew history.

The question that he raises is a question that oftentimes seems to find a time and place within each generation, generation after generation. The question is, "Why is God silent while the wicked succeed?"

There has been some debate about when he wrote. Until recently it was generally agreed that he preached against Babylon, about 600 B.C. But that date and the place of his writing has met with quite a bit of debate. What is not in question, however, is the significance of this book.

As our text indicates, the question of why God allows bad things to happen to good people is a question that remains timeless. And, it is the answer to that question that has strengthened the hearts of people through the ages. The answer to the question in Habakkuk's words is, "Look at the proud! Their spirit is not right in them, but the righteous live by their faith" (2:4).

Indeed, the moral situation inside the kingdom at the time of the prophet was not a good one. Law and justice were being held in contempt; the people had, as in previous generations, turned away from God and turned to pagan cults and all that those cults brought with them. There was robbery and violence everywhere; the bad guys were winning! And it seemed to those who were awash in this misery that there was no way out, there was no recourse. It is in the midst of all of this that Habakkuk presents one of the most daring passages in the entire Hebrew Scripture.

Why call it daring? When you read Habakkuk it is clear that he had protested again and again what was going on all around him. He had prayed over what was happening, pleading with God to make things right, but it seemed his voice was not being heard. Sound familiar? Don't all of us feel like God does not hear us when we pray? Honestly, don't you, like Habakkuk, feel left out from time to time?

In desperation, Habakkuk demands that God explain what is going on. Think about that for a while. Habakkuk is tired and probably more than a little frustrated and he dares to demand that God satisfy his questions. This is a radical departure for a Hebrew prophet who worshiped Yahweh.

A quick glance through your Bibles will tell you that Amos, Hosea, Isaiah, Micah, Zephaniah, Nahum, all of these more famous prophets accepted the world as they found it. They accepted the situation and then responded to it and undertook to explain it in light of their belief concerning God. But Habakkuk was the first Hebrew thinker who ever presumed to question the wisdom or the justice of God's administration of the world's affairs. The fact is that Habakkuk wanted God to explain what was going on! You have to admit that takes more than a little bit of courage. Further, haven't you at some time in your life wanted to do the same? Haven't you had moments when you looked around the world and wanted God to step up to the plate and tell you just what is going on? On September 11, 2001, the world came to a halt as the towers went down. Didn't you want to know from God, why? When the tragic tsunami killed hundreds of thousands wouldn't you have felt a little better if God had made an appearance on the nightly news and told the world that it was going to be okay and that this happened because _____?

386

We all have to remember that, historically speaking, the Hebrew people of that time believed that piety and prosperity went hand in hand. Or more truthfully, that piety and prosperity went together as cause and effect. If the nation pleased God, it might expect God's favor; if the people failed to please God, they could expect disaster. Up to Habakkuk's time all the great prophets had undertaken to explain that the nation had sinned, and in what respect the nation had failed to please God. I hope you see the difference here. Their messages were concerned principally with the question of how God's favor could be won, and how the nation might find itself in a right relationship with God again. In other words, how could they establish their "chosen people" status again? The truth is that Habakkuk takes this discussion to a new level, a very human level.

You see, Habakkuk was very aware of the behavior of the people and that behavior was a major contributor to their problems. He was also keenly aware that the wickedness of the outside world was a major contributor to the problem. Therefore, he asks a thoughtful question of God, "Why do you make me see wrongdoing and look at trouble?" (1:3).

Habakkuk is once again being one of us. His question is not profound, not the question of a philosopher, it is the question of a man who loves God and loves his sisters and brothers in the faith. It is the question of humanity. In the verses between our readings for today, Habakkuk is assured that God is going to do an amazing thing. God is going to use the enemy as an instrument for punishing those who are doing wrong. But, that only serves to confuse Habakkuk, because as far as he is concerned the enemy is the problem. Therefore, Habakkuk challenges God for the second time. How can God show favor to a wicked nation and still call for the worship of good people? It is the enemy that has defied God, again and again. What could possibly be the logic in using one wicked nation to punish another less wicked nation?

It is at this point that Habakkuk describes himself as taking up a position of waiting. Like us, he will wait on the Lord. The Bible does not tell us in what form he expected to find an answer. Would it be a vision? Would God speak with him as with Moses? He does not say. But, Habakkuk is confident that the answer will come, that God will make the answer plain, and God did.

The prophet is told to take tablets and write on those tablets the contents of the vision he is about to receive. Further, he is instructed to write in characters so large that anyone passing by will be able to read even if they are in a hurry, "Write the vision; make it plain on tablets, so that a runner may read it" (2:2b). In today's terms, he is asked to up the font from twelve to fifty. Further, he is instructed not to be impatient, but to wait for God to be revealed. It is important for us to understand that the vision was from God; the record of that vision is Habakkuk's.

It was a very old belief of the prophets that a day was coming when the forces of evil and the forces of good would be locked in a mortal combat. That belief has been taken hostage by movie makers since movies first began. In our own generation, of course, the image of good and evil was portrayed by the good cowboys wearing white hats, and the bad cowboys wearing black hats. The film world then took that to higher levels with science fiction. Today, evil is personified in the image and voice of Darth Vader, of *Star Wars'* fame.

Good and evil are fighting for a place in your life. It is a continuing story, is it not? For Habakkuk, a moment came when he was convinced that God was to emerge triumphant. In his hour of vision, Habakkuk became convinced that the awful brutality and ruthlessness of the enemy was only temporary and the suffering that was being inflicted upon the world was soon to come to an end because the enemy was doomed. The foundational basis for Habakkuk's message of hope was that there was something eternal in righteousness which evil could not destroy, and that those who were righteous would survive because they had that eternal element within them. Their loyalty and faithfulness to God would ultimately save them.

Herein is what must be labeled as a great verse of scripture, "Look at the proud! Their spirit is not right in them, but the righteous live by their faith" (2:4).

The great New Testament writer of Hebrews, picked up Habakkuk's vision when he wrote, "... but my righteous one will live by faith" (Hebrews 10:38). That verse, in one form or another, has become a capstone of the Christian doctrine. The Apostle Paul, likewise, used similar words when he wrote in Romans, "For in it the righteousness of God is revealed through faith for faith; as it is written, 'The one who is righteous will live by faith' " (Romans 1:17). And in Galatians 3:1, "Now it is evident that no one is justified before God by the law; for 'The one who is righteous will live by faith.' "

Today, we are the fortunate recipients of the faith that Habakkuk so brilliantly wrote to us about. Habakkuk knew, as should we all, that the forces of evil will have temporary victories. He also knew that those victories would be empty victories. They would be empty because God would see to it that the right would prevail over wrong.

Habakkuk knew, and we know, that God had been revealed to others in different times and places. That revelation, when it happened, would be such that the people of God would find new life and new hope regardless of their current circumstances. Within the Christian community we find that revelation expressed in the ultimate human vision of God, Jesus who is Christ. It is in the person of Jesus that the final vision has been written and made plain for all to witness. "Write the vision and make it plain." God made it clear and concise for all of us in Jesus. The Apostle Paul saw that vision and wrote about it, and we are the heirs of that vision today.

We owe Habakkuk a great debt of gratitude for his faithfulness and strength. In the final analysis, Habakkuk saw sin and anticipated punishment for those sins. As a great religious thinker, Habakkuk undertook to sort through the evidence and put together a vision of a faith that was both logical and enduring.

Praise God from whom all blessings flow — especially for the prophet Habakkuk who wrote the vision and made it plain to us today, in our time and in our place. The vision is still relevant and timely today.

Amen.

# Building The Temple Of God

Haggai is what has been labeled as the first of the restoration prophets, and he has no recorded history. We are told in verse 13 of chapter 1 that he was "... the messenger of the Lord." As is the case with all of the prophets, those listed as major and minor, the message, not the messenger, is of prime importance. God, not God's prophet, dominates the message. Apart from this book, Haggai is mentioned only in the book of Ezra. His name is usually associated with that of his better known and younger contemporary, Zechariah.

In order to appreciate Haggai's message we need to time travel in reverse. We need to go back to the destruction of Solomon's temple. The Bible is quite clear that Solomon's temple was the pride and joy of the Israelite nation. The temple itself was one of the world's most spectacular structures. It was built with the best of everything that the world had to offer at that time. It was an extravagant structure that stood at the heart of Jewish worship and was therefore a symbol of great importance to the nation. The temple had been destroyed while the Babylonians were in power and the people were in exile.

With that bit of biblical history in mind, we can fast-forward through that time of exile and into the present time of Haggai's life and message. The Hebrew people had finally been given permission to return home. Besides a desire on the part of the people to rebuild the holy city of Jerusalem, they were also given permission to rebuild the center of their worship life together, the temple.

Shortly after the first remnants of the Hebrew people began to arrive back in their homeland, around the year 536 B.C.E., they began to rebuild the temple. It was not long, however, before various problems began to surface and with them a decline in the enthusiasm of the people to rebuild. It is funny, just when you think that things are going to get better, sometimes the slightest problem can slow things down or bring them to a halt. When that happens, someone needs to step up to the plate and take a swing. At the plate we find Haggai. Haggai's mission was to rekindle the faith and the courage of the people so that they would get to work and complete what they had started.

With that information in mind, we can begin to journey with Haggai while he undertakes the difficult task of encouraging and scolding the people of God. He has a very clearly defined job to do. His task differed from, and was in some respects more narrowly limited than, that of either the former prophets or of his contemporary, Zechariah. Circumstances were different from those of pre-captivity days. When earlier prophets delivered their messages, the house of the Lord was there with all its outward glory and honored heritage from the past. The ceremonial observances were rigidly kept, so far as outward forms went. But outward appearances can be very deceiving. When worship becomes so ceremonial that the form is more important than the actual personal investment, problems will surface. Just so during the time of Haggai. The form of worship had become more important than the personal commitment. When that happened, the people turned from inward commitment to outward observance. They began to look with self-satisfaction and deluded pride at their magnificent buildings and those buildings became more important than worship itself.

About a month after the work began on rebuilding the city and temple, Haggai encouraged the people, assuring them that their work was not in vain, and that what they were doing was indeed meaningful and pleasing to God. In verse 3 of the second chapter we read, "Who is left among you that saw this house in its former glory?" Referring to the house in its former glory refers to the temple of Solomon before it was destroyed by the Babylonians. Those who had seen Solomon's temple knew that this new construction would not measure up to the grandness of the original. Ezra recounts the laying of the foundation of the temple shortly after the return of the exiles. In this account we see that there was great rejoicing on this occasion by the younger people, but also weeping on the part of the older priests. Why? Because the older people remembered the laying of the foundation of the original and knew of its magnificence and glory.

What happens today when a church puts on an addition? Or when a church closes one building and prepares to build a new one? Comparisons are made, it is the natural response of people. Our grandparents remember "when" and it is not easy for them to forget the memories of a past that may or may not have been as glorious as it is remembered. Just so with the Hebrew people as they remembered a former time of glory.

The builders began to wonder whether all their effort wasn't in vain since the temple will be so poor by comparison to Solomon's. The new temple seemed to the old timers, like an inferior structure. This poor attitude weakened the resolve of the builders. For, though God is pleased with us if we do our work in sincere appreciation for all that God does for us, it is our own pride that usually gets us in trouble. It is just so human to compare ourselves and our work to what others are doing or have already done. This may sometimes, as in the case of our text, be the fault of older people who discourage the sincere efforts of the present age by constantly reminding the present age that they do not measure up to those who came before them. In the church today we have the famous admonition, "We've never done it that way before."

It is important for us to remember that what has happened in the past can be an encouragement for the present. But the past should never be used to insult the efforts of younger generations and to expose them to contempt.

It is interesting to note that the word, "courage," is used three times in these verses. The use of that word is reminiscent of God's admonition of other crucial situations of the past. Joshua was encouraged with similar words, "I hereby command you; be strong and courageous; do not be frightened or dismayed, for the Lord your God is with you wherever you go." Joshua was never told that he was bound to fail and would never live up to the reputation of Moses. On the contrary, he was encouraged, and as a result he was the one who led the Israelites into the promised land. There are numerous other examples throughout scripture. The point is that when God has ordered a task to be done, God always does God's part. It is for God's servants to be strong and work hard.

This admonition is based upon two different promises. In the first place, we read in verse 4, "... take courage, all you people of the land, says the Lord; work, for I am with you, says the Lord of hosts," and in verse 7, "... I will fill this house with splendor, says the Lord." The first promise is a link to the past, to the covenant made at Sinai. The second is linked to the future, the glory that is yet to come. The fact that God is present with God's people by saying, "I am with you," means that God approves of the work they are doing, and will support that work and protect them. This is no small thing. To the people it means the difference between victory and defeat. If God is pleased, who else is there that they need to satisfy?

A second reason is that God relates their present situation to the upcoming surpassing of the glory of the temple. They needed to know that it was not the structure itself that brought such glory to the people, it was the fact that God was present in it. It was natural to make comparisons between Solomon's temple and Zerubbabel's temple. These buildings were visible representations of the fact that God has seen fit to dwell among the people. The new temple that they were constructing, though less splendid than that of Solomon, is nevertheless God's dwelling place, a place where God's people can come to worship God. Their work, though seemingly insignificant, is nevertheless a part of God's overall plan of establishing God's presence on earth in such a way that not only Israel, but ultimately all nations, will be affected. For those of us gathered in this church on this day, God's purpose was fulfilled in God's Son and our Savior, Jesus Christ.

My brothers and sisters in Christ, the message from Haggai this morning is a powerful incentive to do the ministry that has been placed before us. As long as we are doing that ministry, we remain valued participants in God's great program of making God's salvation known to all who will listen. If we do whatever it is that God has called us to do in sincerity to the best of our ability, we carry with us God's blessing.

We must never forget the example set by those who have blazed the trail before us. Let us never recall the past in an effort to belittle the efforts of those in the present. Instead, let us gather our courage and strength and encourage today's workers in ministry so that they might become the Joshua's and Solomon's of tomorrow.

Amen.

# Isaiah — The Prophet
# Of Gloom And Glory

Of all the writing prophets of Israel, Isaiah stands out above them all. He uses the language like a poet to present to us incredible pictures that lift up God and how God will bring salvation to God's people. In fact, the name Isaiah means, "Yahweh is salvation." But just as the book of Isaiah stands out for its beautiful presentation and powerful message, it also stands out for the controversy surrounding who wrote what within its 66 chapters. One of the reasons for the question of authorship is the life span of this book. Depending on which scholar one reads, the book has a life span of up to 300 years! The traditional view claims that the prophet Isaiah, who ministered during the days of Uzziah, Jotham, Ahaz, and Hezekiah, was the book's sole author. But many believe that Isaiah had nothing to do with the last part of the book, specifically chapters 40 to 66.

What we know without much question is that Isaiah lived at a time when Israel was quite prosperous; both the northern and southern kingdoms knew great wealth and prosperity. And although there were the occasional skirmishes with folks from other countries, for the most part, Israel was at peace.

Having said that, a proper understanding of the structure of this book is essential for interpreting its contents, and it assists in dealing with some of the differences between the two major sections (chapters 1 to 39 and 40 to 66). Rather than spending time in this sermon trying to dissect the entire book, I will be working under the idea that Isaiah chapters 1 to 39 reflect the covenant curses resulting from Israel's disobedience to God's Law, while Isaiah 40 to 66 reflects the covenant blessings promised for the obedient remnant of Israel.

This wonderful book is the first of the writings of the prophets in the Bible, and Isaiah is generally considered to be the greatest prophet. He was probably reared in an aristocratic home and was married to a prophetess. In the beginning of his ministry, he was well liked. But like most prophets, he soon became unpopular because his messages were so difficult to hear. He called the people to turn from their lives of sin and warned them of God's judgment and punishment. No one wants to hear that sort of message. Many believe that Isaiah had an active ministry for sixty years before he was executed during Manesseh's reign (according to tradition).

Like Micah, Isaiah saw the nation, Israel, as a sinful people who, in spite of their material wealth, were really quite poor spiritually. And like Micah, Isaiah sees Israel's spiritual poverty evidenced in their lack of concern for the least of these within their midst. In a very real way, their own self-absorbed concern for themselves reveals the weakness within. The sad reality is that they love neither God, nor themselves.

The chapters in Isaiah that we are looking at this morning are chapters that bring to a conclusion what is sometimes called Isaiah's words of comfort to the people. This message of hope looks forward to the coming of the Messiah. Isaiah speaks more about the Messiah than does any other prophet from Hebrew Scripture. He describes the Messiah as both a suffering servant and a sovereign Lord. The fact that the Messiah was to be both a suffering servant and a sovereign Lord could not be understood completely until the New Testament was put into written form. Based on what Jesus Christ had done, God freely offers forgiveness to all who turn to God in faith. This is God's message of comfort to us because those who heed it find eternal peace and fellowship with God.

The message of the last chapters of Isaiah is the glorious good news that God is at work, restoring what has become broken in our lives and in the world. The passage says quite literally, "For I am about to create new heavens and a new earth" (65:17). The idea here is that God is already at work and that this process will come about shortly.

What is both glorious and troubling about these final chapters is that we discover that God is not going to undo our circumstances immediately. We are faced with the fact that we must live in the world we have created before restoration will take place. God promises help as we do that, but again, total restoration will not come easily.

To better understand why we must live in our own mess, we should take a look at Isaiah's call to be a prophet in the first place. Trees and prophets share at least one important characteristic: both are planted for the future. Isaiah is one of the best examples of this. The people of his time could have been rescued by his words. Instead, they refused to believe him. We must remember that when God called Isaiah to this ministry, God did not encourage him with predictions of great success. God told Isaiah that the people would not listen, but he was to speak and write his messages anyway because eventually some would listen. Notice that only some would listen, not all. Early on, God compared the people to a tree that would have to be cut down so that a new tree could grow from the old stump (Isaiah 6:13).

Today, we who are the recipients of this great prophet's work can see that many of the promises God gave to Isaiah have been fulfilled in Jesus Christ. But what have we done with them?

God does not work with the "what ifs" in life. God is a God of the now, and God's plan is to work with what you have today. God's not interested in your past, except to forgive it. God wants you to move forward with what you have, so that you can now be the person God wants you to be in your current situation.

The same can be said for organizations, including the church. God is not living in the past of this church or any other church for that matter. Isaiah's message across time is that God has plans for what this church should be today, with the people who are here now. History has an important place in the life of the church, but it is history, and the history of the church can inform us and give us some direction, however, it cannot do today what we must be doing.

The key for God's people then and now is to learn what God's plan is for us today. What does God want for me and my family and my church? That question should encompass all areas of our lives. What is God's will for who I am now? What is God's will for our church today? And we must remember that the question is directed at who we are today. Past decisions are just that, past. We all make some good ones and some terrible ones.

The message from Isaiah to us today is to get in touch with God. Get in touch with what God would have us do today. It does not matter what mistakes we have made in the past. The first 39 chapters of Isaiah are filled to overflowing with monumental mistakes on the part of the Hebrew people. To dwell on those errors will do nothing to move you forward today. We will just have to live with the consequences of the bad choices we have made in the past.

It would be fair to ask at this juncture, "But is that all there is?" Is God's final answer that God will help us to cope with our mistakes? The prophet would have us understand today that God wants us to know the joy of living in a right relationship with God, today and every day.

Isaiah chapter 65 gives us a pictorial description of the new heavens and the new earth. They are eternal, and in them safety, peace, and plenty will be available to all of God's children. The message in these last chapters is the glorious good news that God is not sleeping, God is awake and on the job. God is fixing the broken places and making a new path for all of us to follow. "For I am about to create new heavens and a new earth...."

The second part of the verse just quoted says the following, "The former things shall not be remembered or come to mind" (65:17b). The idea is pretty clear that once we get to heaven, once we live within the divine embrace of eternity it will be so good that the former things that seemed so important at the time will not matter any longer.

These verses bring to mind the words of our Lord when he said from the cross, "Truly I tell you, today you will be with me in paradise" (Luke 23:43). Today, not next week, not next month, not next year, but today!

The Hebrew people had traveled a long and difficult road. The chapters in Isaiah leading up to chapter 65 have been filled with all that is good and bad in each person and each nation. But this chapter celebrates life and the great good news that God has accomplished God's plan in the lives of these people, and we can look forward to the day when we will be included in that plan.

The prophet Isaiah was charged with bringing the news, good and bad, to God's children. He did this as no other before or since. He had to tell them about their limitations and how those limitations plagued them all their lives. He also had the great joy of telling them that the things that had held them back and caused such trouble for them would be removed and, once removed, their future was assured by a loving God.

The question that we who are part of the church today must continue to ask of ourselves is, "Do we run the risk of becoming what Isaiah has so thoroughly explained to us that we are not to become?" In Jesus Christ we have been given the example that Isaiah spent his life proclaiming. In him we have a new direction that is filled with good news. In fact, it is "the good news" and that news is that we who are the people of God can look forward to a life filled with the gracious grace of God. We need not make the mistakes of those who came before us. But, we must always be alert that we do not shift into reverse and become that group of people who, because life is good, begin to believe that it is good because of something that *we* have accomplished.

Praise God from whom all blessings flow.

Amen.

**Reformation Sunday**
**Jeremiah 31:31-34**

# Preaching God's Reformation

On this Reformation Sunday, it is useful to look back in time and remember one of the most important elements to come from the Reformation period.

Luther, who is credited with being the first true reformer, was, above all else, a preacher. Luther preached from about 1509 until just three days before his death in February 1546. On Sundays, he preached sometimes three or four times. More than anyone else from that period, he understood that preaching should be central to worship and should be all-inclusive. It is said that Luther preached on the catechism on Monday and Tuesday, and on the books of the Bible the other days. Calvin expounded the Bible every morning. In addition, it is said that large crowds were drawn to the preaching of the great reformer, Zwingli.

Today's lesson reminds us that God offers mercy, justice, and grace. That is something to preach about! The Reformation made the preaching of the Word central in worship. Up until this time, the sacraments were central to worship and the preaching of the Word, although important, was more peripheral and took a backseat to the sacraments. The shift was one of sacramental mystery to gospel proclamation. The preacher is always a reformer in the sense that she or he is constantly fed by the Word and is charged with reminding all who will listen that it is God's desire to bless and not curse!

The prophet Jeremiah was a preacher. He was a youth from the village of Anathoth, one of the original thirteen cities assigned to the Levites (1 Chronicles 6:60), three or four miles northeast of the city of Jerusalem. The Bible tells us that the Word of God came to Jeremiah in the thirteenth year of the reign of Josiah (1:2), which was in 627 B.C.E. If the estimate that he was born in 645 B.C.E. is correct, it would mean that he was eighteen years old when he began his ministry. This may seem young, until we recall that a Hebrew boy was considered to be an adult at twelve. At any rate, he was preaching the Word as a young man, and that Word was often harsh and always without compromise. Jeremiah knew what it was to reform a nation. He may not have identified with the idea as we have it today, but reformation is exactly what the proclamation of God's Word was about.

In our world today, this same spirit of reformation is alive and well. Our reading from Jeremiah tells us that God is in the business of watching over the creation. The God who watched over the people of Jeremiah's day watches over the people of this day. However, as it was in the time of the prophet, God's Word tells us, "And just as I have watched over them to pluck up and break down, to overthrow, destroy, and bring evil, so I will watch over them to build and to plant says the Lord" (31:28).

The Hebrew people who first received this message knew the thoroughness of judgment, but they also knew the promise of better days to come. They, like us, had to toe the line. It is so easy to forget that we are not free agents in our world. We have responsibilities that we must not avoid. In the spirit of reformation, we must be willing to look to God for guidance and trust that guidance in all areas of our lives. God's reformation, God's restoration is not only for our lands and cities, but for our lives as well. God wants to build up and plant, not tear down and ruin the crops. When we learn to follow God's direction for our lives, we will find that God wants to plant us in the fertile soil of God's keeping!

One of the things that happens when the people of God get to thinking about how they got to a certain place in their lives, is a time of reflection. We may begin to wonder if the mistakes of those who came before us have somehow tarnished our own time. It is never fair, though it often happens, that people are blamed for the actions of others. Jeremiah's message to us is that God will no longer hold the actions of those who came before us against us.

Indeed, God establishes accountability. Jeremiah has been preaching to the people that they will be accountable for their own actions. They will be punished for the sins they have committed! In fact, it can be said with clarity that reversing the past is a present choice.

Are we holding the past against ourselves? In the local church, are you blaming the actions of those who came before you for the condition of the church today? If so, you need to reverse the past with good, present choices. There is no use living within the confines of past experience. God calls us to the reality of the present generation. The church of today has the luxury of history. We already know that God will be with us and will restore us. With that knowledge, we would be less than authentic to blame the problems of today on the actions of a few in the past. Only our refusal to seek out God for pardon makes the past look like the problem.

The realistic message of both the Hebrew Scripture and the New Testament is that our help is in an ever-present God. Our God is not confined to the top of a mountain. Our God lives with us, not apart from us. The Bible tells us plainly that God never leaves God's people in bondage or exile. We all need to recognize, as did the early reformers, that our God sees beyond the present reality of our world and is ultimately in full control of all reality. In addition, our God is a God of promise.

"The days are surely coming, says the Lord...." Though reality states that we must live where we are, our reformation preaching must tell all who will listen that this present reality is not our eternal reality. The night can only last so long, and morning must come. Rain may last for a few days, but the sun will surely shine again.

As we look at the prophet and his preaching, it is important to recognize that he became a giant in the way he conducted himself. Jeremiah reached heights of personal religion, moral judgment, and spiritual understanding never before attained by any other prophet. If Zephaniah and Nahum do not always inspire us with lofty idealism and rich spirituality, and if Habakkuk does not reach a solution of his problem but stops with a great, unproven assertion of faith, still the seventh century B.C.E. is redeemed by the exalted preaching of

Jeremiah. To him, as to no other figure of the Hebrew Scripture, we owe the fundamental concepts of personal religion. He is one of the great spiritual giants of all time, and to explore the majestic heights of his mind and spirit by reading and studying his book remains, to this day, one of the great experiences of any person's religious journey. Jeremiah was a thinker, who's preaching shaped a nation and still shapes us today. Jeremiah knew as should we all that God has plans for the future we cannot even begin to imagine.

God is going to make a new covenant with the house of Israel and Judah. A covenant is a legal agreement between two parties. God had a previous agreement with the Hebrew people, but they broke that covenant. Once broken, a covenant becomes null and void. We are told that the new covenant will be different than the old. The most profound difference is that the new covenant will be written upon our hearts. No longer will God be a distant idea of the religion of the Hebrew people. God will be a personal God and unique to each person. No longer will others need to intercede between God and the people as with Noah, Abraham, or Moses. The people can each know God personally. When you think about that fact, is it not exactly what Luther was saying when he posted his "95 Theses" in 1517? Luther was a brilliant theologian and teacher and those "95 Theses" contained many thorough discussions of important theological ideas. But, foundationally, they were a statement that people can know God without the help of indulgences or any other mediator.

In Jeremiah's preaching, we see a move from the external to the internal. God's Word would be written in our hearts. Remember, for the Hebrew mind of that time, the heart was the seat of the conscious decision of the will, and of understanding. It is as if he was telling the people that God would perform a surgical procedure and God's Word would be implanted in their hearts. That is a very personal idea. All people will be able to know God. Not just the Hebrew people, either, but all people, all ages, and all economic levels. God will be known by all the people of the earth. For the Christian community, this has been neatly summarized in the book of Hebrews. "For if that first covenant had been faultless, there would have been no need to look for a second one. God finds fault with them when he says, 'The days are surely coming, says the Lord, when I will establish a new covenant with the house of Israel and with the house of Judah; not like the covenant that I made with their ancestors, on the day when I took them by the hand to lead them out of the land of Egypt; for they did not continue in my covenant, and so I had no concern for them, says the Lord' " (Hebrews 8:7-9).

The new covenant is personal and it brings with it forgiveness. The people will know the forgiveness that offers eternal forgetfulness of sin by God. This is a personal God, who becomes a person to us all.

My sisters and brothers in Christ, the prophet Jeremiah usually had hard news for the people of God. The book is oftentimes depressing because of the difficult days ahead that the Hebrew nation faced. There was also good news in that Jeremiah reports that although God would bring hard days, there would also be help for the helpless and newness of life for the faithful. Jeremiah speaks to them of a time when God will be as close as a loved one. He tells them their sins will be forgiven, not yearly, but eternally. Jeremiah only spoke of what would come to pass some day in the future. Luckily for us, the future is now! The help that he spoke of is already here in the person of our Lord Jesus Christ. We who live on this side of the Hebrew Scripture in the age of the new covenant can know God intimately and have all our sins forgiven. That is not only good news, that is restoration for reformation people. But, because God allows us free will, we can still choose not to listen to Jeremiah, or any of the other prophets who preached God's Living Word. We can still live in the past and complain about the life we have been handed by those who came before. We can avoid facing reality and live with the "what ifs" of life instead of the present reality of living with God as our companion, a close, personal God who will share our journey and never leave us alone.

Reformation Sunday is a day for us all to step forward and claim the resurrection life that has been handed to us by a God who loves us eternally.

You are called this day to be a reformation people who preach the good news that today is a new day and a better day than yesterday. Today we preach a new covenant, a living covenant, and a covenant that restores and reforms our ministry together.

Amen.

# Saintly Visions!

On All Saints, we are visited through the Hebrew Scripture by Daniel. For most of us, Daniel is a book to either be avoided altogether or used sparingly. It falls into that category of books, like the book of Revelation, that is difficult to understand and is often misrepresented.

Daniel is not included in that list of books known as prophets because the authors of the prophetical books were men who occupied a special place in biblical history because of their special relationship with God. Prophets were men who were specially raised up by God to serve as mediators between God and the nation by declaring to the people the words given them directly from God. Daniel, however, was not specifically chosen by God for this purpose. Daniel was a statesman, inspired by God to write his book, and so his book appears in the Hebrew Scripture, but not included with the prophets.

Daniel, like many of the books of the Bible, is not in chronological order. The vision that we are looking at today in chapter 7 was received by Daniel in the first year of Belshazzar's reign and thus it actually occurs in time between the events as recorded in Daniel chapters 4 and 5. The book was edited with the first six chapters dealing with the dreams of Nebuchadnezzar; the writing on the wall for Belshazzar and their exile in Babylon. Each of these events from the fiery furnace of the lions' den demonstrated God's sovereignty in the lives of these people whether they acknowledge it or not. The last six chapters deal with the visions of Daniel and the beginning of their place in history. Yet, throughout this division between the dreams and visions, the overriding theme in the book remains the same and that is the absolute sovereignty of God. Daniel chapter 7 picks up a number of themes that have their antecedents in Genesis and their culmination in Revelation.

And so, to place this chapter in proper context, we are in the first years of the reign of Belshazzar of Babylon. The year is 553 B.C.E. Daniel is around 68 years old, having been taken into exile in 605 B.C.E. at the age of around sixteen. He won't be thrown into the lions' den for another fourteen years. Daniel has previously interpreted a number of Nebuchadnezzar's dreams, now it is his own turn.

The book of Daniel is a part of what is called, "apocalyptic eschatology." That is a fancy way of saying that it is part of what is known as end times theology. The book is filled with symbols and numbers and images and the purpose of these symbols, numbers, and images is to encourage the faithful to continue in the faith and to be assured that God is in control.

The celebration of All Saints is a day in which the church pays attention to the historic connection of the people who have held the church together over time. It is a connection that has no limitations in time. Part of the connection is up to date, remembering and celebrating lives of Christians of our own era, and the celebration reaches back in time and celebrates the faithful of past generations who have contributed so much in helping to fashion a healthy church, a healthy body of Christ.

It may seem as if the vision of Daniel is a strange book to be cited by the church on such an important day. However, our generation needs to be careful to look back and recall how much hope this book gave to those struggling in the vineyards of God's creation so long ago. Daniel's book has many visions that may seem out of place, but the promise at the end of today's reading, specifically verse 18, shines forth as a verse of hope and a future filled with possibilities: "But the holy ones of the Most High shall receive the kingdom and possess the kingdom and possess the kingdom forever — forever and ever."

We, like those who lived in the time of Daniel, live in an uncertain world. People look for security where they can find it. It is especially true in today's world, filled with the threat of terrorism, that people will look for guidance and a sense of hope from our political leaders and our church leaders. We place our hope in them and pray that they will be able to solve the problems that seem so overwhelming as we live our day-to-day lives. Of course, very possibly, the biggest problem we face in our world is ourselves! The placing of our faith in our elected and religious leaders is not misplaced, but we must face the truth that they, like us, are only human. We all have our limitations.

The book of Daniel gives us a glimpse into the relationship between good and evil. It gives us a peek at understanding how that conflict may be resolved.

It is proper to put Daniel into some historical context. Many people during the time of Daniel were sure that God had abandoned them. They had been forced to leave all that they loved and felt secure with. They had left their belongings and shelter and the familiar that we all hold so dear. The temple, regarded by many as the most important symbol of their faith and possibly the most critical link in their relationship with God, had been ransacked and desecrated. In the midst of all of this doom and gloom, they had begun to live in the hope that with the overthrow of the Babylonian empire looming at the hands of the Persians, they would once again gain their freedom and that life would be good. Enter Daniel, who was not quite so optimistic. Early in Daniel's book there is a dream in which Nebuchadnezzar has a vision that things will get worse before they get better.

It is easy for us to understand that the Hebrew people wanted freedom. What they got instead was release from exile under Darius, but that in and of itself did not bring what they were looking for. For the Hebrew people, the idea of salvation was bound up in the idea of national identity and land that they could live on. They were the faithful remnant, the last group from Judah living in exile and ruled by a foreign king.

The people had begun to see that having land to occupy would be wonderful, but what they were really lacking at this point in history was a sense of eternal salvation. This period of exile begins for the Hebrew nation a change in thinking, a shift in the direction they needed in order to begin the journey toward a better life.

Parts of chapter 7 are a bit unusual in that a part of the vision in this chapter was an interpretation of an earlier vision.

No one sermon can properly tackle the visions contained in this chapter. However, a short, abbreviated explanation will suffice. First, and foremost, we must always keep in mind the idea of good battling evil. A modern day analogy would be that of living within the *Empire Strikes Back* model of looking at life. There is the Empire, governed and run by good people and then there is the Dark Side, governed and controlled by the bad people. The Four Beasts in verse 1 represent the unknown, or the dark side, because the ocean was for the Hebrew people a place to be feared. It was unknown by most and therefore not understood. Within Babylonian literature, the sea was a reference to the great abyss. What good can come from such an abyss?

Fast-forward now to verse 15 where Daniel speaks of his fear and confusion about his vision. "As for me, Daniel, my spirit was troubled within me, and the visions of my head terrified me." It is good that Daniel is frightened. Being afraid can do one of two things. It can cause a person to run away, or it can force a person to face their fears.

We should not read into these visions things that are not there. In a previous verse, verse 13 to be exact, there is the introduction of a transcendent agent of God, "... one like a human being coming with the clouds of heaven...," this has sometimes been seen as a statement about Messiah. It would be misleading to think that Daniel had any idea that Jesus was that human being. That would be a real stretch. Further, there is no need for that interpretation. Daniel understood that those who are faithful to God, the "holy ones" of verse 18, will be the ones to exercise authority in the coming kingdom of God.

On All Saints, we should be focusing our attention on how the saints before us and the saints with us concentrate on being the faithful people God has called all of us to be. On All Saints, we celebrate their faithfulness and how they inspire us to be the same strong examples they have become for us. The church celebrates these women and men who have lived through the visions of the world of the book of Daniel and the pages of our local newspapers. You know their names, you learned them in Sunday school and confirmation class and by the singing of the hymns of the church. The names of Jesus, Mary, Paul and Deborah, Ruth and Naomi, Peter, Timothy, Moses, Calvin, Luther, Mother Teresa, Martin Luther King, Jr., come immediately to mind and there are many more that you know within your hearts.

Daniel is a good teacher for us to emulate. He comes to us as one who is deeply troubled because he is aware of the trials and sufferings that await his people. But he, like those named above, knows that God is a God of the living and will not allow the faithful to fall into the abyss. We who look toward the saints of the church for direction should take Daniel's concern to heart. The vision of Daniel raises more questions than it answers about how we relate to one another and to God, our Creator. But it is a vision that causes us to evaluate and re-evaluate those relationships in light of the example of saints like Daniel.

We worship the God of Abraham, Isaac, Jacob, Daniel, and Jesus. In our world of good and evil, there are times when we clearly are not in control of what is going on around us. But we are in control of what is going on inside of us. On days like this, we need to be able to ask ourselves what areas of our lives appear out of our control. Whatever they are, All Saints reminds us that we need to look toward the one who gives us life so that we can live our life as God would have us live it. Our God is the same God who acted in the past, in the present, and will act in the future to protect that which was so carefully created. Our faith needs to mirror that of those who have come before as we struggle today to become the saints God would have us be.

Amen.

# The Shepherd King

Although we are going to concentrate on Jeremiah 23:1-6, it is important to note that these verses are a part of a larger section that is best understood in its entirety. This section contains a collection of prophecies concerning the Davidic kings. It is not important that it be broken down verse by verse, but rather theme by theme. The first section is a lament over Jehoiakim (22:1-9); then Jeremiah's judgment speech against Jehoiakim (22:10-12); a lament over Jerusalem's disaster (22:20-23); speeches against Jehoiakim (22:24-30); and a description of what a false ruler will look like against a true ruler (23:1-8).

How much attention was paid to the maintenance of justice was a major responsibility inherent with being a leader, especially a king. In Judah, the obligation was intrinsic to both the Mosaic and the Davidic covenants. A king must be able to discharge this responsibility in order to gain the stability and continuity of the covenant community. These were no small matters!

In his first recorded appearance at the court as God's prophet, Jeremiah reiterated this basic principle of kingship, probably in the presence of Jehoiakin soon after his accession to the throne. Josiah, who had preceded him, faithfully executed the covenant stipulations in all he did. Jehoiakim, on the other hand was a selfish, heartless tyrant who practiced injustice and unrighteousness. Neither Jehoahaz nor Jehoaikim ruled long enough for a fair accounting of their leadership. Zedekiah and his colleagues did not measure up to the standard that had been set. Our reading for this morning points to a new leader; a leader who will lead the people like a shepherd leads the flock. This shepherd will be like a righteous branch, the Messiah, who will succeed in his service to God and humankind, and will make possible salvation and security for all. This leader will completely carry out all covenant stipulations in his relationship with God's covenant people.

From our reading, especially those verses prior to the ones we are working with today, one would think that such a leader would possess all the qualities that people expect from a king. There are certain expectations of a king. Kings are from royal blood; they are excellent warriors and lead with a sense of dignity and power. But our reading from the Hebrew Scripture for this day tells us of another image; it is not the image we would expect in a leader.

On this Christ The King Sunday let us begin by taking a look at the image of God as our shepherd. I know that the image of a shepherd and a king do not usually go together. A quick look at the early history of humankind will tell you that being a shepherd was one of the earliest occupations ever recorded. The image of a shepherd is not so strange when you consider that the book of Genesis tells us that God gave humankind the responsibility of watching over every living thing that God had created. And what does a shepherd do, but watch over the flocks? In actuality, humankind watched over all the cattle including goats and cows, and other creatures. It was an important job considering that these animals were a primary source of food, clothing, and an important source of income. Having said that, there is no doubt that the sheep were usually the most in numbers. We do well to remember that owning animals was a sign of wealth. The Bible tells us that Job had thousands of sheep, camels, and oxen and Abraham had large flocks that were counted among his most prized possessions. Being a shepherd became an important job with rather large responsibilities. You might even say that being a shepherd meant being a leader.

The truth of the matter is that a good shepherd does not drive the sheep; a good shepherd leads the sheep. The prophet Jeremiah's conviction is that God will raise up a Davidic king whose name will be a sign of his nature. This new leader will lead the people on a new exodus. It takes a king to lead such an exodus.

I know that most of us have an image of a shepherd that has been mentally tattooed on our brains. It is that shepherd that David wrote to us about in Psalm 23. It is a wonderful image to be sure, but it is by no means the only one.

We must be careful to remember that through the prophet, God promised the safe return of the faithful, the flock, and the rise of good shepherds along with the coming of the righteous branch of David who would reign as king. Later, in chapter 31:33-34, Jeremiah paints for us a picture of a future covenant that will be a new beginning for the Hebrew people. This new covenant would be made effective by the wonderful grace of God. It is this freely given grace that will open the hearts of the people to a new understanding of God, a new way of relating to God that had not been present before. God will be their God, and they will be God's people.

It is always a bit dangerous to go directly from the Hebrew text to the New Testament. I do so here only because not to do so would be pulling down the shades on our resurrection minds. There are so many events that are tied to this section of Jeremiah: the return from exile, the rebuilding of the temple, and the temple being destroyed again. Many leaders came along, but none fulfilled all of the requirements as presented to us from Jeremiah. That is, until Jesus. The image of Jesus as a shepherd is a hallmark of our Christian faith. There is simply no way to avoid the comparison.

When you give it some thought you will see the words from Jeremiah that describe what he calls the "righteous branch," are words that fit easily into our understanding of who and what Jesus was and did. There is no need to go into a word count here, but without a doubt the most repeated idea of how we think of Jesus is that of a shepherd. So when the prophet Jeremiah says, "I will raise up shepherds over them who will shepherd them, and they shall not fear any longer, or be dismayed, nor shall any be missing, says the Lord." It is difficult for the Christian community not to make the connection with Jesus.

Remember in Matthew's Gospel the connection is carefully made between David and Jesus. Is that an error? No, it was important to Matthew that his listeners understood the lineage of Jesus. And it is Jesus himself that uses the analogy of the good shepherd

417

in comparison to his own ministry. It must be said here that it is important to understand that Jeremiah did not know who Jesus was. It is often the case that prophets are used and viewed as time machines for religious leaders of our time. It is a mistake to do so. Jeremiah was God's spokesperson for his time. He made promises and helped the people to understand the consequences of their actions. But, Jeremiah was not some kind of a magician, he was a prophet. However, the words of the prophet paint a picture for those of us within the sphere of Christianity, that when looked at from the vantage point of the New Testament, show us a picture of Jesus. The analogy with the shepherd is an analogy that makes sense. Jesus himself, like a good shepherd, fed us with God's Word. Jesus like a shepherd protecting the flock washed us, and when all else failed, gave his life for us. And let us not forget the new covenant that Jeremiah spoke of. Remember, after Jesus departed this world to be with God the Father, his followers were filled with the Holy Spirit, just as Jesus had promised, and through that Spirit they were given the courage and knowledge to go out and tell the story of Jesus to all the world.

Once again, Jeremiah said, "... I will raise up shepherds over them who will shepherd them, and they shall not fear any longer, or be dismayed, nor shall any be missing, says the Lord" (v. 4). Take a moment to look around you, what do you see? We are those shepherds. We are the faithful remnant and we are called to care for one another. We are directed by Jesus to be responsible for all of God's children. Jesus told us to, "Go therefore and make disciples of all nations, baptizing them in the name of the Father and of the Son and of the Holy Spirit, and teaching them to obey everything that I have commanded you. And remember, I am with you always, to the end of the age" (Matthew 28:19-20). Is this not called the Great Commission? Is this not a new covenant that we are called into? We are directed by Jesus to be shepherds. We are directed to care for the flock by sharing the Word of God whenever and wherever we can. Jesus is calling us to action.

Jeremiah was an important piece of the foundation upon which we have built the church. He spoke of things that changed the way

418

an entire people lived their lives. He pointed toward another day, a better day.

Today is that better day. Christ The King is in our midst. The Shepherd King, Jesus, called Peter to action and instructed him to show his love for Jesus by tending to the sheep. Just as Jeremiah saw it, those who love God will love the flock and that love will hold the flock together. We cannot say that we love Jesus while hating the world. We cannot say that we respect the king and continue to be a people that hate. Jeremiah knew, and Jesus showed, that a lack of love for any of God's children cuts us off from any claim to love God.

Finally, on Christ The King Sunday we need to be careful in how we understand what it is to be a shepherd. Too many times we make the mistake of thinking that it is the job of the pastor of the church to care for the church. And as long as we persist in seeing ministry as the singular responsibility of the minister, we will always be linked to the notion of the church as a professional group that employs people to do the caring. When we do that, we make the ministry just another job. And when someone is in need, when someone is sick, or has financial difficulties, or is spiritually running on empty, we call in the professional, the minister, the reasoning being: That's the minister's job.

My sisters and brothers in Christ, God calls on all who love God to love others. Let us learn from today's Hebrew Scripture and step up to the responsibilities that God has placed in our hands. We, like Peter before us, need to answer the timeless question, "Do you truly love God with all your heart — and all your soul — and all your mind?" If your answer is, "Yes," then go and feed God's sheep. If your answer is, "No," then go and sit with someone who answered, "Yes"!

Christ The King is prepared to lead this flock. The question for you this day is, "Are you ready to follow?"

Amen.

# Thanks For
# Receiving Thanksgiving

This wonderful chapter of Deuteronomy speaks to us on this Thanksgiving Day of the forms for the presentation of the abundance of a good harvest. The verses suggest that only those who are in communion with the giver can present the gift with a clean heart. It was the custom at the time of the telling of this story that each year, a basket containing firstfruits of the soil was to be brought to the central sanctuary and presented to God.

The Bible tells us that firstfruits for the people described in Deuteronomy were crops such as barley, grapes, wheat, figs, pomegranates, olives, and dates. The people were to take a basket of these firstfruits to the place they worshiped and present them to the priest.

In today's world, for those of us who are here today, our firstfruits do not come from crops we have labored over. Our firstfruits are not what we gather up and put in a basket and bring to church to be offered to God. Usually, we get a paycheck and deposit that check in the bank and that check represents our firstfruits, and the checking or savings account is our basket.

The Hebrew people's offering to God was done as an act of faith and commitment. When making this presentation to God, the one presenting the gift was to engage in a spoken confession of her or his faith. This confession rehearsed the mighty acts of God in the deliverance from Egypt and the occupation of Canaan.

In our world today, Thanksgiving is a time when we, through a variety of ways, give thanks for all the bounty that we are so lucky to have and then to share. At least, that is what we are supposed to be doing. In reality, however, Thanksgiving has become for many just another day off, albeit with family, and of course, football. The biblical principle of offering God a portion of our good bounty is not exactly on the minds of most people who gather at Thanksgiving tables. The biblical model is one in which the people of God remember how fortunate they are to be out of captivity in Egypt. They, therefore, act out of a genuine faith stance that shouts, "Praise God, from whom all blessings flow!"

Our thanksgiving to God is an action that is commanded by God. God commands the people to bring the offering of firstfruits. It is important to take notice that by this command the people are required to do something physical. They are required to not only harvest the firstfruits, the are required to pick up the crops, put them in a basket and take them to the temple. They become a part of the offering. But thankfulness is not just something we do, or a gift we bring. Thankfulness is a part of the quality of the life we live. Thankfulness should be a daily part of our living. Thanksgiving, therefore, is an attitude which acknowledges that God is in absolute control of our lives. Only with that recognition can we approach God with thankful hearts.

The giving of the firstfruits was a way for the people to say, "Thank you" to God, and to acknowledge that without God, they would have nothing.

For those of you who garden, there should be a special attraction to these verses. There is great joy to those folks who wait patiently for spring and then till the soil and plant the seeds. You watch and water and weed and hope that these tiny seeds will become something special. If you are lucky, in a short while small shoots begin to break the surface of the soil and the anticipation of the harvest begins. There is great satisfaction in reaping that harvest and partaking of its bounty.

It is commonplace for people to think that the first Thanksgiving was when the Pilgrims, who survived that first in winter in Plymouth, gathered together and shared what little they had as a way of thanking God for surviving that first winter. But our text from Deuteronomy says otherwise. For the Hebrew people, giving thanks to God was much more personal than it is for most of us.

We do not think of ourselves, for the most part, as people who have been delivered from slavery into freedom.

A question to ponder this Thanksgiving Day is whether or not twenty-first-century people can think of Thanksgiving as deliverance. The truth is that for the overwhelming majority of people Thanksgiving is a day when we list the many things we have to be thankful for, but not to list those things that we have been set free from.

When we acknowledge that our firstfruits are probably a pay check, the question becomes, how does that check become firstfruits? Now the murmur will go up that here comes another plea for money. The church is always looking for money. Well, sort of.

Thankful hearts come to us as we ponder and appreciate those things in our lives that give us a sense of security and hope. But most people do not think about their good heath, or financial well being, or clothes on their backs, and a roof over their head as firstfruits. Indeed, it could be said that some folks actually think they are owed those things from God, simply because — well, because! When we stop and prayerfully recognize that everything we have in life, those things we have been delivered from, and those things we put into our bank account come from God, one of two results come forward. We either feel like we are actually the reason for those things in life we consider good, or we don't want to admit that God is the giver because we do not want to be beholden to God or to anyone else!

Many people don't want to say, "Thank you," because to say, "Thank you," says, "I am dependent on you." And, sadly most of us, even if we don't want to admit it, are self-centered enough that we do not want to be seen as depending on anyone or anything.

The truth is that saying, "Thank you," or better yet, to admit that gratitude is a good thing, is an action that has its roots in grace. When we are truly grateful, we become keenly aware that we are totally dependent on God and upon one another. When we are really grateful, we recognize that God has given us firstfruits whether we deserve them or not.

Thanksgiving, on our part, in our time, should reflect the knowledge that we have already received from God far more than we can ever offer in return. When you take inventory of your life, you will discover that God has done much gardening in your life. You will come to understand that God has been patient in tending to the needs of your life. You will come to understand and appreciate that God has fashioned you and has provided for all your needs. You will come to accept that those needs may not always be met in a way that you would have them met, but you will come to know they are indeed met.

In returning to our text, it is clear that the Israelites were finally taking possession of the land that God had promised to them. They worked hard to get their crops planted, establishing community, and in doing so, planted their lives as well as their crops. They were laying the foundation for a new life of freedom in this foreign land. One can only imagine how busy those days must have been for them as they went about building new lives. One can imagine that they probably worked long hours every day, and did so with a smile on their face. They might have been tempted to think that they now had it made. They must have thought along those lines, to do otherwise would be contrary to human behavior. The crops are the best we have ever seen. Life is good; we can now live on our own.

But, it appears that they did not get too full of themselves, at least not at this point in their early history. I mean, how many times have we been tempted to rearrange our priorities to reflect a more selfish attitude? When things are going great, it is easy to slip into the self-deception of human pride. And an added problem is that when it is good, we want more, we get greedy.

Our text reflects a different attitude. It is an attitude of gratitude. It is an attitude that says before we get our fill, we need first to tell God, "Thank you." Yes, they had been commanded to do so, but how often has that command been ignored by humankind?

On this Thanksgiving Day let us begin to move into an understanding that we are always to give God our best effort in all things we do. When you think of the firstfruit scenario keep this in mind. The firstfruit was the best and the biggest. It is often from that fruit that the best seed is removed and replanted for the next year. So what does it say when we give our firstfruit to God? It says, "We trust God with the best." Someone once said, "Give God your best, expect God's best." That is a good notion to keep in mind. It would be a tragedy of we neglected the many blessings God has so graciously entrusted to our care. We need on this special day to ask ourselves how it will be with us when God takes stock of our lives. Will we be able to look into God's radiance and say that we have used the firstfruits of our lives in a way that glorifies God? We will be able to say, "Yes, we have used those gracious gifts wisely" when we acknowledge God's grace in our lives.

No matter how hard you have worked, no matter how deeply you are to committed to providing for yourself and those around you; no matter how dedicated you are to making a positive difference for people along the way, the fact still remains: There is nothing that you own. There is nothing that you have by your own efforts alone. It is like the seed that was planted and became a part of the harvest of firstfruits. The farmer works hard to prepare the soil and all the rest, but no matter how hard the farmer works, it is not the farmer that gives that seed life, it is our God who created the farmer and the seed who gives both life.

My sisters and brothers in Christ, we are a people who have been blessed. As you look around the world today, look with eyes of thankfulness. Let us see our blessings and not be jealous, or selfish, or self-centered. Let us, this Thanksgiving Day, be a grateful people, a people that are thankful for our dependency on God.

Happy Thanksgiving to you all.

Amen.

# Lectionary Preaching After Pentecost

The following index will aid the user of this book in matching the correct Sunday with the appropriate text during Pentecost. All texts in this book are from the series for the First Readings, Revised Common Lectionary. (Note that the ELCA division of Lutheranism is now following the Revised Common Lectionary.) The Lutheran designations indicate days comparable to Sundays on which Revised Common Lectionary Propers or Ordinary Time designations are used.

**(Fixed dates do not pertain to Lutheran Lectionary)**

| Fixed Date Lectionaries<br>*Revised Common (including ELCA)*<br>*and Roman Catholic* | Lutheran Lectionary<br>*Lutheran* |
|---|---|
| The Day Of Pentecost | The Day Of Pentecost |
| The Holy Trinity | The Holy Trinity |
| May 29-June 4 — Proper 4, Ordinary Time 9 | Pentecost 2 |
| June 5-11 — Proper 5, Ordinary Time 10 | Pentecost 3 |
| June 12-18 — Proper 6, Ordinary Time 11 | Pentecost 4 |
| June 19-25 — Proper 7, Ordinary Time 12 | Pentecost 5 |
| June 26-July 2 — Proper 8, Ordinary Time 13 | Pentecost 6 |
| July 3-9 — Proper 9, Ordinary Time 14 | Pentecost 7 |
| July 10-16 — Proper 10, Ordinary Time 15 | Pentecost 8 |
| July 17-23 — Proper 11, Ordinary Time 16 | Pentecost 9 |
| July 24-30 — Proper 12, Ordinary Time 17 | Pentecost 10 |
| July 31-Aug. 6 — Proper 13, Ordinary Time 18 | Pentecost 11 |
| Aug. 7-13 — Proper 14, Ordinary Time 19 | Pentecost 12 |
| Aug. 14-20 — Proper 15, Ordinary Time 20 | Pentecost 13 |
| Aug. 21-27 — Proper 16, Ordinary Time 21 | Pentecost 14 |
| Aug. 28-Sept. 3 — Proper 17, Ordinary Time 22 | Pentecost 15 |
| Sept. 4-10 — Proper 18, Ordinary Time 23 | Pentecost 16 |
| Sept. 11-17 — Proper 19, Ordinary Time 24 | Pentecost 17 |
| Sept. 18-24 — Proper 20, Ordinary Time 25 | Pentecost 18 |

| | |
|---|---|
| Sept. 25-Oct. 1 — Proper 21, Ordinary Time 26 | Pentecost 19 |
| Oct. 2-8 — Proper 22, Ordinary Time 27 | Pentecost 20 |
| Oct. 9-15 — Proper 23, Ordinary Time 28 | Pentecost 21 |
| Oct. 16-22 — Proper 24, Ordinary Time 29 | Pentecost 22 |
| Oct. 23-29 — Proper 25, Ordinary Time 30 | Pentecost 23 |
| Oct. 30-Nov. 5 — Proper 26, Ordinary Time 31 | Pentecost 24 |
| Nov. 6-12 — Proper 27, Ordinary Time 32 | Pentecost 25 |
| Nov. 13-19 — Proper 28, Ordinary Time 33 | Pentecost 26 |
| | Pentecost 27 |
| Nov. 20-26 — Christ The King | Christ The King |

Reformation Day (or last Sunday in October) is October 31 (Revised Common, Lutheran)

All Saints (or first Sunday in November) is November 1 (Revised Common, Lutheran, Roman Catholic)

# U.S./Canadian Lectionary Comparison

The following index shows the correlation between the Sundays and special days of the church year as they are titled or labeled in the Revised Common Lectionary published by the Consultation On Common Texts and used in the United States (the reference used for this book) and the Sundays and special days of the church year as they are titled or labeled in the Revised Common Lectionary used in Canada.

| Revised Common Lectionary | Canadian Revised Common Lectionary |
|---|---|
| Advent 1 | Advent 1 |
| Advent 2 | Advent 2 |
| Advent 3 | Advent 3 |
| Advent 4 | Advent 4 |
| Christmas Eve | Christmas Eve |
| The Nativity Of Our Lord/ Christmas Day | The Nativity Of Our Lord |
| Christmas 1 | Christmas 1 |
| January 1/Holy Name Of Jesus | January 1/The Name Of Jesus |
| Christmas 2 | Christmas 2 |
| The Epiphany Of Our Lord | The Epiphany Of Our Lord |
| The Baptism Of Our Lord/ Epiphany 1 | The Baptism Of Our Lord/ Proper 1 |
| Epiphany 2/Ordinary Time 2 | Epiphany 2/Proper 2 |
| Epiphany 3/Ordinary Time 3 | Epiphany 3/Proper 3 |
| Epiphany 4/Ordinary Time 4 | Epiphany 4/Proper 4 |
| Epiphany 5/Ordinary Time 5 | Epiphany 5/Proper 5 |
| Epiphany 6/Ordinary Time 6 | Epiphany 6/Proper 6 |
| Epiphany 7/Ordinary Time 7 | Epiphany 7/Proper 7 |
| Epiphany 8/Ordinary Time 8 | Epiphany 8/Proper 8 |
| The Transfiguration Of Our Lord/ Last Sunday After The Epiphany | The Transfiguration Of Our Lord/ Last Sunday After Epiphany |
| Ash Wednesday | Ash Wednesday |
| Lent 1 | Lent 1 |
| Lent 2 | Lent 2 |
| Lent 3 | Lent 3 |
| Lent 4 | Lent 4 |
| Lent 5 | Lent 5 |
| Sunday Of The Passion/Palm Sunday | Passion/Palm Sunday |
| Maundy Thursday | Holy/Maundy Thursday |
| Good Friday | Good Friday |

| | |
|---|---|
| The Resurrection Of Our Lord/ Easter Day | The Resurrection Of Our Lord |
| Easter 2 | Easter 2 |
| Easter 3 | Easter 3 |
| Easter 4 | Easter 4 |
| Easter 5 | Easter 5 |
| Easter 6 | Easter 6 |
| The Ascension Of Our Lord | The Ascension Of Our Lord |
| Easter 7 | Easter 7 |
| The Day Of Pentecost | The Day Of Pentecost |
| The Holy Trinity | The Holy Trinity |
| Proper 4/Pentecost 2/O T 9* | Proper 9 |
| Proper 5/Pent 3/O T 10 | Proper 10 |
| Proper 6/Pent 4/O T 11 | Proper 11 |
| Proper 7/Pent 5/O T 12 | Proper 12 |
| Proper 8/Pent 6/O T 13 | Proper 13 |
| Proper 9/Pent 7/O T 14 | Proper 14 |
| Proper 10/Pent 8/O T 15 | Proper 15 |
| Proper 11/Pent 9/O T 16 | Proper 16 |
| Proper 12/Pent 10/O T 17 | Proper 17 |
| Proper 13/Pent 11/O T 18 | Proper 18 |
| Proper 14/Pent 12/O T 19 | Proper 19 |
| Proper 15/Pent 13/O T 20 | Proper 20 |
| Proper 16/Pent 14/O T 21 | Proper 21 |
| Proper 17/Pent 15/O T 22 | Proper 22 |
| Proper 18/Pent 16/O T 23 | Proper 23 |
| Proper 19/Pent 17/O T 24 | Proper 24 |
| Proper 20/Pent 18/O T 25 | Proper 25 |
| Proper 21/Pent 19/O T 26 | Proper 26 |
| Proper 22/Pent 20/O T 27 | Proper 27 |
| Proper 23/Pent 21/O T 28 | Proper 28 |
| Proper 24/Pent 22/O T 29 | Proper 29 |
| Proper 25/Pent 23/O T 30 | Proper 30 |
| Proper 26/Pent 24/O T 31 | Proper 31 |
| Proper 27/Pent 25/O T 32 | Proper 32 |
| Proper 28/Pent 26/O T 33 | Proper 33 |
| Christ The King (Proper 29/O T 34) | Proper 34/Christ The King/ Reign Of Christ |
| | |
| Reformation Day (October 31) | Reformation Day (October 31) |
| All Saints (November 1 or 1st Sunday in November) | All Saints' Day (November 1) |
| Thanksgiving Day (4th Thursday of November) | Thanksgiving Day (2nd Monday of October) |

*O T = Ordinary Time

# About The Authors

**Mary S. Lautensleger** is the pastor of Center United Methodist Church in Concord, North Carolina. Prior to entering the ordained ministry, she served for many years as music minister and parish educator in Lutheran, United Methodist, and Presbyterian congregations in southwestern Ohio. Lautensleger is a graduate of the College-Conservatory of Music at the University of Cincinnati (B.M., M.M.), United Theological Seminary (M.A. in theological studies), and Trinity Lutheran Seminary (M.Div.), and she is a D.Min. candidate at Hood Theological Seminary.

**Frank Ramirez** has served congregations in Indiana and California, and is currently pastor at Everett Church of the Brethren in Everett, Pennsylvania. A graduate of LaVerne College and Bethany Theological Seminary, Ramirez is the author of numerous books, articles, and short stories. His CSS titles include *Partners In Healing*, *Lectionary Worship Aids*, *A Call To Worship*, *He Took A Towel*, *Gabriel's Horn*, *Coming Home*, and *The Christmas Star*.

**Stan Purdum** is the pastor of Centenary United Methodist Church in Waynesburg, Ohio. He has served as the editor for the preaching journals, *Emphasis* and *Homiletics*, and he has written extensively for both the religious and secular press. Purdum is the author of *New Mercies I See* (CSS) and *He Walked in Galilee* (Abingdon Press), as well as two accounts of long-distance bicycle journeys, *Roll Around Heaven All Day* and *Playing In Traffic*.

**Lee Ann Dunlap** is the pastor of Pleasant Grove United Methodist Church in Zanesville, Ohio. She is a graduate of Mount Union College and the Methodist Theological School in Ohio.

**John Wayne Clarke** is an ordained minister in the United Church of Christ who currently pastors First Congregational Church in Meriden, Connecticut. He is the author of *What Good Is Christianity Anyhow?* and *A Quest for Silence*. Clarke is a graduate of Bangor Theological Seminary and Providence Theological Seminary (Otterburn, Manitoba, Canada).

**Title:** Sermons On The First Readings, Series II, Cycle C

**ISBN:** 0-7880-2397-7

### INSTRUCTIONS TO ACCESS PASSWORD FOR ELECTRONIC COPY OF THIS TITLE:

The password appears on the reverse side of this page. Carefully cut the card from the page to retrieve the password.

Once you have the password, go to

http:/www.csspub.com/passwords/

and locate this title on that web page. By clicking on the title, you will be guided to a page to enter your password, name, and email address. From there you will be sent to a page to download your electronic version of this book.

For further information, or if you don't have access to the internet, please contact CSS Publishing Company at 1-800-241-4056 in the United States (or 419-227-1818 from outside the United States) between 8 a.m. and 5 p.m., Eastern Standard Time, Monday through Friday.